What Now!

A Pivotal Story of Love, Family, and the Miracle of People

Chrissie Betlach Vinje

BALBOA.
PRESS

A DIVISION OF HAY HOUSE

Balboa Press books may be ordered through booksellers or by contacting:

Balboa Press
A Division of Hay House
1663 Liberty Drive
Bloomington, IN 47403
www.balboapress.com
1 (877) 407-4847

Because of the dynamic nature of the Internet, any web addresses or links contained in this book may have changed since publication and may no longer be valid. The views expressed in this work are solely those of the author and do not necessarily reflect the views of the publisher, and the publisher hereby disclaims any responsibility for them.

The author of this book does not dispense medical advice or prescribe the use of any technique as a form of treatment for physical, emotional, or medical problems without the advice of a physician, either directly or indirectly. The intent of the author is only to offer information of a general nature to help you in your quest for emotional and spiritual well-being. In the event you use any of the information in this book for yourself, which is your constitutional right, the author and the publisher assume no responsibility for your actions.

Any people depicted in stock imagery provided by Thinkstock are models, and such images are being used for illustrative purposes only. Certain stock imagery © Thinkstock.

Print information available on the last page.

ISBN: 978-1-5043-5036-5 (sc)
ISBN: 978-1-5043-5038-9 (hc)
ISBN: 978-1-5043-5037-2 (e)

Library of Congress Control Number: 2016902902

Balboa Press rev. date: 03/29/2016

Contents

Dedication

This book is dedicated to everyone who went through Tom's illness and death with me. There are many, many people who are encompassed by this statement. You will hear some of their voices in the pages that follow; others sat silently, not voicing their personal thoughts and feelings but were present nonetheless. There are even a few people I do not know personally, but because they made their presence known on the CaringBridge or through other friends and family, their impact on me was tremendous.

To the friends and family who enabled me to bring Tom home, you will never know the depth of my respect, love, and gratitude for the time and love you gave to both of us during that period. Thank you for helping care for Tom and allowing me to remain working for the four months he was home. I know you know who you are, but I want everyone else to know as well.

I must start with Virginia Vinje, Tom's mother, who retired from her part-time job to care for her son. She was at our house at 6:30 every morning and stayed as long as she was needed. Tom's family was and continues to be a great support. Thank you to Judy Vinje, Laura Vinje, and Gary Vinje (Tom's siblings) for being here caring for Tom and providing him some much-needed entertainment! Thank you, to Tony Wesley (Tom's nephew and Laura's son) for taking the entire night shift and keeping a watchful eye on your beloved uncle. Thanks also to Eric Wesley (Laura's son) and Ty Vinje (Judy's son) for taking shifts during the weekdays, often pairing up with the ladies of my family. Thanks to Drae Vinje for helping when he was home with us. I also want to thank M'Kenzie Vinje for helping out with things around the house.

My family, too, has been amazing. Many thanks to my mother, Sherrill Betlach, and my aunt, Marlene Trombley, for being here every Monday and taking on the duties of the day with Virginia. To my sisters, Beth Timm, Theresa Betlach, and Jessica DuCharme, I thank you for your willingness to care for Tom and support us. Many thanks to my niece, Nicole Betlach, who (while living in the apartment in our house) got up every four hours during the weekend nights to help care for Tom.

I also want to express my gratitude to one of my very best friends, Karrie Cable, for being willing to drop anything at a moment's notice, run across the alley, and help or lend an ear whenever I needed it. I have a wealth of gratitude for our other friends who helped out at the house or provided some much-needed moral support both during Tom's illness and after his death; thank you, Krissy and Barry Grupe, Wendy Kreps Peterson and Keith Kreps, Lisa Berry, Shannon Bielke, Pam Larson, Jackie Thomas, Jodi Hystead, Lynn Robson, and Carolyn Rudi. Another round of thanks also to the Buds: Bill Bishman, Steve and Jodi Campbell, Chris Heimerl, Bill Larson, Kent and Kim Peterson, and Mark Peterson.

I would like to give some special shout-outs as well. First, a big thank you to my friend Candace McCown, who took our girl Bailey out to play every day during Tom's illness and continues to give her a much-needed break away from the house three days a week. Also, to Kelly Ayd, nurse extraordinaire, thank you for your unconditional caring and support while we were on 6A and beyond. You will never know the level of comfort you were for me during that most trying time. And last, but most certainly not least, my therapist, Paula Becker. My God, I have no idea where I would be mentally or emotionally without you. You had quite the undertaking when I showed up on your doorstep this time! I am so glad you get me.

If it had not been for all these people, I would not have had the capacity to carry on during the seven months of Tom's illness. I would like to thank each and every one of you for your unconditional love and support. You all are so amazing, and you were the greatest gifts Tom and I received when we needed it most. There is a special place in heaven for each one of you. I love you all.

In loving memory of

Valerie Ann Hassler

Preface

This book is based on my journal entries and the guest book entries on the CaringBridge website for Tom Vinje. The CaringBridge is a website designed to keep people updated on health issues or situations of friends and family members. My husband, Tom Vinje, was diagnosed with a glioblastoma brain tumor in March 2008, and on the pages that follow, you will be witness to all that encompasses such a diagnosis, including the effects on me as well as family and friends. The entries were created as life was unfolding and have been copied and pasted with the original dates and times from the website and put into chapters to keep the love, energy, and passion intact.

There were a few people who put the idea in my head about writing a book based on this experience. At first I thought, *Yeah, right. It sounds like a great idea, but how could I ever pull that off?* Then, as time passed, I thought, *How could I not write this book? If I have an opportunity to reach out to someone and touch him or her in a way I couldn't otherwise, who am I to not make that happen?*

So, from the words of Tom's former boss, John H. (who was the first to mention this to me), "It'd make a helluva book, Chrissie," to now, I hope you agree and that I have done my husband, our family, our friends, and myself justice by telling our very real and emotional story for everyone to hear.

Tom's CaringBridge page remains active.

If you care to visit the page you will find
it at the following address:

www.caringbridge.org

You will need to type in thomasvinje at
the site name to reach the page.

You may also have to create a CaringBridge
account if you do not already have one.

Prologue

December 25, 2011

It is Christmas morning, and there is no snow on the ground. Don't get me wrong, it doesn't really bother me, but it is true that snow makes it feel more like Christmas. Something else that makes it feel less like Christmas is your absence. It has been three years since you left me, and this is my fourth Christmas without you. This is the first year I have allowed myself to wish others a merry Christmas. It's also the first year that I have looked forward to the holiday, if only a little bit—not pushing it away so I wouldn't have to feel, see, or hear the fact that you aren't here with me.

I miss you so very much. I miss our holiday tradition of opening presents in the morning, indulging in champagne and cheese before we set out for the day. I miss us watching our dog Bailey open her presents and laughing at how she would shake the hell out of it to get the toy out. I miss being together at the family Christmas gatherings. I miss your smile, your laugh, your sense of humor, your companionship, and so much more. I miss you every single day, and I don't expect that will ever change. There will always be a void that only you can fill, and you are not here.

I am grieving the greatest loss I will ever experience. That, my love, is you. I know you are near, and I feel you with me a great deal of the time. This brings me great comfort, but of course it's not the same as having you here. That is both my problem and my reason for writing.

Writing is my greatest ally as I attempt to move on with my time left on earth. It will help me to express to others how much I loved you and how much you meant to me. And hopefully along the way, our story will help others to be more prepared if tragedy strikes. It is also my hope that our story will help people appreciate and nourish what they have. Believe me, do not take what you have for granted; it will not last forever. If I can help just one person with our story, it will be worth all the time, energy, and emotion spent getting it on paper. My desire is that the gift of this book will bring people a greater understanding of how precious life is—all the more so because it can change in an instant. Life is all about change, learning, and loving one another.

I will love and miss you forever, my love, and I am doing the best I can until we meet again.

Chrissie

Chapter 1

The Phone Call

It was St. Patrick's Day of 2008, and I was standing in line at the grocery store, waiting to pay for my things. As I was working my way to the front of the line, my cell phone rang. It was my mother-in-law, calling to tell me that my husband, Tom, had been in a car accident. (He had taken her car in to work to be fixed and was bringing it back.) Ginny said he had called her to pick him up and bring him home. (*Strange,* I remember thinking, *that he didn't call me.*) When she arrived at the intersection where he had instructed her to meet him, he wasn't there, and no one in the area recalled seeing a man of his description.

She wanted to know what to do next. To prevent panic from setting in, I tried to think of a logical scenario. I hoped that maybe he had started walking home from the site of the accident, which wasn't too far from our house. So I suggested that she head toward my house and meet me there. I arrived home to find Tom standing in the alley, talking to our neighbors. He had, in fact, walked the mile and a half home. Ginny was not far behind me and drove up to see that he had made it home. (I will never understand why the police let him walk away from the accident.) He seemed disoriented and had blood on his face. I hugged him with tears in my eyes, happy that he was okay. Yet he barely hugged me back, and it was clear that he was not himself.

I asked him what had happened, and he told me that as he was driving south on Cedar Avenue he had noticed a school bus about a block away, heading north. Then, he said, the bus had suddenly turned in front of him, and he had hit the side of it. When I asked him what had happened to his face, he said he had hit it on the seat belt. I guessed that he meant the steering wheel, as it was apparent that his face had hit something hard, pushing his glasses into his face and cutting him.

While Tom continued talking with the neighbors, I went inside and started dinner. When he came into the house, he stood in the back hallway, looking around. I asked him if he was okay, and he didn't really answer. I helped him take off his coat and told him to go into the bathroom and wash the blood off his face. After a few minutes, I went to check on him and found him standing at the sink, running water over his hands and then slowly rubbing his face. I helped him clean up, and then he said he was going to lie down. He went into the living room and lay down on the couch. I finished making dinner and brought him a bowl of chili. He started to eat lying down, and I quickly made him sit up to eat. His behavior was very strange. I wasn't quite sure what to do, so I let him rest.

The next morning, I tried to wake Tom as usual so he could get ready for work. For weeks it had become increasingly difficult to wake him, and something told me to stand in front of him until he answered me. I kept waking him every ten minutes until I left for work. As I was leaving, he said he was going to call his boss to tell him that he would be late. Once I got to work, I called Tom every hour or so to see if he had gotten up and gone in to work. Finally, I called his mom and asked her to call Tom and report back to me. When she called to say he was not himself, I felt panicked. I knew something was really wrong, so I rushed home.

When I arrived home, Tom was lying on the couch with his arms crossed on his chest, watching television. I sat down on the couch next to him, and I asked him if he was okay. He replied with a very unconvincing, "Yeah." He then looked at the clock and said, "Boy, it's late." (I had known for at least a couple of months that something was going on with him and had only recently wondered if he might be depressed.) I then asked him if he thought he was depressed, and he answered that he didn't know. Once again, he looked at the clock and said, "Boy, it's late." That was it. After a bit more dialogue, I asked him if he wanted me to call his mom, and he nodded.

After Ginny arrived, we decided that he needed to go to the Riverside Hospital ER. Tom then started to throw up bile while he was lying on the couch. We quickly sat him up and grabbed a bucket. As we were dressing him, he continued to vomit. Once he was dressed, we stood him up to go out to the car. Although hours earlier he had taken our dog for a walk, he was now unsteady on his feet. We got him outside, and while I was pulling the car out of the garage, he threw up again on the driveway. On the way to the hospital, Tom's odd behavior continued. He refused to fasten his seatbelt and was extremely agitated that the car was beeping for this reason, but there was no time to argue about it.

Upon arriving at the hospital, I dropped Tom and Ginny off at the ER entrance, where he proceeded to throw up once more on the sidewalk. The security guard noticed us and quickly brought out a wheelchair and had him admitted immediately. After parking the car, I went to take care of the paperwork before going back to his room. It was there we were told that the doctor thought Tom had a concussion and wanted to treat him quickly. Why hadn't I thought of that?

In his room, the doctor asked all three of us a battery of questions before taking him for a CT scan. After the scan, they brought Tom back into the room, and we waited for the results. All of a sudden, the doctor whipped open the curtain and said, "I apologize for the hastiness of this, but the CT scan showed that your husband has a brain tumor, and he is being transferred to the University of Minnesota Hospital. Lifelink is on their way; they will be here in minutes." She then told us that we could drive over to the U and meet him there. These are words I will never forget.

I looked at Tom, and then I looked at Ginny and said, "Who is she talking to? Does she have the right room? She's not talking to us."

Never in this life did I think that we or anyone else we knew would ever be in a situation such as this. It just couldn't be true. Thus began our descent into hell.

Chapter 2

Tom and Chrissie— the Beginning

How did we get here? Tom and I were in our midthirties when we met in December 1995. I had started working at a local car dealership where Tom had worked for nearly fifteen years. After a few months of getting to know each other we discovered that while I was growing up, I had known his uncle and cousins and that my aunt had worked with his dad at Honeywell. What a small world! It wasn't love at first sight—not at all. As a matter of fact, I was in the process of getting over a past relationship when I met Tom.

As the months went by, I knew Tom was smitten with me. A group of us occasionally went out for drinks after work, and eventually, Tom and I got to know each other a little better. Still, I was not ready to date. Then one day I noticed that I had started liking Tom the way he liked me. Since he was not aware of this new development, it was clear that I was the one who had to make a move. I knew that he and his "buds" went to the block party in downtown Minneapolis every year, so I decided to head down there that Friday night to see if by chance we would run into each other. It was not to be. As I found out the following week, he and his friends were out of town on one of their "bud weekends" instead.

No matter. Soon after, the dance started. That fall, I had a party at the townhouse I was living in. On our lunch hour, Tom went with me to the liquor store to pick up and set up the keg for the party that evening. Later, after everyone had left, Tom stayed, and we ended up talking until the sun came up, discovering all that we had in common. The list was quite extensive! Not long after, he asked me out to dinner and a movie. (On our first date, we saw *Copland* with Sly Stallone.) The date went well, and we were off and running. We never looked back. From the minute we started dating, that was it. We were together; it was meant to be.

When I say "meant to be," I feel like I am not doing our relationship justice. We had a connection. We had chemistry. We were soul mates. We had a once-in-a-lifetime love that many people never experience. We had all of this and more.

****

Tom grew up in a south Minneapolis neighborhood with a lot of kids his age. The guys from the 'hood are all friends to this day and are known as "the Buds." There were a few guys they met along the way who became Buds too. It is a rare thing in this day and age when a big group of guys remain friends for life.

When Tom and I started dating, I was informed that the Buds had three annual outings a year. The first was a weekend golf outing in May. In July, the "Bud Annual" was held. For this drunk-fest, the guys would rent cabins or trailers for the weekend and use them as their home base. Eventually, a couple of the guys obtained their own cabins, and they finally had their own home base. The last but certainly not least event of the year was the September golf outing. This was usually a one-night trip, and the tradition actually ended the year Tom and I got married. Our wedding fell on that weekend, and for whatever reason, they never did it again after that. If I were to take a guess as to why, I would say that it was due to life changing. The guys were in relationships or getting married and having kids and decided to partake in the outings that were the most enjoyable.

****

In October of 1998, Tom and I went on a trip to Lake Superior in Duluth, Minnesota, a trip we had taken the year before. We were to leave on Friday morning, but at the last minute he wanted to leave the night before, which I was not prepared for. It had been a long week at work, and I didn't want to deal with the long drive that night. But Tom's powers of persuasion being what they were, he talked me into it, and away we went.

The next day we went to Superior, Wisconsin. The changing colors of the leaves and the shining sun were incredibly beautiful. We then drove to Bayfield. Having just discovered we missed the Apple Festival by a week, we decided to take the ferry to Madeline Island. The tourist season had recently ended, so things were quiet. We decided to just hang out in the new, still-unfinished bar and restaurant and have lunch and a cocktail until it was time to take the return ferry to Bayfield. Upon hearing that it was time for us to depart, me, Tom, and the rest of the people waiting for the return trip made our way to the dock. As the ferry was approaching, Tom realized he had forgotten the camera case on the back of the chair in the restaurant. He bolted back to get it, and thankfully, the waitress had given it to the bartender, who had safely tucked it behind the bar. He grabbed it and high-tailed it back to the ferry, making it just in time!

Later that night, back in Duluth, we went out for dinner and then came back to our hotel to listen to some music in the bar. Tom asked me if I wanted to go for a walk along the shore of Lake Superior. I wasn't really in the mood for a walk at that point, but after a while, we left the bar and set out for the boardwalk. As we were walking along there was a fairly strong dead-fish smell, and I had no problem pointing that out once or twice. Soon, we started the long walk down the pier and up the stairs to the lighthouse on the north pier in Canal Park. We were alone as we made our way around the lighthouse, and suddenly Tom stopped. He pulled a ring out of his pocket, got down on one knee, and proposed. I was completely surprised! Of course I said yes! Just then we noticed a couple of teens lurking around the lighthouse. We did not have a good feeling about the situation, so we got out of there. As we were on our way back to Canal Park, Tom told me that he had been trying to propose all day and couldn't find the right time. He also told me that he had hidden the ring in the camera case earlier in the day. No wonder he was freaked out about forgetting it! Then he planned to propose as we walked along the shore, but I was too busy complaining about the fishy smell. I sure didn't make it easy for him, poor guy!

After we returned to Canal Park, we were just giddy and decided to go to Grandma's Sports Garden to celebrate with a pitcher of Long Island iced teas. We told everybody we saw that we had just gotten engaged. We were on cloud nine!

For the rest of Tom's life, he referred to that lighthouse as "the scene of the crime." What a funny guy! On our subsequent annual trips to Duluth in September we bought a picture of the lighthouse and a couple of ornaments with an image of our lighthouse on them. To this day, I can't look at that lighthouse and not think of it as the scene of the crime and remember the role it played in our lives.

The next day we started to discuss our wedding party. I soon came to the realization that this was going to be one huge-ass wedding. With all of his Buds, his brother Gary, and my brother Tony, we figured there would be nine attendants on each side. I was stunned! I almost felt embarrassed about it, and he said, "I can't cut anybody out. Who would I leave out?" Knowing that I, too, could easily fill those spots on my side with my four sisters, his sister Judy, and my friends, I said, "Okay! Let's do it!" I wasn't embarrassed for long. It was pretty darn cool! We had nine attendants on each side, four ushers, a flower girl, and a ring bearer. A wedding party of twenty-four! Such is life with big families and a lot of friends. Let the games begin!

****

We were married on September 18, 1999. It was a beautiful day, and we were surrounded by our families and friends. The wedding procession came to be known as "the Parade." It was a truly magical day, and we tried to hang on to it as long as we could. The next morning we were bummed that our day was over, but we were happy because we had another party for gift opening that day. The Monday after our wedding we took off on our honeymoon to the Cayman Islands. What a nice, relaxing time after eleven months of planning a big-ass wedding like ours! Still trying to hold on to the magic of our day after the honeymoon, we were looking forward to getting our pictures back. After that, you just have to accept that you had your day.

Settling into our new life together wasn't always easy. Both of us had been single for most of our adult lives, and adjusting to living together was not without its challenges. We had talked about having children, but I wanted to be married for at least a year before we brought that dynamic into our lives, and Tom did not object. I was about forty when the subject resurfaced—this time after having tried unsuccessfully to conceive. We tried various methods to become pregnant, including six months of in vitro fertilization, to no avail. It puzzled me because our family histories didn't provide any explanation; it had to be my age. After we found out that the last round of in vitro didn't work, I had a brief mourning period. Then one night I came home to find Tom sitting in the garage with the TV on, just hanging out. As I joined him, I asked, "We're okay, aren't we? Are you okay with the fact that we are not going to have kids?"

He was more than okay with it. In fact, he said, "Of course! I didn't marry you to have kids." We briefly discussed adoption, but then the subject just kind of faded away. In retrospect, I believe it happened the way it was supposed to. They say God doesn't give you more than you can handle. All I can say to that is, "Thank you."

****

Although Tom and I did not have children of our own, it all worked out as was intended. It left the door open for us to help others when they needed it. There was a period of time when my niece Nicole stayed with us. Tom's brother Gary also stayed with us for a time. And then there is Drae. Drae is the only son and youngest child of Tom's oldest sister, Debbie. Drae frequently came over and spent weekends at our house. He would hang out with the neighbor kids who happened to be his age. At one point, while Debbie was in the hospital, Drae was at our house on a nearly permanent basis. After she returned home, Drae continued to stay with us and consequently went back and forth between our house and his Mom's house frequently.

Tom enrolled Drae in soccer and baseball and was very supportive in his school and park board activities. He became a father figure to Drae, disciplining and teaching him life lessons as any father would. They had quite a bond.

Tom was great with kids! All the neighborhood kids loved him. Tom called out their names as they rode down the alley on their bikes. When our neighbor girl, Olivia, would ride by, he would yell loud and clear dragging her name out as long as he could. She acted like she hated it, but, I think she secretly liked it. He gave the kids nicknames, such as "Big D" for Dylan. Tom was talking to one of our neighbor boys, Lewis, about pickles one day and was telling him how much he would like Zingers, a slightly hot pickle. Once Lewis tried a Zinger, he wanted one just about every time he was over. The kids even came to Tom to put air in their tires or basketballs. And talk about uncle of the year—Tom was very special to the nieces and nephews from both of our families. Ask them; they'll tell you.

****

Traveling was a big part of our lives. Tom was big on taking a winter vacation every year, which was something I never did before we started dating. His favorite place on earth was Negril, Jamaica. I was there three times with him and never quite understood his passion for it. I told him that he must have been Jamaican in all of his previous lives. As I mentioned, we honeymooned on the Cayman Islands and took subsequent trips to Chicago, Costa Rica, Key West, Puerto Vallarta, Nevada, Arizona, and of course, Vegas. Apart from going to Vegas for our dear friends' (Kris and Barry's) wedding, we traveled to Las Vegas in November five years in a row with a group from 92KQRS, a popular classic rock radio station in the Twin Cities. As it happens, 2015 was the last Vegas broadcast for the radio station, they moved the trip to Punta Cana in the Dominican Republic. In its day, the trip to Vegas included a couple thousand listeners following along to attend the broadcast. It was quite the drunk-fest, with people staying up all night as the broadcast began at 3:40 a.m. Las Vegas time. On our first trip out with the KQ bunch in 2002, we were on a flight at 8:00 a.m., and the plane was out of vodka and rum by the time we landed! At the broadcast on the second day, I turned to Tom and said, "We're coming back!" And come back we did, for five years in a row, bringing friends and meeting new ones along the way. We decided not to go on the trip in 2007 to save money. Our plan was to go out for the ten-year anniversary of the Vegas broadcast in 2008, but that was not meant to be. Tom had passed by the time KQ was in Vegas that year. I finally made it back out there for the KQ party with friends and family in 2012. It felt good to be in that environment again with the people from the radio station and friends I had not seen in a while. It was the right time to go back.

There were also the out-of-town trips to our friends' cabins and resorts. They were all great times, but my favorite tradition was our anniversary weekend. Every year around the weekend of our anniversary, we would go to Duluth. We would visit "the scene of the crime" and sometimes head further up the North Shore, visiting Split Rock Lighthouse and Gooseberry Falls. We soon noticed that the weekend of our anniversary trip coincided with the Northshore Inline Marathon—a marathon on inline skates that follows the same route as Grandma's Marathon. It wasn't too long until Tom decided he had to do that too. And for five years in a row, do that he did. I was so proud of him for skating the entire route that I got choked up every time he crossed the finish line. It became part of our tradition.

****

Let me tell you about the farm. Tom, his brother Gary, and their cousins Ted and Warren inherited the farm from their uncle Kenny who passed away in June of 2001. The farm where Tom's mother was born and raised, is located north of Hibbing, Minnesota, a four-hour drive from Minneapolis. As children, the Vinje boys spent summers there with their uncle Kenny. When Kenny passed, it had been years since Tom had visited. Soon after, we were traveling to the farm every chance we got. It had not been a working farm for quite some time, but its 140 acres of beautiful land situated next to a state park make it perfect for four-wheeling, hunting, and bonfires. In 2004 we held a family reunion at the farm in honor of the hundredth anniversary of the homesteading. It is a truly magical place to get away from it all for a few days. When you sit around the bonfire at night, surrounded by complete darkness, you can actually see all the stars and their constellations. Not to mention, the light of the moon is so bright you can walk far into the fields and not get lost. Did I say magical?

****

Party much? Yes we did. We loved to entertain by having our family and friends over for barbeques, fires, and get-togethers on the deck or for a full-blown keg party. When I first met Tom, he already had started a traditional after-Thanksgiving party, which was held every

Saturday after Thanksgiving. It's a tradition I carry on to this day. After we were married, another party evolved, the Fourth of July block party. This one involved several neighbors, blocking off the alley, a band, a moonwalk for the kids, a port-o-potty, and a fire truck. Good times were had by all. One year it rained and we put up a tarp between the garages, and the kids would stand underneath it until the rain collected and dumped all over them. I got caught underneath once too—so much for that hair-do! As we know, life changes, and a few years after Tom's passing, neighbors moved on, interest waned, and the party fizzled out. It's a shame too because it was quite the event!

****

When I met Tom he had two cats, Bud and Pal. We lost Pal to cancer when she was five years old. I've never been a cat person, but Tom and the cats were a package deal. I grew to love them, though; it's hard not to love a little being running around your house. Animals are hilarious. Tom always spoke about getting a dog. I had grown up with and liked dogs, but I didn't think we necessarily needed to have one, especially with our frequent travel. One Sunday evening (it happened to be Halloween of 2004), our friend Karrie came over with a puppy named Boston. It wasn't long before Tom got the itch to get one of his own. He found out where Boston came from, and then it began. He would call me at work every day to talk about getting a puppy from the same litter. Every day for a week he'd call and say, "What about the puppers?"

He finally wore me down. I figured since we weren't going to have children, we might as well get a puppy! He took the following Friday off, and with Drae, our neighbor Larry, and his son Tyler in tow, they made their way to Pequot Lakes (about three hours north of Minneapolis) and came home with Bailey. It was love from the very first minute. Tom took her to various dog parks and walked her around the neighborhood. That lucky girl got to go out for walks twice a day. He would play with her whenever an opportunity presented itself. That opportunity was usually Bailey finding a stick the size of a small tree that she would bring to him to throw for her. They would clean up the stick together by breaking off the branches, and he would hold it up so she could jump for it. Then he would throw it for her to bring back to him. He would also throw tennis balls in the alley with a Chuk-It that allows the ball to go further without having to touch it. He loved her so much, and he was the best daddy any puppers could ever ask for!

Chapter 3

Surgery to ICU

Ginny and I arrived at the University of Minnesota Hospital and found Tom in the emergency room. He was quite agitated and at one point had to be restrained in his bed, a sight that was quite startling and unsettling. Our friend Steve Campbell met us at the hospital. (I had called him as we were leaving Riverside Hospital, updated him on the situation, and asked him to please check on Ginny's car.) Tom's agitation was escalating, and he asked Steve to get him out of the hospital.

The plan was to do an MRI on Tom's brain, but he was completely uncooperative. They tried to do the test twice, and he was extremely belligerent during the process. The technicians had had enough of him, and they refused to try again. (A decision that proved detrimental.) We were then sent to the neurology floor, 6A. When we finally got into a room, the nurse turned on Tom's bed alarm so a staff member would know when Tom got up; this was for his own safety. Again he was put in restraints, this time to prevent him from getting out of the bed. He was still too unstable to stand on his own. He kept repeating that he wanted to go home. It was breaking my heart and scaring me at the same time. Finally, around 11:00 p.m., I realized he wasn't going to settle down until we left. That night would be the last time I saw my husband stand or talk normally.

My plan was to be back at the hospital by 6:00 a.m. for rounds. I needed to be there when the doctors came so I would know what was happening. The next morning, when I walked into Tom's room, he was sleeping. Pretty soon the doctors arrived, and they quickly realized that they could not wake him. They suspected that the tumor was swelling and cutting off the flow of spinal fluid to Tom's brain. They immediately took him down for an MRI and inserted a shunt to restore the flow. After they had determined the location, size, and other critical information about the tumor, they scheduled him for surgery at 5:00 p.m. that night.

There were literally thirty or more of us in the waiting area during the surgery. I am sure we were quite a sight! I know it got a bit loud at times but what can you expect when you have a small army waiting for the outcome of such a surgery?

The surgery ended around 10:30 p.m., and his surgeon, Dr. H (the head of neurology), came out to speak with us. My memory of that moment is a little fuzzy, but the gist of the conversation was that the tumor was near the part of the brain that controls sleep regulation and that they had removed most of it. (That explains why it had been increasingly more difficult to wake Tom up in the morning.) The doctor did not yet know what type of tumor it was or even if it was cancerous. He also did not know if or how Tom would be affected physically from the surgery. No further information would be available until he woke up. The doctor also informed us that Tom would have a drainage tube from the site of the incision on his head. We were not permitted to see Tom until the morning, so we all headed home to try and get some sleep.

The next day just broke my heart. There was my beautiful husband in the intensive care unit, lying in a hospital bed with tubes coming out of his body. He looked around the room at us, looked down at himself, and then started to cry. I thought someone had ripped my heart in two. I just wanted to stop everything and make it all go away for him. It was so painful. What was also painful was the fact that he had pretty much lost the use of his right side. Although he still had feeling, the muscles were extremely weak. His speech had also been affected. Sometimes when he spoke it was unintelligible; other times it was fine. Within an hour, he started doing different things with his left hand, like trying to unbuckle my belt! Nice try, my love! The next day he held my hand for over half an hour and wouldn't let go. I told him that the guys were at our house working on the basement bathroom so he wouldn't have to do the work himself. His reply was, "What the fuck!" Yes, a few colorful words escaped his lips during this time. Why the hell not!

The next week had its ups and downs. On the down side, a few days after the doctor removed one of the catheters that drained fluid from the tumor site, the fluid buildup reoccurred, and he was not responding as well as he had been in the previous days. Another catheter had to be inserted. In addition, an internal shunt was also inserted to assist in the drainage. This procedure did allow him to be transferred out of ICU to a regular room, where he could move forward with eating, rehab, and treatment.

The speech, physical, and occupational therapists had been visiting Tom since a week after the initial surgery. The speech therapist had been most impressed with his speech, and that was a hopeful sign for all of us. The physical and occupational therapists came in to assess Tom to see where he was at physically. The best they were able to do at this time was to get him to perform very minimal tasks.

On the up side, we put Tom's glasses on him, and he was able to watch the Minnesota Twins' home opener. Baseball was his favorite sport, and the Twins were his favorite team. Tom was also able to give a thumbs-up as well as a good squeeze with his right hand when the nurse prompted him to. The problem was that he was unwilling to do that for the doctors. He just laughed at them. That's my honey.

On Thursday, April 3, 2008, after more than two weeks in the ICU, Tom was finally moved to a regular room in unit 6A. We were hopeful, taking another step in the process. He had swallow testing on deck in order to determine when he could start eating solid food again and have his feeding tube removed. That would be nice.

Guest Book Entries

Written March 24, 2008, 11:06 a.m.

Tommy,

My dearest cousin, you are so special to me. My heart goes out to you. I wish you the very best. I am looking forward to visiting when you are feeling better. You are in my thoughts and prayers. I have always thought it was so cool that when we were kids, people thought we looked so much alike. Take care.

Much Love,

Cheri Lagerquist

Written March 24, 2008 4:59 p.m.

Hello, Tom,

Sorry to hear about you being in the hospital. You are such a wonderful nice person. And I see you are getting better and that it sounds like you're heading in the right direction. I will be seeing you soon; my prayers are with you and your family. PS: Chrissie, keep your head up also. It will get greater later.

Love and Peace,

Rese Patton

Written March 24, 2008 8:15 p.m.

Hi, Tommy,

Cheri and I went to Linda's house for Easter. You were in our thoughts and prayers. I understand that you are doing much better. We're so glad to hear that. You are a strong person. I love you very much. I remember the day that you stopped in IKEA when I was a greeter. It was great that you gave me a hug because I really felt special being your cousin. You and Chrissie always make me feel part of your family.

Take care.

Love,

Susan L.

Written March 25, 2008, 4:14 p.m.

Hey, Tom,

I wanted to stop by and say hello! I hope everything is going better for you. I'm happy to say that I have been hearing nothing but good news lately. I pray for you and the family. You are one of the most upbeat, fun, and *hilarious* people in the family, and everyone loves it. We have faith in you and know in our hearts everything will be okay. Get well soon.

Love,

Cristina Melzer

Written March 26, 2008, 11:31 a.m.

Hi, Tom,

We have never met … I work with your sister, Judy. I want you to know you are a loved man. Your family thinks the world of you, which says a lot about a man's character. You and your family are in my prayers. Get better soon … all my best!

Lots of Love,

Bonnie Versboncoeur

Written March 27, 2008 12:46 p.m.

Tom,

Every day you're making huge progress! We can't wait to have you back at home. It just isn't the same without you harassing the neighbors!

We love you and miss you!

Karrie, Ian, and Tyler

Written March 28, 2008, 3:58 p.m.

Tommy, Tommy, Tommy,

Thank you for coming into my sister's life and for accepting us as part of your family. Thank you also for fighting the fight you have in front of you so I don't have to be so mushy anymore! Just to make it quite clear … I love you, dammit!

Your *real* favorite sister-in-law,

Beth Timm

Written March 28, 2008, 6:10 p.m.

Tom (and Chris),

Beth has been e-mailing me about your situation with updates … I have been in shock ever since she let me know. My heart goes out to you, and there are many prayers coming your way. You have been in my thoughts ever since Beth told me the news. Please know there are *many* people praying for you. Prayer is a very powerful thing! I will continue to send prayers your way. Knowing who you are, I know you will fight your way through all of this.

Thinking of you in this difficult time,

Kris K.

Written March 30, 2008, 10:28 a.m.

Hey, Tom and Chrissie,

I am so very sorry that you two are going through this right now—we all are. I don't have any words to tell you that are going to make your fight any easier. But I can tell you that you are *not* fighting this battle alone! We are all here to help you through this any way we can. Please remember that, and know that we are all praying for you ... *Miracles* do happen, and I choose to believe that there is one in this as well. Stay positive; attitude is everything ... and when the time comes where you feel a little down, lean on us—the ones who love you *both*! We are here for both of you!

We love you both so much!

Steph Wettstaedt

Written April 1, 2008, 9:13 a.m.

Hey, Tom! (That was from Tyler C—you know how he would yell at you from across the alley!)

So how 'bout them Twins! Sorry we didn't make it to watch the game with you last night—but we are glad that you were able to watch it. Sounds like things are gettin' better and better. Keep it up!

All the best,

Karrie, Ian, and Tyler

Written April 1, 2008, 10:06 p.m.

Hello, Tom-a-seena,

Let me start off by saying what a beautiful bald head you have, my friend. Ahh, who needs hair anyway? Wait a minute, I know I do. Thanks to Britney Spears, I will never shave my head. I would like to get all sappy on you, but that's not going to happen. I know once you read this you will appreciate my humor as I appreciate yours. Anyway, I know you like to lay around all day and everything, but for God's sake, man, this is a little extreme. I can't wait till you pull out of this little setback so we can make some more wacky memories. I know you don't need to know you are loved and appreciated because we are all falling over each other in the hospital trying to get to you "Mr. Popular." So while you are here, I wish you sweet dreams during your life vacation and a speedy recovery d---it. I love ya.

Theresa Betlach

Written April 1, 2008, 10:12 p.m.

Hey, Tom! This is your favorite person ever ... Catey, of course! I miss my bald-headed uncle! Whose head am I gonna make fun of now? I'll find someone. Well I can't wait till you get better and I get to see you again! I love you lots!

Love,

Catey Kushinski

Written April 2, 2008, 9:41 a.m.

Hey, Tom,

Just so you know, I have a cold, so I won't be able
to visit until it's gone. Would sure hate to pass it on
to you or Chrissie! You guys really need each other
right now, and the last thing you need right now is a
cold! So I'll keep my distance until it's gone, which
really sucks! I look forward to coming to see you and
seeing the progress you make every day, so this is
going to be hard for me. I'll just have to bug Chrissie
for updates. :) Anyway, I love you lots. See you soon.

Love,

Judy (your favorite sister)

About a week after Tom's surgery, we had "the meeting." Yeah,
that meeting sucked. Never in my life could I have fathomed I
would be part of such a meeting. We were told that Tom's tumor
was cancerous. It was a glioblastoma, the worst of the worst. In
addition, Tom's tumor was one of the most aggressive the doctors
had encountered. We were told that people with this diagnosis had
a life expectancy of no more than five years. What! Are you freaking
kidding me? Again, are you talking to me?

The next topic of discussion was treatment. They informed us that
whether the tumor was cancerous or not, they would still have to
treat it. We were told that after the incision on Tom's head healed,
he would start radiation. Following the radiation treatments, and
if the results were dramatic in nature, they would administer the
chemo pill. This is the standard protocol for this type of tumor. Tom
would be fitted for a radiation mask, and the radiation would be
administered to his head and spinal column (to target the cancer
cells in his spinal fluid) for ten minutes a day, Monday through

Friday, for six weeks. The doctors wanted to begin the radiation as soon as possible due to the weakness on his right side. Their goal was to shrink the tumor as much, and as quickly as possible, in the hopes to have the best chance at regaining mobility and use of the weak side. We were also informed that radiation was the only reasonable hope for change. What a helluva way to phrase it! Then, depending on how Tom recovered, there would be rehabilitation for approximately six weeks.

After the meeting, Ginny said to me, "Well, at least you had nine good years." I did not want to hear that. I couldn't accept that, and I didn't. There had to be something we could do. There had to be more. I was not going to sit there and let them tell me what was going to happen. I just couldn't. This is my husband we were talking about, the person I was sharing my life with, the love of my life, my every day! How could this be happening? How could our lives be forever altered? Why couldn't we go back to a time and place when this was not a reality? Why, indeed.

Chapter 4

6A—the Journey Continues

Now that Tom was out of ICU, the real progress could start. Below is my journal entry from the CaringBridge from Tom's first full day in 6A.

Friday, April 4, 2008 6:28 a.m., CDT—
Chrissie's journal entry

Happy Friday, everyone,

Tom had a tiring day yesterday. Physical therapy had him standing up next to the bed for several minutes. He was extremely alert and laughing with the staff. He wasn't so alert later in the day by the time people started visiting. I suspect that's how his days will go as they work him during the day. (I did give him the fabulous SpongeBob that was signed by his friends at work.) He spent about ten minutes reading the messages people wrote to him, and when I left last night, SpongeBob was catching a few ZZZZs in bed with Tommy. Thank you, guys. That was too cool for words!

As we found out yesterday, his right leg is doing pretty well; it appears that his right arm is the weakest spot. Hopefully rehab will take care of that. He is a strong man. We have a consultation with the radiation team today, so I will keep you updated on that subject.

That's all for now ... Until tomorrow.

XOXOXO

Chrissie

Guest Book Entries

Written April 4, 2008 7:52 a.m.

Tom and Chrissie,

Much love and many, many prayers are heavenward for you both. God is watching over you.

I love you,

Patty Betlach Russell

Written April 4, 2008 7:57 a.m.

Tom and Chrissie,

I sure miss seeing you both on a daily basis; you have such shining personalities that made each day better. It sounds like every day is getting better for you, Tom, so keep reaching forward. My daughter and I have you in our prayers. Believe me, a two-year-old's prayers are super-powerful. :) God bless.

Tammy Anderson

Written April 4, 2008 8:57 p.m.

Dearest Tom,

Wow … I was so disheartened by the news that Beth told me about your condition. It sounds like there has been a lot going on and that there is progress, so I am so happy to hear about this. This is a tough battle, and knowing the strength you have, I think you will duke this one out and win! You have a wonderful wife who loves you immensely, and I'm sure that makes the battle worth it even more. We are sending many prayers your way, and our thoughts are with you every day. Keep up the good fight.

All our love,

Sarah and Scott

In an effort for you to experience the energy and emotion as it was happening, I am going to let my journal entries and the guest book entries do the talking.

Saturday, April 5, 2008 7:16 a.m., CDT—
Chrissie's Journal Entry

Hello,

Well, yesterday was a long day. You wait four hours for the doctors to come talk to you for four minutes. Anyway, it sounds like Tom may start radiation as early as Tuesday of next week. His surgeon, Dr. H, is also working on the bridge between the hospital and rehab that could happen as early as next week. The waiting game continues.

Tom is *very* tired. He slept a good part of the day yesterday and is not yet awake enough to perform the swallow testing that will allow him to eat food again. I asked about this, and they said that this is not uncommon. Dr. R said that his brain is injured, and it takes longer for it to bounce back (from the surgery on Tuesday). He is not talking like he was before they put the shunt in on Tuesday. Hopefully all the deep sleep will help him heal fast, and he will surpass what he was doing just a few days ago. They keep saying this recovery is going to take a *long* time and that it does not just progress. There will be peaks and valleys. It is hard to take when you are just waiting to see new improvements every day and there aren't any. You just want him to get better so badly, to be the Tommy we all know and love. Then you have to remember the one word they keep saying … *time.* I guess it's something we have to learn to deal with no matter how much it sucks.

Until tomorrow, take care, and much love to you all.

Chrissie

Guest Book Entries

Written April 5, 2008 10:57 a.m.

Thomas,

I'm sorry to hear about your new struggle. You have my support in any way you need. I cherish the friendship we have developed over the years. You made me feel like one of the buds ... and for that I thank you. I have a lot of respect for you as a man. I know you'll pull through this. You have a strong will and love for life. My heart goes out to you and Chrissie (and Bailey) for the struggle you have to endure.

Much love,

Matthew Smallman

Written April 5, 2008, 11:06 a.m.

Hi, Tom and Chrissie,

We are so sorry for the crap you have to deal with right now. You are in our thoughts and prayers for a speedy and complete recovery.

With best wishes,

Victor, Dianne, Luisa, and Lydia

Your neighbors

Written April 5, 2008, 11:07 a.m.

Uncle Tom,

This is Aaron, your coolest great-nephew. It was funny when you made chicken wings and you said a bad word. Hope you get better soon. That's all ...

Love,

Aaron

Written April 5, 2008, 2:19 p.m.

Tom,

I just wanted to let you and Chrissie know that you are in our thoughts and prayers. We are waiting to see you back in the alley for our daily drive-by wave sooner, rather than later! Keep up the strength and determination!

Your neighbors,

Heather and Asher

Written April 5, 2008, 8:43 p.m.

Hey, Tom!

Ever since we learned of your illness, you've been in our thoughts and prayers. I can imagine the days ahead will seem long. Sounds like there have been triumphs each day—make sure to celebrate each one. Stay strong, Tom (and you too, Chrissie)!

Love,

Jeanne Galle Franklin

Sunday, April 6, 2008 8:21 a.m., CDT— Chrissie's Journal Entry

Good morning,

Tom was still sleepy yesterday, but he was keenly aware of what was going on around him. He was lying in bed with his eyes closed (he did open them occasionally) just listening. Krissy and Barry came to see him yesterday, and as Barry started talking about cleaning up dog poop and the fact that Krissy wouldn't know what that was all about, Tom started cracking up (with his eyes closed). Naturally then there were conversations about sweat and puke, etc. Tom was cracking up at all of it. Karrie came up for a while, and as usual, he was snoozing. Later, after everyone left, Tom was listening to his roommate and his wife and just cracking up at their conversations. That was dang funny!

The doctor came in yesterday and took some stitches out of his head, and as he was leaving, he told Tom that he was doing well and to keep fighting. Tom said, "Yep!" and the doctor was most pleased. That's always nice.

Anyway, that is about it for now. I suspect that this next week is going to bring some big changes, and I will keep you posted.

Have a great Sunday!

Love,

Chrissie

Guest Book Entries

Written April 6, 2008, 12:55 p.m.

Hi, Tom and Chrissie,

I just wanted to say to stay strong and that I have been praying for you every day. I also wanted to let you know that I plan on visiting again sometime this week. It was great to hear you laugh last time I was there. Keep up with the humor!

Love,

Katie Anderson

Monday, April 7, 2008, 6:20 a.m., CDT— Chrissie's Journal Entry

Morning, all,

Good news—Tommy is becoming more alert every day. He was laughing with his visitors yesterday with his eyes open. They had him sitting in the hospital chair a couple of times; of course he was pulling at the Velcro strap. He can't leave that stuff alone. He is always undoing and pulling at things. The nurses don't care for that so much.

More good news—he is starting to say people's names now. Last week when his mom was leaving he said, "Bye, Mom," and then yesterday when his brother Gary walked in, he said, "Brohamski." (Vinje-talk for brother, dontcha know.) So, woo-hoo, things are progressing. Hopefully tomorrow I will have more fun stuff to tell ya!

Much Love,

Chrissie

Guest Book Entries

Written April 7, 2008, 9:16 a.m.

Tom,

We are not a sappy couple, so I will just get this out of the way ... we love you and are praying for you. Be strong! Now for the real message ... kick this cancer's a** so we can get back to partying! Vegas, baby!

Git 'er done!

Love,

Renee and Brandon Olson

Written April 7, 2008, 11:24 a.m.

Good to hear you're moving ahead! With your shining, positive personalities, you'll have this thing on the run in no time and we can get back to more important things like partying at Timbo's! Look forward to seeing you soon!

You're in our prayers.

Tim Hanley

Written April 7, 2008, 10:25 a.m.

It was great to see everyone at the hospital yesterday. The support Tom is receiving is indescribable. I hope he can feel the love (he so … loves mushy). He will be shaking his head at me for that one! Oh well!

I wish we could visit more, but at least now that I have the CaringBridge logon, I can at least check in and find out what's going on, which is great.

Chrissie, you take good care of him for us and stay positive.

Love you both,

Kim and Kent Peterson

Written April 7, 2008, 3:47 p.m.

Hi, Tom and Chrissie!

I am so glad you are getting better every day! The power of positive thinking, strength, and positive prayers *works*!

I have been taking Bailey Babee to the park with us, and *wow*, that girl has energy! I do throw the stick, throw the stick, throw the stick, and sometimes Whitney wants the stick! Ha-ha!

Keep on truckin' and getting better. I have complete faith in you, Tom, and in Chrissie to get through this and come home to play!

Candace McCown

Wednesday, April 9, 2008 8:00 a.m., CDT—
Chrissie's Journal Entry

Morning everyone,

Sorry I missed yesterday, but I was at the hospital all day as they wanted me there when they took Tom down to radiology to get him set up for radiation. As it turned out, they could not do what they needed to do because he was too sleepy. They were worried about him falling off of the bed, as it were. So they will be bringing him down today at 1:00 to try again.

As it stands right now, he is not able to begin the chemo pill because he is still on the feeding tube. Everything is pretty much on hold waiting for him to become more alert. I asked the doctors about this last night, and they said that medically, everything is fine. All his vitals are normal, he has not run a fever at all, and they did another CT scan on Sunday morning to make sure his spinal fluid was draining properly. All is okay. The doctor said that he has been through a lot and the fact that he does wake up and is alert is good. It would be a problem if he wasn't waking up at all. I might be just freaking out, but I wanted to hear them say that all was fine.

It looks like he may still be moved to rehab this week. They wanted to do it yesterday, but they were not able to because the nurses had him wearing a mitt so he would leave his feeding tube alone. Rehab considers that to be a restraint, and they would not take him. He has not worn the mitt since noon yesterday, and he has not messed with the tube. Sweet. Once he gets to rehab, I am going to bring Bailey up to see him. When I mentioned that to him the other night, he nodded his head. It will be good for both of them to see each other. Maybe when it gets warmer he can throw the stick for her on the grounds of the rehab center. I've got it all planned out!

I just have to say, once again, I am so touched by all of the cards, visits, guestbook entries, well wishes, and positive energy from everyone. Words do not describe the feeling. All of you are so awesome. It is unbelievable. I'm sure when he is able; Tom will tell you the same. You guys are the best!

Love,

Chrissie

Guest Book Entries

Written April 9, 2008, 6:56 a.m.

I am so happy to read about the progress these last few days. I think about him all the time and love hearing about how he is laughing … just like Tom.

Take care of yourself, Chrissie, and we will be visiting Tom again soon.

Love,

Kira Martin

Written April 9, 2008, 9:04 a.m.

Hi, Tom and Chrissie!

It is great to hear of your progress, Tom. It sounds like you are doing a great job getting stronger and giving the doctors a hard time! Thanks for all of your updates, Chrissie. It is important for all of us at work to read about Tommy. We miss you at the store, Tom!

Julie Warrick

Written April 9, 2008, 1:03 p.m.

Hello, Tom,

Is it all right to scream and say F&%# (Sorry, Virginia) when you write a letter and lost all you wrote? LOL, anyway I was very happy and pleased to see that you have some progress in your rehabilitation process, and it was good to see you and your wife. And I can see no matter what, you have the same personality and strong will about you. That really shows progress in itself, and all the family and friend support will really help with your strength and recovery process. I remember all those great parties you have and miss going to them. Thank you for those good times. You and your family have been a very important part in my life. Thank you very much for those good times. My thoughts and prayers are always with you and your families.

Love and peace always,

Rese Patton

Thursday, April 10, 2008, 7:29 a.m., CDT— Chrissie's Journal Entry

Good morning,

Thanks for tuning in for another installment of the "Tommy Update." Tom did not go to radiation yesterday because Dr. H came in around 1:00 p.m. to check to see if he was awake. He was not, so he ordered some tests just to make sure there were no infections and that everything is as it should be medically. As of 7:00 last night when I left, some of the tests had come back and all was okay. They were still waiting for the results of the fluid they tapped from his shunt. I will find out about that today. If all is fine, the plan is to move him to the rehab center today at 11:00 a.m. I do not have word on when the next radiation appointment is.

He was awake for a bit (mainly with his eyes shut again). He was chuckling and laughing, *and* he actually gave Lisa E. a hug. Cripes, he hasn't even hugged me yet! How does she rate? I do know she was most proud of herself! That's okay; I won't take it too personally ... yet. We'll see how things unfold in the coming weeks.

Anyway, if they move Tommy today, I will update to let you know. In the meantime, I need to find out how to find him once he gets over there! Always a new challenge!

Love to all,

Chrissie

Guest Book Entries

Written April 10, 2008, 12:52 a.m.

Tom and Chrissie, we want you to know that Karen, Lydia, and I are praying for you every day. We serve an awesome God that answers prayers. It is great to hear of your progress. Please do not hesitate in letting us know how we can help you.

God bless,

John and Karen

Written April 10, 2008, 1:16 p.m.

Hey, just wanted to let you know we had our luncheon for Tom today, and I ate his burger. I needed to tell you to avoid the guilt! Were glad to hear he's laughing even with his eyes closed, I'm sure he'll be a hit over at rehab! Thanks for the update. Rock on!

Tim Hanley

Written April 10, 2008, 8:21 p.m.

Tom and Chrissie, sorry to hear what's happening to you both at this time. Jim is keeping me updated while selling tickets and raising money. You have a lot of good friends pushing for you, waiting to hear the laughs again. Take care and will chat again.

DeAnn

Friday, April 11, 2008, 8:00 a.m., CDT— Chrissie's Journal Entry

Hello,

Well, yesterday Tom was supposed to be moved to rehab. He was not, but it sounds like it may really happen today. On the other side of the coin, we have his sleepiness. Finally, they may have it figured out. I have been telling them for almost a week that he has not been as alert as he was in ICU. The last couple of days he has been even sleepier. He did not wake up for me at all yesterday. The results of the testing from Wednesday were good. As far as the tapping of the spinal fluid from the shunt, they could not get enough to test, which means that it is draining and working properly. So, they did another

CT scan yesterday and found that the left side of his brain (where the surgery was) is very swollen. They started him on steroids again to reduce the swelling in the hope that he will "perk up," in the words of Dr. R. I do know that he was on steroids in the ICU and he was way more awake then. What I don't know is when and why he stopped getting the steroids. I need to find that out.

I found out from his wonderful nurse, Elizabeth that they gave Tom a "loading dose" of steroids. A loading dose is a higher dose to kick it in the pants and get it moving. That dose was 10 mg, and going forward he will be getting 2 mg three times a day to keep it going. Please pray real hard that this will pull him out of it. We need to move on and get him back!

I will leave you with the words that Dr. R. has said to me a couple of times now. The road to recovery from brain surgery is up and down and up and down for a long time, and the most important thing to remember is this: *the bad things happen fast, and the good things take time.*

Last night he told me to *always* remember that. Those are words he got from medical school.

Until tomorrow, keep the thoughts and prayers coming; we really need them now.

Thank you so much,

XOXOXO

Chrissie

Saturday, April 12, 2008, 6:01 p.m., CDT— Chrissie's Journal Entry

Hi, everyone,

They just took Tom in to remove the feeding tube from his nose and put one in his stomach. They did this so he can move over to rehab. It will also be more comfortable for him. They are doing this just in time too, because his spring allergies have started and with all of that going on it could get pretty gnarly! Grody to the max! I let the doctors know that he takes Allegra 180 for his allergies, so they started him on that last night. He will be feeling better soon.

Last night the radiology docs came in to check on him, and I told them about the swelling on the left side of his brain. Dr. Lee checked the dosage of the steroids they are giving him and told them to kick it up a bit, which they did today. Sweet! I want my honey back!

The physical therapists had him sitting up on the edge of his bed for the last couple of days. He does really well for them. I tell them to wake his butt up, but of course, it tires him out and he sleeps afterward. Can't win for losing, I tell ya!

It sounds like the benefit for next Sunday is really pulling together. It will be a *really* amazing day. I am just so amazed, elated, touched, astounded, and truly grateful to everyone for putting this together as quickly as they have. Everyone has been working so hard. Tom and I are truly blessed to have so many people around us who care about us like you do, and for that I thank you. Who could ever ask for anything more in life? Truly. Words could never express the emotions going on inside of me. I wish you all could know.

Much love,

Chrissie

Saturday, April 12, 2008, 6:18 p.m., CDT—Chrissie's Journal Entry

Thank you, Jaguar Landrover Mpls!

I want to take this moment to thank everyone for their kind donations of money and vacation days for Tom. We knew we loved you guys! This has touched me so much that I tear up every time I think about it. It just gives me chills. You guys rock! I can't wait to tell Tom about it, and there is *no* doubt he will feel the same.

Love to all!

Chrissie

Guest Book Entries

Written April 12, 2008, 7:53 p.m.

Tommy, Chrissie and the Vinje family,

I just wanted to let you all know that we've been thinking of you. I've been reading your wonderful updates on Tommy's condition, Chrissie. Your positive attitude is great. Keep hanging in there, all of you.

Oh, and my dad says "ditto."

Teri V.

Monday, April 14, 2008, 7:29 a.m., CDT— Chrissie's Journal Entry

Good morning,

Well, they were not able to put the feeding tube in his stomach because his stomach would not drop below his rib cage, so they could not get to it. (They are saying he has a hiatal hernia.) So, they will have to do it surgically today. I *really* wish he didn't have to go under again, but we have to move on from this phase.

As of yesterday Tommy was waking up more. He had his eyes open more and was just overall awake even when his eyes were shut. I know he was well aware of what was going on because when I was talking to John and Jenny Ruoho yesterday about the swelling in his brain, he started crying. I had told him when I first got there about the luncheon they had for him at work and he shook his head like he couldn't believe it, but when I told John and Jenny about it, he started crying. I told you he would feel the same as I do! If I had known that Ms. Jodi H. was going to visit yesterday, I would have let her tell him!

Just to let you know how alert he was, I found the Twins game on TV and put his glasses on him; damned if he wasn't checking out the game! Too bad we came in at the fifth inning. I need to get a Twins schedule so I know what time the games are!

Until tomorrow, take care!

Love,

Chrissie

Guest Book Entries

Written April 14, 2008, 10:04 a.m.

I am so glad to hear he was interested in the game. That reminds us that even though he isn't able to fully communicate with us, Tommy is still there!

Chrissie, we know this is very difficult for you and you want him to move on to the next phase. Just stay strong; he will get there.

Love you both!

Karrie Cable

Written April 14, 2008, 1:29 p.m.

Uncle Tom and Auntie Chrissie

My *godfather*, I'm going to make you an offer you cannot refuse … Get better soon or you'll definitely feel the wrath of your goddaughter! Tom, you have always been very special to me, ever since I can remember. And adding Chrissie into the Vinje family has truly been one of the biggest blessings in my life! I really can't express how I feel about the two of you other than *I love you* both more than you'll ever know! I, my children, my Bible study group, and my pastor are all praying for you on a daily basis! Keep your spirits high and know that you have a whole bunch of friends and family that are here to support you both with anything you could possibly need. I've already told Auntie Chrissie the funny stories about Bailey Cuz, and the story about Uncle Gar and the fabulous nickname "Lizardbreath." I'll tell you in detail when I come to visit! Remember *"We are the Vinjes, the **mighty, mighty** Vinjes!"* We will get through this. God bless the both of you for being in my life!

Elizabeth AKA Lizardbreath

Tuesday, April 15, 2008, 7:27 a.m., CDT— Chrissie's Journal Entry

Greetings,

Tom had the feeding tube removed from his nose yesterday and placed in his stomach. This should work a little better for him. I found out that once you put a tube in the stomach, you have to keep it in for six weeks even if it is not being used. I guess the stomach forms a seal around the tube (it takes six weeks), and if you were to pull it out before that time, there is a risk of infection. It makes sense. I was expecting him to be really sleepy last night after the procedure, but he wasn't. Woo-hoo! We got to joke and laugh with him.

My guess is that he will be moved to rehab at the earliest on Wednesday. I know they are eager to get him over there. We also have to deal with the treatment portion. Elizabeth (Tom's nurse) lit a fire under the surgeons yesterday to move forward with his treatment, which is our next step now. Keep your fingers crossed and your prayers flowing.

Love to all,

Chrissie

Guest Book Entries

Written April 15, 2008, 9:21 a.m.

Yeah … good to hear. I know he was pretty much done with that tube in his nose, and if they didn't remove it, he was going to. Keep up the good work! I'm glad the nurse is stepping up and telling them what he needs. Since she's there every day, they should listen to her.

Hope to see everyone at the benefit on Sunday at Whiskey Junction!

Love,

Kim Peterson

Written April 16, 2008, 5:54 p.m.

Dear Chrissie,

We just heard the news. Our prayers are with you and your family. We all know that Tom is going to kick this tumor's ass and be better soon!

We'll make sure to toss a few balls to Bailey!

Irene and Dave Peterson

Written April 17, 2008, 6:40 a.m.

Chrissie and Tom,

This is wonderful news! And just from my own experience, nurses rock! It sounds like Tom has some amazing ones!

My kids just bought some raffle tickets with their own money last night, and we are *all* so looking forward to Sunday!

Love to you both!

Kira and Dave Martin

Friday, April 18, 2008, 5:51 p.m., CDT— Chrissie's Journal Entry

Okay, we just received some not-so-good news. It seems that the reason for Tom's growing sleepiness and lack of alertness is because the tumor has grown in between the places where the spinal fluid isn't. They found this with the MRI that was done. Tom did receive his first treatment of radiation today, but next week when it commences, they will be doing the whole brain and not just the tumor site as was originally planned.

In the meantime, they will be doing a spinal tap to see if there are tumor cells present. Everything, at this point, hinges on how he takes to the radiation. If they are able to get this under control, he will be able to still have chemo. If not, there is no point in attempting chemo.

What we need from you right now is lots and lots of prayers and positive energy. Please pray that Tom's brain accepts the radiation treatment and shrinks that damn tumor into nothingness. Pray also that there are no tumor cells present in his spinal fluid. Beyond that please pray for all good things for Tom and that he comes through this to the best of his ability. Please pray.

Thank you so very much.

Love to all,

Chrissie

Guest Book Entries

Written April 19, 2008, 10:08 a.m.

Chrissie:

Keep the faith, Chrissie! We all think of you every day. Tom has a strong desire to get well and is doing everything he can to get healthy. We love you and are praying for you each and every day. Stay strong.

Lynn and David Robson

Written April 19, 2008, 10:11 a.m.

Dear Uncle Thomas Vinje,

What in the world do you think you were doing getting into a car crash like that! You had me worried sick! Just to let you know if you haven't figured out who this is, it is your one and only little niece, M'Kenzie Alizabeth Vinje!

Man this is so messed up. You are my only Uncle Tom left in this world because my other Uncle Tom just died in February 6, 2008, along with my great-grandmother. That uncle who just died was my great-uncle too, and they were brother and sister.

Well I can't wait until this school year is over so then I can come and see you more often and so I can sleep in too.

Anyway I'm going to wrap this up here by ending it with get better and *I love you*!

Love yours truly and yo little niece, the daughter Lizardbreath,

M'Kenzie Vinje-Smallman

Written April 19, 2008, 10:23 a.m.

Chrissie, Here's the good news! If what you need are lots and lots of prayers and positive energy, then there should be plenty of both this weekend surrounding the benefit in Tom's honor. So stay strong! Keep your feet on the ground, but let your spirits fly high! Let's keep this weekend's prayers and positive energy soaring on! Hope to see you. Keep the faith!

Tim Hanley

Written April 19, 2008, 2:10 p.m.

Tom,

My family and I are praying for your recovery and healing. May God bring you the strength, grace, and peace you need during the difficult journey. Keep fighting!

God Bless,

Melinda

(Friend of Tammy Anderson)

Written April 19, 2008, 2:22 p.m.

Tom and Chrissie,

The following gives me hope that we are not invincible! You are both in my thoughts and prayers, and I look forward to Sunday.

Just a little something I wanted to share with you, for those times when you don't feel quite like yourself and everything seems crazy out of control (and experience tells me you have some of that ahead of you).

(Inserted here was a writing entitled, "What Cancer Cannot Do.")

The road to recovery can be long, but your sense of humor, Tom, will make it a brief journey. Keep up that great laughter you've always had that makes me find you in the most amazing places.

The best to you both! You will overcome!

Lory Ruggles

Written April 19, 2008, 3:42 p.m.

Chrissie and Tom,

We are praying for you! Hang in there and be strong. A little attitude goes a long way toward fighting these kinds of things, and if anyone has attitude it is you guys!

Can't wait to see you,

Renee and Brandon Olson

Monday, April 21, 2008, 8:59 a.m., CDT— Chrissie's Journal Entry

Holy Hannah!

Yesterday was as phenomenal as I knew it would be! Everybody worked their tails off to pull this together, and it could not have been more perfect. Thank you to everyone from the bottom of my heart. Tom and I are truly blessed to have all of you in our lives. I really feel like these words do not justify how I really feel inside about everyone involved in the planning and execution of Tommy's benefit and to everyone who came! I think I am as speechless as I was on stage for cripes sake! Mikey Anderson called me this morning, and I think he nailed it. He said, "What a class act that was, just phenomenal!" I agree 100 percent, truly amazing. Thank you, thank you, and thank you!

I have spoken with the hospital a few times this morning, and they should be done with the spinal tap by now. This will tell us if there are any tumor cells in his spinal fluid. They did not see anything on the MRI they did on his spine on Friday, which is why this procedure was necessary. We will know the results probably tomorrow. He will then be going to radiation. My poor honey. I wish I could make it all stop and he would be fine.

Also, Tommy is moving to rehab today at eleven o'clock. Once I go there and figure out where he is, I will post it here. I do know that he will be on the third floor for a couple of days, and then the whole rehab department is moving to the fourth floor on Tuesday and Wednesday. More info to follow …

Once again, thank you everyone for a truly amazing day. I can't wait to see the pictures and footage taken by our friend Shane and the pictures taken by our friend John Ruoho. And, I especially can't wait for Tommy to see it all!

Much love to all,

Chrissie

Guest Book Entries

Written April 21, 2008, 8:18 a.m.

Tom and Chrissie,

I cannot believe yesterday! (But really it is no surprise!) Tom … it was soo amazing how many people showed up to support and show their love for the two of you. And the organization and hours and dedication it took to pull all of that together! Dave and I are in absolute awe of it all …

What a huge success!

Love,

Kira and Dave Martin

Honored neighbors

Written April 22, 2008, 8:59 a.m.

Hi, Chrissie and Tom,

Awesome benefit! Wow! What a turnout and excellent, positive energy for you both! Glad to be a part of it!

A few of us at the dog park want to bring Bailey to visit Tom. I know we had spoken, Chrissie, and you were worried about having to bring Bailey back home if they would not let her in. We could meet you at the hospital with Bailey and bring her back if she can't visit. That way might work. Just let me know and we will do it!

Candace McCown

Written April 22, 2008, 11:10 a.m.

I just wanted to take a few moments to *thank* everyone on behalf of the Vinjes to everyone who attended the benefit. All the support was just awesome! When we were on the stage looking at all of you, it was so overwhelming. It brought tears to my eyes to see so many people who support my brother in his time of need. I know with all the energy and prayers you all send his way he feels it, and it makes him stronger. So thank you again from the bottom of my heart!

Judy Vinje

Chapter 5

Transitional Care Unit—Rehab

**Tuesday, April 22, 2008, 8:59 a.m., CDT—
Chrissie's Journal Entry**

Morning, all,

First of all, Tom was moved to the transitional care unit (TCU) at Fairview Riverside yesterday morning. Currently he is in room 321. That will change tomorrow when the whole unit moves to the fourth floor. I will let you know his room number when I find out.

We had a meeting with the doctors yesterday about the growth of the tumor and the treatment going forward. Due to the early regrowth of the tumor, it is necessary to radiate Tom's whole brain. They are anticipating that the cancer cells have spread to the spinal fluid, but we will know for sure hopefully on Wednesday. If they are, they will also be radiating his spine. Given the aggressiveness of the tumor at this point, we have elected to be more aggressive with his radiation. What this will entail is radiation for three weeks instead of six. While they say this may cause brain damage years down the road, it was the only course of action that would give Tom a chance. We could have: A) done nothing (yeah, right); B) kept with the current radiation schedule, or C) be more aggressive with the radiation. The choice was clear to all of us. It would be one thing if he was not there at all, *but* he is. He is so there. The doctors have a hard time with that because they don't see it.

Yesterday I was telling Tom about the benefit, and when I told him about all the people, he shook his head. Then, when I told him about the money that was raised, his lifted his eyebrows up as if to say, "What now?" I think a great testament to who Tom is that four of his nurses were at the benefit on Sunday. They have only known him in his current state, but they think he is pretty special. Tell me that it is not our job to fight for him right now! He would fight for us. I already told him that we have a long road ahead and we will do it together. I am certain you all would agree.

Thanks again for all your love, support, prayers, and positive thoughts. It helps to know everyone out there is thinking of us and pulling for us.

Love to all,

Chrissie

Guest Book Entries

Written April 22, 2008, 7:54 p.m.

Chrissie and Tom:

I just wanted to tell you how amazed I was with the work, time, and planning that went into the benefit. It was first rate! What a testament to you two and the relationships you have. The support group is very deep, very strong, and very committed to you.

I am so proud of you with your decision for Tom's care. I felt that same way when I saw him. We are all here for you, and not a day goes by that we don't think of you. You are in our thoughts and prayers.

Hugs, kisses, and prayers!

Lynn Robson

Written April 22, 2008, 10:29 p.m.

Chrissie and Tom:

You are making the right decisions. Stay strong! I miss being in the neighborhood and am thinking of you all the time. Maybe Savannah can write some more letters and send some more good cheer your way.

Jeanne Galle Franklin

Wednesday, April 23, 2008, 7:43 a.m., CDT—
Chrissie's Journal Entry

Good morning,

Tom will be moving up to the newly remodeled fourth floor today. I won't know his room number until I get there. I have already found that he will be in a private room (woo-hoo) close to the nurses' station. I have brought his cards, stuffed animals, SpongeBob clock, and pictures with me today so I can put everything back up for him. But tomorrow is the big day. Bailey gets to go see her daddy. We had been telling him repeatedly last night that Bailey was coming up on Thursday, but when I told him before I left that Bailey was coming up to see her daddy, he got a huge smile on his face. Everything is good to go to bring her; they took copies of her current shots (which she got on the twelfth) and records. Bailers will probably pee on the floor she will be so happy to see him.

A few of the workers yesterday asked me if Tom was unresponsive. I'm like, *no*! I told them that he has a tendency to not respond to staff, but when it comes to his friends and family, he is totally there. At one point last night when we were laughing, one of the nurses stepped in to see for himself, and Tom had a huge smile on his face and his eyes were open. I think I need to make it my mission for them to see how he is with us and for them to know how "with it" he is. I was almost getting angry with one nurse when I was trying to explain how alert he is at times. I just want them to understand and witness it for themselves. I did find out that he is in this facility only while he is doing his radiation treatments unless the therapists want him there longer to work with him. Currently they have twenty-one radiation treatments set up, and they started yesterday. (Radiation is only done Monday through Friday.)

Keep the prayers and good thoughts coming. We will take them all.

Love,

Chrissie

Guest Book Entries

Written April 23, 2008 10:47 a.m.

Chrissie, Good to hear Tom is moving along. Hopefully the incredible positive energy from this past weekend and the impending Bailey visit is helping! Great seeing you and everyone. It was a super event. Stay strong and rock on!

Tim Hanley

Wednesday, April 23, 2008, 9:15 p.m., CDT— Chrissie's Journal Entry

Hello,

I just came from seeing Tommy, and despite the radiation, he was pretty alert this evening. It took him a while to wake up, but once he did, he was paying attention to all the banter between Kent, Kim, his Mom (Virginia), my sister Theresa, and my mom, Sherrill. It went on for quite some time with Kent telling childhood (and adulthood) stories of their escapades. Like the time Tom and Kent and the other "Buds" were out of town for their Bud annual drink-fest when Kent asked Tom what shirt he should wear to the bar. Tom then told Kent what shirt he should wear. Later when they got to the bar, the two of them got out of the car and Tom turned to Kent and said, "You're not wearing that, are ya?" Total set-up! Good times!

I have not heard yet about the results of Tom's spinal tap. I need to make a few phone calls tomorrow apparently, updates to follow. In the meantime, please keep up the positive thoughts. I told Tommy tonight that he needs to hurry and get well so he can come home. *Word*! Keep hope alive, baby!

xoxoxoxo

Chrissie

Friday, April 25, 2008, 8:12 a.m., CDT—
Chrissie's Journal Entry

OMG!

Yesterday, when Drae and I walked in with Bailey, Tom's eyes were wide open. (I wasn't expecting that!) I walked over to him and said, "Hi, baby!" a couple of times. All of a sudden Tom said loud and clear, "Hi, baby!" That was the first time he has acknowledged me verbally since everything started, and the first time I have heard him speak in over a week. After he said a couple more words, his nurse came in and asked him if he remembered her from yesterday, and he said yes. She told him that she would be in and out all night, and he chuckled. That was the most I have heard him say at once in almost three weeks. Also, as I was looking at his eyes, it appeared to me that his left eye was starting to straighten out; it was more inward than it has been in two weeks. I am going to take a stab and say that there will be dramatic changes due to the radiation (which is what I have thought all along), and that he just may be able to swallow that chemo pill soon.

On Tuesday Debra, a social worker at the TCU, brought a CD player and a couple of CDs in for Tom to listen to. She told me on Wednesday that I should bring some CDs from home. Well, of course I was all over that like a cheap suit, so I brought in about seventeen CDs yesterday, one of which is Tommy's favorite. That, of course, is Bob Marley. Let me just tell you that my hubby was lying there mouthing the words to the songs! He had his puppers and Bob Marley! Ya, mon!

So now, about Bailey; she was not sure exactly what was going on. We brought her over to Tom so he could pet her. He had a smile on his face as he was petting her. We had kind of a hard time getting her to stay in one place for long so, we had to keep bringing her over. Tom did give her a couple of treats in his usual manner. Once she tried to jump on the bed, which they are okay with, but I made her get down because I did not want her to get near his feeding tube. That would not be good for anyone, especially him. I plan on bringing her up just about every day. We will see what happens.

Now for the last bit of good news; I called yesterday to get the test results for the spinal tap they did on Monday, and it was negative for cancer cells! Woo-hoo! I did find out yesterday that they planned to radiate his spine based on the results from the MRI they did last Friday. I need to find out today if the results of the spinal tap mean that they don't have to radiate the spine. More phone calls! Maybe I should stop in to unit 6A and see if I can talk to someone.

Anyway, finally some good news! I still have to remember that this healing is going to be slow (bad things happen fast, good things take time), and that he is still not out of the woods. We still need prayers and positive thoughts and energy from everyone for some time to come. Thank you for providing us those things. It will never be forgotten!

Much love to all,

Chrissie

Guest Book Entries

Written April 25, 2008, 8:56 a.m.

Chrissie and Tom:

I just read your journal about Tom's baby's visit. His response was exciting news! Let's see if Bailey can stay there all the time. Keep up the good work, Chrissie. We are all behind you.

Lynn Robson

Written April 25, 2008, 10:51 a.m.

I was so happy to see Tom and Bailey together again last night. I know when Tom was at the U we would mention Bailey, and he would light up. Also Chrissie forgot to mention that last night Kent said something to Tom about thumb wrestling, and Tom grabbed Kent's hand, put out his thumb, and they thumb wrestled; so good to see. He definitely knows when people are visiting and also who is visiting … very cool! Chrissie, I will stop in tonight for a short visit. It is hard to stay away, especially when we can see the progress.

Love ya,

Kim Peterson

Written April 25, 2008, 11:42 a.m.

I am so glad to read that there are some major improvements with Tom's speech and alertness levels. You must be in heaven, Chris, to see some progress (and *big* progress, might I add) starting to emerge. I am so glad that the benefit was such a huge success … You deserve it!

You continue to be in my thoughts many times during the day.

Kris K.

Written April 25, 2008, 1:47 p.m.

All I can say is *amen,* sister! I wish I could have been there when Bailey was there yesterday. Larry called when he was bringing Drae home. Drae was in the background going nonstop about Tom's reaction and saying her name and giving her treats!

Kudos to you, Chrissie, for keeping that positive energy going! It's important for you and Tom to only have positive energy around you at this time. I am so very proud of you with how you have handled everything that has been thrown at you in the past five weeks.

So here's a little line from one of my all-time favorite movies: "Stay gold" (from *The Outsiders* … I know I am dating myself here, but who gives a rat's a**!).

Stay strong—you know we all love you both very much.

Karrie Cable

Written April 25, 2008, 4:55 p.m.

Chrissie and Tom,

I am so happy to hear the amazing progress that Tom has made and am truly inspired by your positive spirit and energy. You and Tom have been and will remain in our thoughts and prayers. You are both inspirations to us all!

Your neighbors,

Heather and Asher

Monday, April 28, 2008, 11:15 a.m., CDT—
Chrissie's Journal Entry

Hello,

Sorry this is so late, but I am feeling slightly under the weather and trying to get enough rest to stay healthy. I cannot afford to be away from Tom for any amount of time as I feel like I have to watch everything to make sure he is getting all the care he needs. A lot of the people up there are still under the impression he is unresponsive even though I have been telling everyone I come into contact with that he is very much there. I also make it a point to tell them that he does not always respond so well to staff. If they want to see how he really is, they need to peek in when we are there. So far no one has done that. (Also I have month end coming up at work and have no time to be sick!)

After this weekend, it is clear to see that he is more awake than not. Suzanne from speech therapy was in on Saturday and Sunday asking him questions and such. On Saturday he actually told Suzanne my name! Woo-hoo! As she was asking him things like, "What's your birthday?" and "How do you say your last name?" and he didn't respond, she told him, "I see, you only respond to humor or sarcasm!" Of course, he laughed then. As she left the room, she said good-bye to him, and he waved at her with his left foot. (He can wave with his left hand, he just chose not to.)

While he was entertaining earlier on Saturday, he reached a point where he just hit the wall and became very tired. He was still pretty tired yesterday as well. He said a few words to Suzanne yesterday, but it was a pretty quiet day. It will be interesting to see how this week progresses given that he will have a full week of radiation. It can only get better from here. I think a good indicator of that is that he is awake most of the time now instead of sleepy like he was before. I am just looking forward to him doing things like changing the TV channel and stuff like that. It is probably a little ways away yet, but that's what hope is all about!

Until tomorrow,

Much love,

Chrissie

Tuesday, April 29, 2008, 8:29 a.m., CDT—
Chrissie's Journal Entry

Good morning,

Yesterday I was so worried about the cold I have (that I have been taking Zicam for) that I stayed home to sleep and rest. Then when I went to the hospital to see Tom, he already had a cold. When he kept coughing yesterday afternoon, I asked him if he had a cold and he nodded yes. My poor honey. I suppose the radiation will reduce the immune system. Yesterday, Judy mentioned to his nurse that Tom had a cold, and he listened to his chest. Fortunately, he only heard sounds in this throat and not his chest, so they suctioned out his mouth to get out the mucous he coughs up.

Nothing much new in other news except that he was pretty tired yesterday given the cold and starting radiation for the week. One of the nurses' aides said he got goose bumps yesterday because he heard Tom speak, and when they turned him, he grabbed the side of the bed with his left hand to help them out. (I didn't have the heart to tell him that he has done that for weeks.) I was just glad he witnessed what he did. I think I need to have a chat with my husband and tell him that he needs to start performing for the staff so they don't misdiagnose him or write him off as it seems some have already done. Hopefully he will listen to me. If he doesn't, I'm sending his mama in! He *cannot* refuse her. I've seen it!

Keep us in your thoughts and prayers as Tom's treatments progress. I know he can feel them!

Love to all,

Chrissie

Guest Book Entries

Written April 29, 2008, 9:15 a.m.

Chrissie, that's great news about the test results and the initial radiation. Hope this week goes well! So he still responds to humor and sarcasm; I guess some things never change. Also, are you sure you want to let Tommy get ahold of a remote control? Be careful what you wish for. Seriously though, prayers and positive energy will sustain you, and keep the updates coming. Oh, by the way, get some sleep. You need to stay strong and rock on!

Tim Hanley

Wednesday, April 30, 2008, 8:00 a.m., CDT—Chrissie's Journal Entry

Good morning,

Well, try as you might, it is hard to keep from getting sick even while in the hospital. Last night Tom was coughing constantly, so the nurse suctioned him a couple of times (Bailey was not down with that whole scene) and finally decided to have a chest x-ray taken. The nice thing is that they came to him. They didn't haul him over to the hospital or anything; they brought the machine to him. The results were not yet back by the time I left last night at 8:30.

Despite not feeling well, he was awake the entire time I was there, even actually watching the NBA playoff game. I asked him if he wanted to watch baseball or the NBA and he chose the NBA. Go figure! The Twins are his favorite! I left the baseball schedule tacked to the bulletin board in his room. That way if anyone is visiting, they can check the schedule to see if a game is on and turn it on for him if it's not already.

While his sister Laura was there last night, we had a little chat about "performing" for the staff. He, of course, shook his head at me and rolled his eyes. Laura backed me up (thanks for the assist, Laura), and we reinforced the point that if he didn't listen to me that his mama was on deck to have the next chat. We will see what happens. At least we have the nurse's aide, Jim, who is noticing more every day. He was most pleased with Tom's reactions last night, especially when he told him that if he was a Packer fan, he could not guarantee the level of care he was receiving would remain the same and Tom laughed. Forward—we just need to keep moving forward.

Love to all,

Chrissie

Guest Book Entries

Written April 30, 2008, 10:36 a.m.

Hello, Tom and Chrissie,

I am one of the nursing assistants from 6A. I came to the benefit with Kelly, Elizabeth, and Joanne. I just wanted to let you know that we have been thinking about you and Tom, and keeping up on the journals. From what I've read, it seems like the radiation is helping, and that is *great*! We miss Tom on 6A, but we're glad he's moving in the right direction, and we hope to hear more good news! We're praying for you.

Monica Lang

Thursday, May 1, 2008, 8:57 a.m., CDT—
Chrissie's Journal Entry

Good morning,

The results of Tom's x-ray showed a small amount of fluid in the very bottom lobes of his lungs, so they are having him sit upright in a chair twice a day and have started him on an antibiotic to nip that in the bud. On the up side, he was able to sit in the chair for three hours yesterday in the sunset room, as they call it. When Judy and I were in there with him, I ran down to his room and got the CD player. For our listening pleasure I chose a little Earth, Wind, and Fire (as Judy had just seen an ad for them and it happened to be one of the CDs I brought from home).

Once he got back into bed, he wanted to rest before Tony came up to shave his beard again. So I went down to the cafeteria for dinner. About a half an hour later as I was approaching his room, I heard all this laughter! I was like, *Dang! Is that coming from Tom's room?* Oh yeah! He had two speech therapists in his room, and he had them cracking up. Imagine! (So much for letting him rest.) I think the therapists have been warned that he responds to sarcasm and humor because it was certainly flowing in that room. They actually had him talking more than I have heard in six weeks. Also, very exciting, they started his swallow study. They had him chewing and swallowing ice chips. They wanted to give him applesauce, but given his allergies to raw fruit and vegetables, I didn't think that would be wise, so they opted for pudding instead. Tom ended up not wanting the pudding. It's not his favorite, so I wasn't surprised. Anyway, I was *most* excited to see them doing that. If he is able to start eating and drinking consistently, he will be able to take the chemo pill and get that feeding tube removed after the six weeks have passed. (He did make a move for the feeding tube yesterday, but I had to put the kibosh on that! I told him he could get a serious infection if he were to pull that out. Thank God he listened to me … so far!)

Woo-hoo! We've got progress! Thank you, thank you, thank you! Keep the positive thoughts and prayers coming. They are working!

Love,

Chrissie

Guest Book Entries

Written May 1, 2008, 10:43 a.m.

Yeah! Great news! What else is there to say!

Keep up the good work; we are all proud of both of you.

Kim Peterson

Friday, May 2, 2008, 8:10 a.m., CDT— Chrissie's Journal Entry

Good morning,

Tom was in the chair in the sunset room again yesterday for about four hours. He was mainly lounging, not sitting up, because he was extremely tired yesterday. Being that he was so alert for so long on Wednesday, I am not surprised. These are the ups and downs they keep telling us about.

He only said a few words yesterday, mainly when Jodi and Julie from Jaguar were there. They were telling him things that were going on around the dealership and telling him to hurry up and get back to work. (*Word*!) I think it is awesome for him to hear those things to keep him in the loop and make him feel like a part of what is going on in the outside world (apart from those of us he sees every day). I am hoping it gives him continued motivation. It is what I hope for.

We will see how he is over this next weekend. I am curious about the weekends to see how he does on the days he does not have radiation. Last weekend he was pretty tired. We will see how this weekend shakes out. Of course, I will keep you informed of every little move my honey makes. He might not like that so much, but as we keep telling him, there are *so* many people out there who care and are concerned about him that he wouldn't even believe it.

I know I sound like a broken record, but please continue with your positive thoughts and prayers as we go forward. We need *all* of them.

Love to all,

Chrissie

Guest Book Entries

Written May 2, 2008, 9:40 a.m.

Hey, Tom and Chrissie!

I'm thrilled to read about Tom's continued progress— great news indeed! Special thanks to you, Chrissie, for updating this journal so often. With being spread so thin with work and hospital visits, everyone appreciates the precious time you spend sharing the news with all of us!

Sending all the mojo the Andersons can muster! Take care, and give Tom a big hug from all of us.

Peggy

Written May 2, 2008, 8:37 p.m.

Hi, Tom and Chrissie,

It sounds like baby steps are being made, which is absolutely a wonderful sign. I think about the two of you every day, and you are on our prayer list! I am so grateful for this website. It's a great way to connect with everyone instead of playing telephone tag!

Continue to stay strong, both of you. I wish you continued progress and peace of mind. I hope Bailey gets to visit Tom often so he gets his daily hugs from him.

Chris, you are a great strength for Tom, and I'm happy to hear of the progress he has made.

You are in our prayers every day.

All our love,

Sarah and Scott

Saturday, May 3, 2008, 9:40 a.m., CDT—
Chrissie's Journal Entry

Morning, all,

Yesterday I got a phone call about one o'clock in the afternoon from the TCU telling me that Tom took a tumble out of bed. As I was freaking out, they were telling me that it could either be a seizure or that he was alert enough to try to get out of bed. They also assured me that he was okay at the moment. They took him down to get a CT scan to make sure there were no fractures. Fortunately, it didn't take them long to call me back with the results. As I was driving they called me back to tell me that there were no fractures and they believed he fell trying to get out of bed. There wasn't any evidence of seizures (which would make sense because he is on antiseizure medication and has been since the surgery). *Also*, they told me that by looking at the CT scan, they saw that *the tumor is shrinking*! Woo-hoo! You want to talk about some happy/relief tears after I got off the phone with them ... Holy Hannah!

When I finally got up there yesterday, I asked him if he was okay, and he did not really respond. Judy, Karrie, and I were all asking him about the fall, and he simply would not address it. My thinking is that he may have just realized his limitations at the moment and was having a hard time with it and/or he was embarrassed. Either way, it shows he is waking up more and more and starting to be mobile. Thank God! It will be that determination that will get him through therapy.

I just want to thank everyone who takes the time to read the updates every day. (As Julie W. tells me, everyone at Jaguar rushes to their computers in the morning to get the latest! Rock on, you guys!) (Thank you, Tim.) Sometimes it's not easy to say the things I have to say, and other days I can't wait to tell you what's going on. It's a process ... for all of us. So, thanks again. We love you guys!

Chrissie

Guest Book Entries

Written May 3, 2008, 9:03 p.m.

Wow, Chrissie and Tom, such great news. I say a prayer every night for you both. Prayer is such a powerful thing. I read your entries, and I have tears with each one. At least we can say that most of them going forward have been happy tears for you guys. Your strength gives us all strength with our little challenges to your great challenge. It's all about just having faith! Hugs to you both!

Julie S.

Monday, May 5, 2008, 7:30 a.m., CDT— Chrissie's Journal Entry

Hello,

Jackie and I were there yesterday when Tom was having physical therapy, and he did really well. Bailey was also there, and he got to pet her while he was sitting at the edge of the bed; very nice. She was having him do things with his upper body to build the strength in his stomach muscles and the old butt muscles (which he is really good at flexing normally). The therapist said that he is really flexible, which is good.

My main focus at the moment is getting Tom to start helping himself. The whole deal he has going on with not responding to the staff is really not helping his situation. It is seriously hurting it, as I am finding out. The fall he took last Friday did something to his psyche. Friday night and most of Saturday he was even unresponsive (at times) to those of us who saw him. I really wish he could tell me what he is thinking, but since he can't yet, I am going to ascertain that he is either embarrassed by the fall or he has now realized that he has limitations and is trying to avoid dealing with it. We have to get him to realize it is time to start fighting for himself. I have had a couple of different conversations with him since Thursday about what he needs to do. Right now, what I need all of you to do is to pray that he accepts all the positive thoughts and prayers and finds the strength within himself to fight for his life. Pray that he gets past his very stubborn attitude and faces this thing head-on. It is time. His life depends on it. Pray also that all of the staff begins to see the progress we know he is making. Please, just pray, pray, pray.

Thank you for all the thoughts and prayers.

Love,

Chrissie

Guest Book Entries

Written May 5, 2008, 1:01 p.m.

Hi, Chrissie,

I read your journal daily and say a prayer for you and Tom each time. I believe you have many silent friends who are wishing only the best for you and Tom. And please remember to take care of yourself too ... I often find a glass of wine or a brewski at the end of the day is a perfect antidote to a tough day. Please let me know if there is anything we (the Block Club) can do.

With best wishes,

Dianne, Victor, Luisa, and Lydia

Written May 5, 2008, 2:01 p.m.

Chrissie, thanks for the update! This is one of those times when you need to stay strong in your faith, believe in the best, and keep only positive thoughts. Prayers and positive energy are being sent your way. You know you have the support of others. Fight! Fight! Fight! How's that for cheerleading? Rock on!

Tim Hanley

Written May 5, 2008, 9:28 p.m.

Hi, Chrissie,

I read your updates every day, and I want you to know that you and Tom are in my thoughts each day. I admire you, your positive attitude, and your unconditional love for your husband. You are a true inspiration. Keep the faith!

Love you,

Amy Loughrey

Tuesday, May 6, 2008, 7:06 a.m., CDT— Chrissie's Journal Entry

Good morning,

Yesterday was kind of exciting. After they put Tom in the chair, his nurse told us that we could take him outside if we did not leave the property. So Billy and I went outside with him for a short time. It was still slightly chilly yet for him. From there, we checked out the sunset room on the fourth floor, and that was too hot. They had the temp set at eighty degrees! Dang! So we just went back to his room as he sat in the chair for a few hours.

When I got there yesterday, the doctor was in his room, and she talked to me about his fall. She said she thought it was a good sign, and of course, I agreed with her. It was nice to hear she thought the same.

Other than that, Tom was awake the whole time I was there yesterday, resting his eyes occasionally. Then, when I left, he reached up and gave me a hug! Woo-hoo! That's the first time he's done that without me asking. Rock on!

I do believe all the positive energy is working. Keep it coming!

Love,

Chrissie

Guest Book Entries

Written May 6, 2008, 10:44 a.m.

Awesome! With the nice weather hopefully he will be able to throw the stick for Bailey Girl! If anything would help his motivation, that would be it!

Chrissie, you continue to do an amazing job of staying positive and strong ... Tom is incredibly blessed to you have a wife like you! *Word* (to the wife)!

Love you both,

Karrie Cable

Wednesday, May 7, 2008, 6:14 a.m., CDT— Chrissie's Journal Entry

Good morning,

After being extremely alert on Monday, Tommy was pretty tired yesterday. He was in the chair in the lounge for about five hours until his booty couldn't take it anymore. (Even though he was as tired as he was, he was trying to adjust himself in the chair.) It was a good thing we were in the lounge because he had a constant stream of visitors all day, and it would have been way too cramped in his room. After we got down there, I ran back to his room to grab the CD player so we could play some tunes. If we continue at this pace, I will have to bring some fresh musical selections from home!

I have some good news to report in that the doctors now believe he is progressing! They are also encouraged by the shrinking of the tumor. Hooray! It's about dang time. It hasn't been easy to get them to realize that you can't walk into a room, see that the patient's eyes are shut, and then walk out because you think he is sleeping, and then *assume* that he is sleeping all the time. This is just one of many battles. I have a care conference tomorrow morning at the hospital; hopefully we will be able to get some more information going both ways. I did talk to his speech and occupational therapists yesterday about his participation in his therapy, and they say it is not consistent due to his alertness but he is participating when he is alert (which I have seen). Pray that with the further shrinking of the tumor that this will no longer be an issue. We need Tommy back, dang it!

Thank you for your continued love, support, and prayers.

Love to all,

Chrissie

Guest Book Entries

Written May 7, 2008, 6:56 a.m.

Chrissie,

I read this journal right away every morning, and I am thrilled to hear about Tom's day-by-day, continual progress. Just like you said, "Bad things happen fast, good things take time."

I can't say enough how blessed he is to have you at his side. You *rock,* woman!

Dave, Olivia, Quinn, Lewis, and I are all praying and cheering for Tom and you. Lewis is still is talking about those Zingers pickles!

All our love,

Kira Martin

Written May 7, 2008, 10:58 p.m.

Hi, Chrissie and Tom,

We're your neighbors, Victor and Dianne and Luisa and Lydia down the road. Just want you to know that I think about you every day as I drive past your house through the alley. We check this site every day and are thrilled that things are looking up. Our good vibes and energy will continue to come your way. Keep up the good fight. Chrissie, you're doing an amazing job. Keep it up; all the best, guys. Please know that there are a lot of people sending prayers your way. May the force be with you.

Victor Zupanc

Thursday, May 8, 2008, 5:55 a.m., CDT— Chrissie's Journal Entry

Hello, everyone,

I must say, yesterday was pretty cool. Tom had physical therapy around three o'clock, and they had him sitting on the edge of the bed for his longest time yet, fifteen minutes. The best part about that was he was holding himself up for most of that time! One of the therapists was behind him to catch him if he faltered, while another one was in front of him working his legs and arms. At first he didn't want to raise his leg because he knew he would lose his balance, but he did it and managed to catch himself and pull himself back up with his stomach muscles. He did this several times while he was sitting up. They have to keep reminding him to keep his head up and straighten up, but as he gets stronger, that will be easier for him.

The other cool thing that happened yesterday while I was sitting next to him reading was that all of a sudden he hoisted himself onto his right side and grabbed the railing (setting off the bed alarm) because he was uncomfortable. He was lying completely on his right side, which is the first time I have seen that! Holy Hannah! I ran around to the other side of the bed to make sure he wasn't going to fall out. Needless to say, he was somewhat tired after all of this activity.

After I got home last night, I heard the doorbell ring. At the door was our neighbor girl Fiona with Pastor Jeff and her church group. They stopped by to give us a check for money they raised for Tom. Pastor Jeff told me that the kids had gone out to get donations and within twenty minutes had gotten almost $400, which they split between us and another family that had a very premature baby. They also brought a bouquet of balloons, which Drae, Bailey, and I will bring to him tonight. Surprises like that are so touching and mean so very much. I know I hugged you last night, but thanks, Fiona! You are a special girl. I will make sure to tell Tom that you miss him in the alley!

We are making progress! A little bit each day ... good things take time, good things take time ...

Much love to all,

Chrissie

Guest Book Entries

- Written May 8, 2008, 9:09 a.m.

  It's a small world. Chrissie, I've never met you, but I've known Tommy my whole life. My brothers were in Boy Scouts with him, and I grew up with Michelle. I'll never forget playing "Nuts" with Grandpa and the rest of the Vinje clan. I've been reading your updates every day and praying for Tommy like crazy. I also attend church with Fiona. I knew the youth group was collecting money for two families. I had *no idea* that *your* family was one of those families. Just know that you guys are loved and prayed for by *many, many* people. Keep up the great progress!

Ilse Rolf

Friday, May 9, 2008, 6:22 a.m., CDT— Chrissie's Journal Entry

Hello,

I have more good news today! Yesterday, at our care conference, his speech therapist told us that they had had their best session ever, just that morning! He had swallowed five ice chips and four spoons of pudding, and everything went down as it should. He followed all the commands and responded appropriately to questions he was asked, and when he spoke, his voice was clear! The session went so well that they are doing a "video swallow" today. This is where they give him different thicknesses of barium and watch him swallow it on an x-ray. If he passes this, he can move on and begin eating again, and we can lose the feeding tube when the time is right! Rock on!

Another exciting and unexpected (to me) tidbit is that last night, as he was sitting in his chair, I had my hand on his right knee and told him I was going down the hall and would be right back. All of a sudden, I could feel the muscles in his knee contract, and he bent his knee! I looked at him, and as you can imagine, got very excited. Then he did it again, with a slight smile on his face! Later on he did it about three more times. I told him to keep on working it!

It appears as if we have gotten through to him about it being time for him to start working and take his life back. I certainly hope that in the coming days I will have new and exciting reports on his progress for you. Nothing would give me more pleasure! In the meantime, keep the positive energy and prayers flowing (as I know you are), as I do believe they are working.

Much love to all,

Chrissie

Guest Book Entries

Written May 9, 2008, 11:28 p.m.

Hi, Tom and Chrissie!

So glad to hear of all Tom's progress. I knew he had it in him! Keep up the good work. Everyone on 6A misses you guys.

Kelly Ayd

Sunday, May 11, 2008, 4:01 p.m., CDT—
Chrissie's Journal Entry

Hello, all,

Since I had a few minutes, I thought I would update on Sunday afternoon instead of Monday morning. Over the weekend Tom started eating food! He is not eating a lot, but it's just the beginning and he hasn't eaten in seven weeks. I don't think that I would jump right into that myself. It is progress at any rate, and I will take it! Maybe soon he will be able to start that chemo pill.

His therapy is going well. He is moving his right knee even higher than he was the other day, and he was using it to lift up and push out during one of his sessions. When I asked the therapist if she was helping, she told me to stand up and watch his quad work! Very nice!

Bailey and I are in his room at the moment, but he is very tired today. He was more awake yesterday. The therapies and radiation are taking a toll, as you can well imagine. Also, he has started to lose his hair. There are many little hairs all over his pillow for evidence.

Well, I must run; my honey needs me. Happy Mother's Day to all mothers out there!

Love to all,

Chrissie

Guest Book Entries

Written May 12, 2008, 6:51 p.m.

Chrissie, yeah, I wouldn't say he's ready for cooking on the barbie yet, but it is a good sign that he's eating again! Good to hear the therapy is working. I'm sure Bailey is keeping a close eye on him. As far as the hair goes, now he'll be able to complete his Yul Brynner look! Thanks for the updates. Stay strong and keep your spirits up. You're in a marathon, not a sprint. Rock on!

Tim Hanley

Tuesday, May 13, 2008, 7:11 a.m., CDT— Chrissie's Journal Entry

Good morning, all,

Yesterday I walked into the TCU and almost walked right past my honey! There he was sitting straight up in his chair by the nurses' station looking around. He really doesn't like sitting there in the middle of everything, so we took him down to the lounge, where we camped out and played tunes, and he ate some dinner. For about the first fifteen to twenty minutes I was there, he didn't even have a pillow behind his head (just his back), and he was doing a damn good job of holding that head up for that period of time. That is the longest he has done that since this first began! As we were sitting there listening to some tunes, I looked down at his feet, and there was his right foot moving to the beat just like his left foot was, looking perfectly normal. He was moving it all around, from side to side, up and down just like nothing ever happened. I got way excited, and he looked at me and just gave me the nod with a big smile. The look on his face said, "That's right, here we go!" He was pretty proud of himself!

He has one week left of radiation, so hopefully he won't be as tired as he is now and he will really be able to progress. Now that he is eating, we have to find out when he will be able to start the chemo pill. Let's just keep the treatment coming, along with the positive thoughts and prayers. As you can see, they are working! Thank you!

Much love to all,

Chrissie

Guest Book Entries

Written May 13, 2008, 8:11 a.m.

Well happy birthday to you, Chrissie!

What a way to start your birthday by having great news to share about Tom! Hopefully something else spectacular will happen today to make your birthday really special because you certainly deserve it!

Love,

Beth Timm

Written May 13, 2008, 8:53 a.m.

Christina J-M V,

Happy birthday, my darling! So thrilled with your news today. Sending birthday love and prayers your way ...

We love you huge,

Wendy H-K P

Written May 13, 2008, 9:21 a.m.

Good morning and happy birthday to you, Chrissie Vinje!

It was great to see Tom eating last night. Every bite of "real" food will make him that much stronger! Tom has made and continues to make great progress. He smiled so big last night, and he is giving those looks more and more. It is just awesome to see more of the Tom we all know and love!

Have a wonderful day—you certainly deserve it!

Love to you both,

Karrie, Ian, and Tyler

Wednesday, May 14, 2008, 7:34 a.m., CDT— Chrissie's Journal Entry

Sweet!

Tommy had a couple of really great therapy sessions yesterday! In OT he had to take his socks off and put them back on both feet, which he did. While he was taking a slight break in between, he was holding his right leg on top of his left one all by himself for about two to three minutes. Sheila, his therapist, told him that he was using his muscles to hold that leg up, that she was not helping him! Very nice! Sheila also had him throw a ball to her. Overhand was the preferred method, but every once in a while, Tom would just take and throw it to the ground underhand, just to mess with her. He was cracking himself up on that!

The most exciting news came during PT when they got him standing. The first time, the therapist didn't realize that he could grip with his right hand, so they didn't have him grasp the bar. So, after a little break and some leg exercises, they got him up again and he stood for two and a half minutes! Woo-hoo! Rock on! Every so often he would start to slump, so we had to remind him to squeeze those butt muscles, and then he would straighten up! Nice job, honey! That was the best birthday present ever. He was dang tired afterward. It is really cool to watch him in therapy and see his progression.

I have made a phone call to inquire about the possibility of Tom starting the chemo pill now that he is eating. I will not know anything until next week sometime.

One really cool thing I will leave you with is something Jim, a nurse's aide at the TCU, said to me as I was leaving last night. On my way out, he asked how Tom was doing (I had told him earlier as I passed by him in the hall that Tom had stood up for two and a half minutes). I told him he was doing really well in therapy, etc. He then said that Tom was in pretty rough shape when he got to the TCU, but watching him over the last few weeks, he now thought that Tom was going to be one of their success stories!

I told him that I had thought that all along ...

Love to all,

Chrissie

Guest Book Entries

Written May 14, 2008, 8:30 a.m.

This is the best news ever. I knew my brother was going to pull through this, and this great news just confirms it. Next thing you know he'll be walking down the hall! And then walking right out of there! You rock, Tom. I'm so proud of you!

Love,

Judy Vinje

PS: Chrissie, you *rock*. Your dedication to Tom is so heartwarming. It's hard to put it into words how grateful I am.

Love ya,

Judy

Thursday, May 15, 2008, 7:38 a.m., CDT— Chrissie's Journal Entry

Good morning,

Tom had another good day in therapy yesterday. In OT he put on and took off a t-shirt (I am bringing up some of his own clothes today for him to start wearing.), and he was working his arms by doing tasks that would spontaneously need both arms. He did things like gripping a homemade apparatus with both arms and moving it forward and back mostly with his left arm but taking his right one with it, working it at the same time. His therapist, Sheila, says that the muscle tone in his arms is there; he just needs to build it back up. In PT he stood again, twice, for two minutes each. His therapist, Barb, has to put her knee against his right knee to lock it into place as he is standing or it will buckle, but he is getting stronger each day. He stood up a little straighter yesterday than he did on Tuesday.

In other news, Tom is finished with radiation! He had his last session yesterday. Hopefully he won't be so tired now and will be able to participate even more in his therapies. It really is cool to watch him in therapy. I get so excited with each new thing he does. (Especially when he is a smart-ass while he's doing it!)

Last night he had many visitors, and it was the most I have heard him talk in eight weeks! He seems to really respond to people he hasn't seen in a while. If there is anyone who is thinking of going to visit Tom and you either haven't or it has been a while, please do! This is a really good time to do it. I also think it would be a really good thing for him to see some of the guys that he works with, so if any of you want to visit, I think that would be awesome. He is going to be at the Fairview Riverside TCU (2512 South Seventh Street) until next Wednesday. I do not know yet where we will be next Wednesday. That is being worked on. He is in room 422, but a lot of the time we are at the end of his hallway in the lounge. That room is much bigger and brighter, and we crank the tunes. He has been having therapy between 2:00 and 4:00 this week, so any time after that would work. Hope to see you there!

Love,

Chrissie

Guest Book Entries

Written May 15, 2008, 9:23 a.m.

Hi, Tom,

> It's your neighbors, Victor and Dianne and Luisa and Lydia. Wow, all great news. We think of you all the time. Keep strong, and *keep sassy*. You'll beat this thing if you just plain kick it in the ass! We're looking forward to seeing you up and down our street with your dog really soon.

Peace,

Victor Zupanc

Friday, May 16, 2008, 7:41 a.m., CDT—
Chrissie's Journal Entry

Morning, all,

While yesterday was a really good day, there is something that we all have to pray for, *really* a lot. On Monday I had noticed that Tom's left arm was swollen. I mentioned it to his therapist, who mentioned it to a nurse, who mentioned it to his nurse for that evening. They elevated his hand on Tuesday night and the swelling went down (for a while), but it was back on Wednesday. Finally, yesterday, the doctor came in while he was in therapy to check him out. She said she would do an ultrasound to see if they could find anything. Well, they found a blood clot in his upper left arm. The problem with this is that he cannot take blood thinners right now because the recent radiation could cause bleeding in his brain. (Later on, the further away from the radiation we get, I don't yet know the time frame, he will be able to take blood thinners.) Another option at this point is to put in a "filter" to block the clot from getting to the heart, lungs, and brain. They usually do this when the clot is in the lower arm, not upper, of course. The other option, as of this moment, is to do nothing and just watch it. They have put him on a machine that monitors his breathing so they will know right away if it moves to his lungs. The doctor I spoke with last night (at 11:00 p.m.) said he was letting his doctor know and they would be consulting with more doctors today to see if they could, in fact, put the filter in even though the clot is in his upper arm, or what our next step should be. There is also the chance that the clot could dissipate on its own and he will be fine. I pray that it will be. My lord, there is some new complication at every turn.

On the up side, Tommy had an awesome day in PT when he stood twice for two minutes, and then his therapist had him standing for six minutes at a standing frame for a total of ten minutes! With this contraption, they put a strap around his booty that hooks on to a metal part on the frame and then crank him up to a standing position with a frame in front of him that he can lean on; pretty cool. His therapist, Natasha, wanted to take a picture she was so excited! She repeatedly told Tom he made her day! I am bringing my camera today to take a picture, and I will put it up on this website when I get a chance.

The other cool thing that happened yesterday was that after therapy, Tom, his mom, and I went and sat outside in the meditation garden for two hours. Tom even ate dinner out there! Hopefully we will be able to go out again today. I don't know about that breathing machine though. Damn.

Tom also is talking more and more every day. He told his friends from Jaguar last night that the radiation has been tough on him! I looked at his mom and went, dang! Thank you, Paul, Jim, and Nick, for coming to see Tom last night! I knew it was what he needed!

Please keep Tom in your prayers and think more positive thoughts to get us through this new complication. They are all *greatly* appreciated.

Much love to all,

Chrissie

Guest Book Entries

Written May 16, 2008, 2:23 a.m.

Hey, Uncle Tom and Auntie Chrissie,

It's me, Little Michelle ... I guess I just stopped by to tell you both I love you very, very much. I'm praying nonstop, and I think God might be getting a little annoyed, LOL. Auntie Chrissie, I know this isn't necessary, but I wanted to tell you how great I think it is that you found my uncle. You two are more than perfect for each other, and I couldn't imagine this happening without you. Just know in your heart you're the number-one reason why Uncle Tom has the strength to do what he's doing, and I thank you for that! You're such a wonderful person, and I love you. Well I guess I'll see you both soon enough.

I love you.

Your flower girl,

Michelle Vinje

Written May 16, 2008, 8:31 a.m.

I just wanted to say thanks for making me cry, Michelle!

I agree that Tom and my sister were lucky to have found each other, and I believe this scare will strengthen even more an already strong marriage. As Tim H. would say … Rock on, Chris and Tom!

Beth Timm

Written May 16, 2008, 9:45 a.m.

Yeah, thanks, Michelle. :) Love you, Chelle Bell.

Remember: "Bad things happen fast, and good things take time."

Judy Vinje

Written May 17, 2008, 1:00 a.m.

Hey, it's me again, little Michelle. Sorry, I didn't mean to make you cry, and I love you too Auntie Juicy. ;)

That's horrible to hear about his arm. You should tell the doctor to just cut it off so he can't hold me down to fart on me anymore! Besides, he can always just use the other one, right! Oh, my mom and Christine say hi … And I love all of you very much. And Auntie Chrissie, again, thank you. I can't even begin to tell you the words that you make me feel because they wouldn't serve you justice. Thankful, happy, grateful, hopeful—those words are not even close. I think that God must be doing this for a reason. Maybe he wanted you and Uncle Tom to spend more time with each other. He might have thought you two worked too much and a little time "off the job" (in the hospital) was the only way for you two to spend some quality time to rethink why you love each other so much. I mean, after all, everything does happen for a reason. (That's just the best one that I could think of.)

Michelle Vinje

Written May 17, 2008, 10:54 a.m.

You're right, Michelle, everything happens for a reason, although sometimes it's harder to understand why. Again, Chrissie, just like a marathon, you don't know what's around every corner, but if the positives outweigh the negatives then you're winning, and I believe this to be the case. Nothing's perfect, but if you stay strong and have each other, you'll cross the finish line together! So rock on!

Tim Hanley

In the middle of May 2008, my family had a garage sale at my mom's house with all of the proceeds going to Tom and me. My sister Theresa spearheaded the event, and in an effort to give you an idea for a fundraiser, should you need to have one, I wanted to share the following e-mail she sent out after the event was over.

From: Theresa Betlach

Sent: Sunday, May 18, 2008, 8:06 p.m.

Subject: Garage Sale Results!

Hello, all,

The garage sale was a huge success. We earned $1,917 for Chrissie and Tom. Oh yeah! I thought we would earn maybe like $500. I guess I was just a little off. I want to extend a huge *thank you* to all of you who donated and/or helped at the sale. We couldn't have done it without you. The brand new school supplies and hats and mittens went like crazy.

Thank you for those, Karrie and Larry. On Saturday (yesterday), as a teaser we gave Chrissie a $1,100 cashier's check that she wasn't expecting. The reaction she gave was worth every hour spent toward the sale. She'll get the rest very soon. I have to say, nothing feels better than giving all you have to someone who really needs and appreciates the gifts that they receive.

Once again *thank you,* and much love to you all!

Theresa Betlach

Monday, May 19, 2008, 7:39 a.m., CDT— Chrissie's Journal Entry

Greetings,

Tom had his first fast food on Friday night. We thought maybe if he had food that he really liked he would eat more so, Judy stopped by McDonald's on her way to the hospital and got him the number 2 (two cheeseburgers, fries, and a diet coke … for me). He ate half of the cheeseburger (using his left hand to feed himself for the first time) and a fry or two. Karrie got him a solo pizza from Davanni's on Saturday for lunch, and he only had a few bites of that. So, all in all, he is not eating much. I think that might have something to do with the fact that his mouth hurts and/or things taste weird to him at this point. I have explained to him (a few times) that as he starts eating more and more, he will be able to lose that feeding tube. Maybe he just needs a little more time …

As far as the blood clots (there are two) in his left arm, they are not going to do anything until they do another ultrasound on Wednesday. At that point they may or may not put in the filters. One thing Dr. H (from the TCU, not his neurologist) told me was that one of the other doctors told her, "If it were my brother, I wouldn't put them in." That is because they have a tendency to migrate to places they shouldn't go just as clots do. In the meantime she suggested that I do a little "healing hands" exercise. She says to put your index and middle fingers together (or the bottom of your palm) and point to the trouble area and say a few words with intent and purpose. Things like, "No toxicity and the blood clots will dissolve," etc. I am kind of into the whole "energy" thing anyway; I believe it is very powerful. The same goes with being positive and having the right attitude. I think it all goes hand in hand. So I have been doing it. I swear, there were a few times yesterday when, while he was sleeping and I was concentrating, that he woke up with a start and looked at me. He seemed a little restless. I don't know … as Dr. H said, "It couldn't hurt!"

Also, something that is really bothering me is that he was pretty sleepy on Saturday and most certainly yesterday. When I got there about 2:45 yesterday afternoon, they told me he had been sleeping all day and had not eaten. They said he had not even opened his eyes for them. As my stomach is in knots, I pulled that blanket off of him, washed his face, and told him it was time for therapy so he better get himself up and ready to go. He got through therapy, but it was not gang-busters. Part of the problem may have been because Sheila, his OT, put tape on the left eye of his glasses to try and help his vision as we believe he is seeing double in that eye. We have to watch to see if he closes his left eye to focus with his right like he has been doing. We are not sure that we can yet rely on the answers he gives us regarding what he is seeing. Hopefully soon though … Also, part of me is wondering if he is depressed after hearing about the blood clots. I asked him if he was, but he said no. Yesterday, when people were around and talking, he would open his eyes, but for the most part he was sleepy. At one point I asked him if I could work his legs like they do in therapy, and he said yes, so I did. I worked his calves and knees for little bit; the more the better. The stronger he will be.

I am hoping this is just a stumbling block and we will get past it. I will not let him rest, that is for sure. In the meantime, I am asking for more positive thoughts and energy and prayers for Tommy. I think he is really in need at the moment.

Thank you and much love to all,

Chrissie

Guest Book Entries

Written May 19, 2008, 8:50 a.m.

I hadn't yet had the chance to tell you, Chris, but Bob and the kids stopped by and saw Tom yesterday before you got there (maybe around 1:30?). He was asleep when they walked in but then woke up. They said he did a lot of talking. I thought this might make you (and everyone) feel a little better that he wasn't just sleeping the entire time. We will, of course, keep praying!

Beth Timm

Tuesday, May 20, 2008, 7:41 a.m., CDT—
Chrissie's Journal Entry

Morning, all,

I was a little upset last night because Tom was really sleepy. He would wake up at times but not like he has been. I am way gun shy because of the last three scares due to his sleepiness.

1) His spinal fluid backing up because it wasn't draining.
2) The swelling of the left side of his brain.
3) The growth of the tumor.

Last night the charge nurse told us that as long as he does wake up at times, he should be okay. (Plus he is not fully sleeping because he hears what is going on. If you tell him to move his foot or his knee he will, with his eyes closed.) She said that he has had a lot of stimulation, and his brain is constantly taking in all the sounds, etc., all around him and is just trying to repair itself. Not to mention the radiation that it is still dealing with after the fact. I intend to double check with radiology today about the after effects of the radiation now that he has been done for a week. While the nurse's words helped me get through the night, I am still freaking out a little bit (okay, maybe more than a little).

As far as the blood clots, they are limiting any vigorous activity with his arm, so he was not able to stand in therapy because it involves him grabbing the parallel bars and holding himself up. Dang! One step forward, two steps back. Maybe we can do some strengthening exercises so that when he is able to stand again he will be that much stronger.

I had a consultation yesterday with a doctor from the Pain and Palliative Care Center. They are a resource for things like pain management, hospice care, etc. They have two doctors, a chaplain, and a social worker. She kind of torqued me off right away with her slight condescending attitude and telling me that by reading Tom's chart (mind you, she has not met him and had just met me) that it was her "guess" that Tom's time was short. I wanted to deck her and walk out of the room, but I sat there and listened while she spewed her venom. I guess I don't have to use their services if that's how it's going to be.

On the flip side of that attitude is the attitude of the people at the TCU. Over the weekend, Dr. H told me that she thought the CaringBridge was such an awesome tool for spiritual healing and that we were all really cool people. Yesterday, another woman who works in administration told me and Judy that Tom had come so far, and it was because of all of us and our energy. She was most excited about his progress. *Word*! Thank you very much!

For the moment, make me feel better and pray for those clots to dissolve and for him to get through his post-radiation healing and wake up so we can jam on some therapy. We have to move on so we can go visit our friends on 6A and they can see the Tommy we all know and love. It will happen!

Love to all,

Chrissie

Tuesday, May 20, 2008, 11:52 a.m., CDT—
Chrissie's Journal Entry

Hello again,

Just a quick update for ya; I just heard from Chris H., who had just come from seeing Tom, and he told me that Tom was wide awake and talked more to him than he has since this whole thing began. As a matter of fact, Tom had his eyes closed when a nurse walked in and said, "Oh, he's sleeping." When Chris told them that he wasn't, Tom said, "Shhhhhhh!" That little sh*t! I know I feel better now!

Love to all,

Chrissie

Guest Book Entries

Written May 20, 2008 10:11 a.m.

Hey, Tom and Chris,

What a small world! Mike and I ran into Mike's cousin (well actually a second cousin; he has no first cousins) at Kohl's last night. She said she saw my name in the guestbook and that she works with Tom. Her name is Jennifer D.

Keep up your spirits. We are still praying.

Shari

Written May 20, 2008, 12:34 p.m.

Tommy, Tommy, Tommy, what the h*ll?! :) I feel way better too! I'm glad I didn't jump on here this morning after reading about that doctor from the Pain and Palliative Care Center. I was pissed! How dare she! She apparently doesn't know my brother! I was ready to vent. :) Nothing but positive energy when around and when speaking of Tom!

Judy Vinje

Written May 20, 2008, 1:19 p.m.

Holy Hannah! Okay, so we all know that Tom isn't the most cooperative patient, but c'mon, man, quit stressing your wife out. :) Chrissie, it's just one more way the real Tom is shining through. You have so much positive energy surrounding you both. It's amazing, and you are truly the driving force.

Keep on keepin' on. We love you both!

Karrie, Ian, and Tyler C.

Written May 20, 2008, 1:53 p.m.

Hi, Chrissie,

A while back (before the benefit) I had talked to Terry on the phone. She told me what had happened to Tom. Terry also gave me this website, where I have gone to almost every day. I wish we would have kept better contact with each other through the years. Tom sounds like a great guy! The two of you are so lucky to have each other, and I know you will get through this difficult time in your lives. You are both truly blessed to have so many friends and family by your side.

Thinking of you,

Gail

PS: Woody and Jerry C. say hi

Wednesday, May 21, 2008, 10:35 a.m., CDT—Chrissie's Journal Entry

Good news!

Okay, sorry about that! I was at the hospital and I had my whole entry done, and when I hit save it said I was not authorized to update on that server. So I did a little test run with the "Good News," and well, you know the rest. Anyway, sorry I didn't write earlier today, but Tom had an appointment with Dr. H (his neurologist) at 9:30, and I did not get a chance to update before I left. It worked out for the best as I do have good news to share. First of all, Dr. H said that he was healing beautifully; Tom then said hi to him for what I think is the first time ever. He would always mess with him in the hospital. Then Tom squeezed Dr. H's hand with both of his. But the best news of all is that the doctor said that his sleepiness is right on track! He actually said that he was pleased he was as alert as he was! *Rock on!* Also he and Patti (from neuro-oncology) said that he could be this way for up to three months. They also said that there can still be changes from the radiation for up to one year.

As far as the chemo goes, they have to wait three to four weeks for Tom's brain to "settle down" from the radiation. The next step is to do an MRI on the brain and then one on the spine. They then assess the scans, along with his functionality, to determine what type of chemo to do, if any.

I still do not yet know where we will be going later today, but I will be certain to let you know tomorrow. Hopefully it will be Providence Place, which is seven blocks from our house. Tommy will be getting closer and closer to home.

I was most excited to see our friend Tim (rock on) H. visiting last night. I know it was good for Tommy, and besides, I have had people ask me, "Who is Tim H.?" (Because of his entries in the guest book.) Now they can put a face to the name.

Well, I must run back up to the hospital (I had to leave to update "the Bridge") to pack up his room and see what is going on. Until tomorrow, everyone take care.

Love,

Chrissie

Thursday, May 22, 2008, 9:37 a.m., CDT—
Chrissie's Journal Entry

Greetings,

Today is moving day. We are going to Providence Place, which is seven blocks from our house. My days of paying to park every day are over! Woo-hoo! As a matter of fact, I can park at home, grab Bailey, and take her for a walk to go see her daddy. That will be nice. The address for Providence Place is 3720 Twenty-Third Avenue South in Minneapolis, of course. I do not yet know his room number as he is scheduled to be moved at two thirty this afternoon. I will let you know the details tomorrow.

Tom was pretty sleepy for most of the day yesterday. He was more alert at the end of the day. He was messing with his nurse, and then I caught him messing with me and I called him on it. I was telling him that while I knew he was tired from the radiation, he has to do his part with the staff and during therapy so that he can get the most out of his recovery. He proceeded to do the head drop like he was falling asleep right in the middle of the conversation, and I pushed his head back up to the middle and said, "Bullsh*t, you are not asleep!" He opened his eyes and smiled and chuckled. He was most proud of himself. Now I know I need to watch him every minute. Like I don't have enough to do!

Anyway, I really need him to cooperate so we can move forward. If you would not mind, please pray for Tom to realize it is time to do his part and fight as hard as he can. I told him I was working my butt off out here trying to keep everything together, and it was time for him to step up. I also told him he could mess with the staff but not in a way that would hurt us or hinder his recovery. Let's hope he gets the message!

Much love to all,

Chrissie

Guest Book Entries

Written May 22, 2008, 10:28 a.m.

Tom, Chrissie,

Great work, you guys. Keep it goin'. We're rootin' for you, both of you. Chrissie, you're amazing, and Tom, you too. You're doing great, but *listen* to Chrissie! One day soon you'll be really glad she's kickin' your ass. We want to see you out front of our house with your big puppy soon. Really soon! Our prayers keep coming.

Victor, Dianne, Luisa, Lydia

Chapter 6

Providence Place

Friday, May 23, 2008, 8:19 a.m., CDT—
Chrissie's Journal Entry

Hello,

Tom is back in the hood! He is in room number 1122 at Providence Place. It was a rough day yesterday. He didn't want to leave the TCU, and he did not say a word or smile the rest of the day after we left. It was like a wall went up. At least he would shake and nod his head when I needed him to. I can't imagine what he is going through, leaving a place where you have gotten to know the people who are helping you and then being swept away to a world full of unknowns. (The therapists are all going to miss him, and they even did a little dance for him before he left yesterday while they sang, "These boots are made for walking." That was so awesome! Thanks, you guys!) I tried to reassure him and tell him that hopefully he will like the people at the Providence Place TCU just as much as the people at the Fairview TCU. He, of course, nodded, but who knows what he really wanted to say. For me, this whole week has been one of the roughest since the first few weeks of our ordeal, for various reasons. I really need for this week to be over, and I am glad it is a three-day weekend. I'm ready.

The most important thing that I can say today is that I would be most appreciative if everyone could please pray for Tom to tear down the wall, open up to healing and rehabilitation and keep moving forward. After yesterday, I know he really needs a boost of strength, willpower, and determination. My guess is he is tired of hearing it from me. Cripes, he might even tune me out by now, who knows. Some things don't change!

Have a great Memorial Weekend!

Love,

Chrissie

Guest Book Entries

Written May 24, 2008, 9:45 a.m.

Chrissie, it was great visiting with all of you last week, and I plan on making it to the hood. After talking to you, I knew the week would be tough, but I also realized how blessed Tom is to have you in his corner. You are his strength, and you never let up! So keep the faith, and I hope you have a great memorial weekend. You deserve it! Rock on!

Tim Hanley

Tuesday, May 27, 2008, 7:46 a.m., CDT—
Chrissie's Journal Entry

Good morning,

Things have definitely changed over the weekend. Tom is absolutely sleeping off the after-effects of the radiation. He woke up briefly on Friday night to talk to our friend (and his former controller) Angie W. That was the most he talked all weekend. Proof, once again, that he tries to entertain the people he hasn't seen or doesn't see very often. With those of us who go see him regularly, he is more comfortable sleeping and letting us just be there. After our visit with him on Friday night, I realized that I need to find out from the doctors today what Tom needs the most. Does he need to sleep right now, or is it okay to proceed with some kind of therapy during this time? These are answers I need to get in the next day or two. From what Dr. H said, he could be like this for as long as three months. He also said this is the most difficult time for the families. He wasn't kidding. It feels like we are at the beginning again. It really sucks because I don't want him to lose what he has already gained in therapy.

Still at issue are those blood clots. On Sunday and Monday I was all over the people at Providence Place making sure they knew about them and asking if there was a plan in place to monitor them. I got an answer (I think) from a nurse on Sunday but, I couldn't understand him. So I asked again yesterday. Then as I mentioned to the nurse's aide that his arm is definitely more swollen (it goes past his elbow now), she called the doctor yesterday, who put him on a water pill, and they scheduled an ultra sound for today. I have to say, this situation really freaks me out, especially as I watched as his arm got bigger over the weekend. It's obvious that the clots are not dissolving as they should.

I guess we are (and have been) in the middle of a cruel waiting game, and the hardest part is that there is nothing we can do about it except watch (to make sure he is okay and has everything he needs) and wait. I really hope this doesn't last the three months they say it can. In the meantime, there are times when he opens his eyes, briefly, and will nod or shake his head. You know he is at the surface and listening to you as his body works through the radiation. I don't pretend to understand it or like it, but you have to work through it and hope and pray he comes out all right on the other side. Until he does, please keep the positive energy and prayers coming. The road ahead seems to get longer and longer some days but, we'll do what we have to do.

Much love to all,

Chrissie

Guest Book Entries

Written May 27, 2008, 11:06 a.m.

Hi, Chrissie,

You are an amazing woman! I can only imagine the frustration you feel in dealing with the staff and the doctors to be proactive with Tom's care. Every day, I look for your journal entry. Your very positive attitude is very uplifting to me. Cheri, Linda, and I stopped in to see Tom early Sunday evening. He was sleeping, so we didn't attempt to wake him. We were impressed with Providence Place as it was by far the best short-term care facility we have been in. We love you so much and are amazed every day of your fight for Tom. We hope and pray that his current condition won't last for three months, as we know how difficult and taxing it is being a caregiver.

Love,

Susan L.

Written May 27, 2008, 2:49 p.m.

Dear Chrissie

Keeping up to date on Tom's progress, it seems, is like watching corn grow. The progress seems very slow when I know you are looking to see something positive each day. I have a close friend in Arizona who has cancer of the brain, discovered in February as we were driving down to spend some time with them, and the progress is not much different than Tom's. (His name is also Tom.) Your aunt Jeanne and I continue to offer daily prayers for him, and other than that, we can only send you our love ... Uncle Harold.

Harold Trombley

Written May 27, 2008 5:05 p.m.

Hi, Chris,

Tom *will* come back and be strong. Positive energy and prayers are what can make a world of difference. I am living proof of that. One day, one moment is all you can deal with at a time. Take a moment to breathe for yourself.

Love ya,

Roxie Chudy

Wednesday, May 28, 2008, 8:41 a.m., CDT— Chrissie's Journal Entry

Hello,

Not too much new to report other than last night we had a visit from the Storm family, and during that time was the most I have seen him awake and talking in well over a week (except for when Angie visited)! Through all of this, it is so nice to see these bright spots. While I know he will be extremely sleepy or somewhat sleepy at times, it *really* helps me to see him wake up, speak, laugh, and give me "the look" for the occasional visitor. It just reinforces what I already know to be true—that he is there, working through his treatment, and he will come out of this on the other side to be the Tommy Vinje we all know and love. Mark and Colleen could not get over how good he looks! They came in expecting to see him looking very sick, but instead they saw that he looked like himself with just a little less hair! That's my baby!

We have already passed the two-week mark since the radiation stopped. That's good news. The further away from it we get, the better. The issue of the blood clots I am still dealing with. Apparently a nurse practitioner came in yesterday and decided not to go along with the ultrasound ordered by the doctor the day before. She did not think it was needed. The doctor herself will be in today and will hopefully go ahead with her original decision. I have asked them for three days what their plan is, and it seems I cannot get a straight answer. It also seems that I have to go through the nurses to talk to the doctor, which is BS. I can call his brain surgeon and talk to him, but I can't talk to a nursing home doctor! Please! They haven't heard the last of me! Word.

Love,

Chrissie

Guest Book Entries

Written May 28, 2008, 10:11 a.m.

Stay strong, Chrissie Vinje! You know we are all out here pulling and praying for both you and Tom. Though you may be getting resistance or obstacles while you are there with Tom and dealing with some of those doctors and nurses, you have tons of support from all of us out here. That won't stop.

Love to you both!

Karrie Cable

Written May 28, 2008, 11:19 a.m.

Hey, Chrissie and Tom! I'm so happy to hear you've moved closer to home and you're improving daily, despite those nasty blood clots. I have to chuckle when I read your posts, Chrissie; it's just like having you sitting here in person with your funny lingo … Word! Ha, ha! Keeping both of you and your families in our prayers. Let's keep the steady progress going and show this cancer who's boss! Hey, a shout out to Roxy (Clark) too! Long time, girlfriend, hope things are good with you!

Peggy

Thursday, May 29, 2008, 8:29 a.m., CDT— Chrissie's Journal Entry

Good morning,

The bummer of yesterday was that Tom barely woke up for us. He had a few moments when you knew he was listening and he would nod or shake his head, but not much more than that. I did find out from the doctor yesterday that they are upping his Ritalin dose today. He has been on 5 mg twice a day, and they are doubling that to 10 mg twice a day. Maybe this will help. It would be nice.

Behind the scenes there is a lot happening, and it is a little stressful, to say the least. Due to the after-effects of radiation Tom is experiencing, he is not able to participate and progress in therapy like he was previously. This translates into no insurance coverage in a skilled nursing facility. So the options are to private pay to keep him in Providence Place, which means pay for *everything*, including medications, or bring him home and at least have medications (and I don't know what else yet) paid for, and then I am not paying for a facility. Tom will still need care 24–7, and all of these details will have to be worked out. The good news is that once he is able to participate in therapies again, he will be assessed and then therapies will be covered again. We have a lot of things to work out. I am sure there are things I have not even thought of yet.

A real bummer on the nursing home scene is that Tom already had some things stolen from his room. He had a yellow basin we brought over from Fairview full of toiletries and some lotions we had bought and even some stuff they brought in for him that was sitting on his window sill; all gone. Then, as I was filling out the report, I noticed that his hospital socks (with the grippers) were gone, along with his prescription sunglasses. Nice. I guess it's time to remove a few things from his room and bring them home.

As far as the blood clots go, there will be no ultrasounds because they cannot treat them at this time. We just have to pray that they dissolve and become a nonissue. I'm ready. They freak me out.

Bad things happen fast; good things take time. Bad things happen fast; good things take time, etc.

Love,

Chrissie

Friday, May 30, 2008, 8:22 a.m., CDT— Chrissie's Journal Entry

Good morning,

Tommy is still sleepy. He woke up enough to have a few bites of dinner last night, and there were times when we knew he was listening to us. We have a care conference this morning at Providence that he will attend; hopefully he will be awake for it. In the meantime, there will be a few meetings over the weekend with friends and family so we can get a plan of attack.

At this point, I am extremely tired and I am just trying to keep it going, but I need some help from him. I found out the other day that while he is in this state, we can push him to do therapy to a point that is reasonable but also within his abilities. Right now, I am not sure what that is. I keep thinking that if we bring him home, he might thrive and start moving forward. I also found out that it is common for people to not react to staff and just to their loved ones. Good to know. That is why I think he might just do better at home. We will see.

Please pray for strength for Tom to rise above his current condition and take charge to get his life back, because he can. He just has to realize it himself because currently, I am not sure that he does. Prayers and positive energy are what it is all about. Let's go!

Have a great weekend!

Chrissie

Guest Book Entries

Written May 31, 2008, 11:40 a.m.

Dear Tom and Chrissie: Just a short note to let you know you are in my thoughts and prayers. Love you both. I would be honored if I could help in some way. I'm available Fridays, every other Saturday night, and every other Sunday. Keep the faith!

Robert Notch

St Paul, MN

Monday, June 2, 2008, 9:28 a.m., CDT— Chrissie's Journal Entry

Okay, I am feeling a little overwhelmed at the moment. There are so many things running through my head that I can barely focus. We had a great powwow yesterday. We got a lot of information out there from all sides. There are still *a lot* of things I need to find out from Providence Place and the insurance company about what is covered and what is not when he comes home. Some good things that happened at the meeting yesterday were that our nephew Tony and my brother Tony both have hospital beds available. My brother also has a wheelchair and a commode. The guys were all over measuring and figuring out how to build the ramps at the house. I truly don't know what I would do without any of you, and I mean that from the bottom of my heart.

As far as the care conference last Friday, I was pleased at the way they seemed to get on board to care for Tom once we told them what he had accomplished before he got there. They are scheduling his therapies in the afternoon when I am there, but I have a feeling he will not wake up for them. He has not woken up for the last couple of days, and they are upping his tube feeding to be more than just at night because he is not waking up to eat. When I got there on Friday morning before the conference, Tom was lying there with his eyes open, and when I walked in he shut them and did not open them again. I don't know. It freaks me out a little that he is not waking up at all right now. I tried placing a call to Patti B. this morning to see if this is par for the course, but she is on vacation. I will have to call Dr. H. I just want to be sure.

The next couple of weeks are going to be something. I cannot even fathom what will be around the corner on any given day. It tires me out to think about it. I guess we just need to take it one moment at a time and forge ahead. In the meantime, pray for Tom to wake up and come out on the other side with smiles for everyone. I can't wait!

Love to all,

Chrissie

Guest Book Entries

Written June 2, 2008, 8:32 a.m.

Dear Chrissie,

I talked with Marlene last evening, and she gave me this site.

Please be strong, dear! Know that my parents and I are praying for you and Tom!

I am so blessed to have your mom and your whole family as my friends as long as I can remember!

Most sincerely,

Laura S.

Written June 2, 2008, 12:11 p.m.

Hi, Chris,

Hang in there … I know all the red tape and rules of insurance and all is so aggravating. I was talking with Sandy; she has worked her whole career in skilled nursing facilities. She said that if there is a care that they provide on all shifts, for example, taking a blood sugar, they will do it so all shifts will have to take it so the patient will remain covered. I am sure you have checked into all avenues, but in case that was not brought up, just thought I would throw it out there.

I do know, on the other hand, that when I came home I did better after being in the hospital for so long. I had a nurse come every day, plus my sister and Chris … Tom has more cares than I did at that point. I am not sure what to tell you. There are pros and cons on both sides of the coin.

I am praying and sending positive energy for you. I know you are exhausted. If there is anything I can do, please let me know …

Love and hugs to you … keep plugging along. Tom will overcome this.

Roxie Chudy

Tuesday, June 3, 2008, 8:13 a.m., CDT— Chrissie's Journal Entry

Good morning,

I bet y'all didn't realize you'd be on this rollercoaster with me for so long. Yesterday I got to PP (short for Providence Place from now on) in time for the therapists to come in. When I walked in with Hanifa (speech therapist), I asked him if he was awake, and he nodded. We tried getting a little more out of him for a few minutes and didn't get too much. About fifteen minutes later, the physical therapists came in. Tom (physical therapist) stayed and showed me some range of motion exercises to do with his legs and feet. On about the third exercise, Tom started to participate. It was kind of sporadic. Then, before Tom left, he told him he would be back tomorrow, and Tommy nodded his head. (This is the most activity they have seen with him since we got there.) At Tom's parting suggestion, we put on our Bob Marley CD, and as I sat there with Tommy he slowly woke up and was awake (except for dozing here and there) until I left around eight o'clock.

At six o'clock they put him up in the wheelchair, and Tom wanted to go for a walk around the joint (although he did not want to go outside). So as Judy got there, we went walking around the first floor about four times. We went into the lounge but the TV was up too loud for him, so we moved on. He is not too keen on loud noises and bright lights these days. I'm guessing it could be that way for some time. He was also opening his eyes much more than I have seen in a while. You could see that he was just drained, but he is coming around. I guess that four-day sleep he just had worked the way it was supposed to. One thing that happened (that I will tell the therapists about today) is that when we went back to his room, while we were sitting in there waiting for them to put him back to bed, his back started to spasm. He kept trying to move himself around in the wheelchair, and he started grabbing the front of the chair and pulling himself forward so I could rub his back. He must have done it about five times ... very good for the stomach muscles! He would sit forward until he got too tired, and then after a short rest, he would pull himself forward again. Yeah baby!

For some reason, he was really sweating yesterday. That is the first time I have seen that. Yes, it is a little warm in there, but I don't know if that's the reason. I brought it up to his nurse, who put a cold washcloth on the back of his neck as he was in the chair. I was also washing his face and head with a washcloth to cool him off and to help take off some of the peeling skin on the top of his head (from the radiation). It has been three weeks today since the radiation ended. Hopefully this is the beginning of his waking up period. Of course, he may have a few more weeks of sleeping for a day or two. It's all a mystery at this point.

In other news, I did find out that the medical equipment is covered by insurance. Hopefully the Heuer (lift) is also covered. We are checking on that. In-home physical therapy is also covered as long as he is progressing (of course). The thing I am most concerned about (except those blood clots) is that he gets all of the therapy he needs. I was told yesterday that after he goes home, I would have to get a doctor to write an order for therapy so he can be reassessed. It could be any doctor. Weird. Do I call his primary physician, or do I call the Neurology Department? I am uncomfortable with this situation. I don't want to pull him from PP until I know more.

Thank you everyone for your continuing positive thoughts, prayers, and offers of help. It means so much that you are all hanging in there with me. I know that I sometimes don't react the way I would like to when someone helps me/us or does something nice for us. I really want to jump up and down and scream and be most appreciative. Let me just say that I appreciate *everything* everyone has done! I just can't always express it in the right way. I think I am just numb. There has been too much information in and out of my brain in the last eleven weeks. So, thank you, everyone.

Much love to all,

Chrissie

Tuesday, June 3, 2008, 2:58 p.m., CDT—
Chrissie's Journal Entry

Hey, everyone,

This is Judy. I'm writing on behalf of Chrissie. Tom is being transported to Fairview Riverside. When Chrissie got up to PP to visit Tom, she noticed he was having a hard time breathing (he nodded his head yes when she asked), and he looked bloated and was sweating a lot. We wanted you all to know right away so you could send all prayers and positive energy his way. Chrissie will keep you posted once she knows more.

Thanks,

Judy Vinje

Tuesday, June 3, 2008, 3:25 p.m., CDT—
Chrissie's Journal Entry

Remember: bad things happen fast, and good things take time.

Tuesday, June 3, 2008, 7:15 p.m., CDT—
Chrissie's Journal Entry

Hello, everyone,

Here is the situation. When I got to PP this afternoon, the nurse was in his room putzing around doing what he does. After he left the room, I was sitting with Tom, and in less than two minutes I knew something was not right. He was breathing really heavy, he was really bloated, and he was sweating profusely. I walked out to the station and told them that something was wrong. They came in and took vitals and found that his heart rate was elevated. They called the doctor and then called for an ambulance.

After an x-ray, a CT scan, and several other tests, it has been determined that the very large clots have been breaking off. There are currently one clot in his right lung, two in his left (taking up approximately three-quarters of his lung), and one in his left arm still. He is currently in stable but critical condition. We are at Fairview Riverside ICU at the moment for observation. I am not sure if he will stay in ICU or go to the main part of the hospital from here. The problem, of course, has not changed. They cannot treat the clots with a blood thinner because of the radiation and the cancer because it could cause bleeding into the brain. He also is not a candidate for the filter. All we can do is wait, hope, and pray that these things dissipate. It is our only chance with these.

The other negative part of this is that it is another setback and could affect whether he receives chemo. But let's pray that through this he will sleep off the radiation and those damn clots. They are keeping him sedated so he does not move around and break off more of the clots.

I guess, once again, we need lots of positive energy and prayers. I know everyone has been continually praying, and I thank you. Let's just keep it going!

Love to all,

Chrissie

***

I would like to interject here that hindsight is, of course, twenty/twenty. As I figured out the next day, when Tommy was grabbing the wheelchair and pulling himself forward and sweating, his back was not having spasms. The blood clots were moving. And they were moving for hours upon hours. If only I had known that the night before. But hell, they didn't even see anything was wrong with him the next day when I knew instantly. You have to watch everything and everyone. I cannot stress that enough.

***

Guest Book Entries

Written June 4, 2008, 7:32 a.m.

Hey, Chris and Tom,

My constant thoughts and prayers are with you. I visited my mom yesterday, and she is my reminder how precious life is. I know you know that, so just take deep breaths and have faith, and Tom will get through this somehow … His love for you shows you that already. I know that deep down my mom is also saying prayers for you both … I tell her and update her on what's happening with Tom and you, and before I left she reached out and held my hand. I know that it was not just for me but both of you also! *Lots* of *hugs* sent your way also!

Julie S.

Written June 4, 2008, 9:32 a.m.

Chrissie,

We just wanted you to know how amazing we think you are! Please know that you and Tom are in our prayers every day. If there is anything we can do, please let us know.

Love and prayers,

Mark and Colleen Storm

Written June 4, 2008 11:50 a.m.

Hi, Tom and Chrissie,

My sister just told me about this site, and I think it's great that you can keep people updated every day on Tom's progress. I am sorry to hear that Tom has blood clots, and I hope this is a mere bump in the road to his recovery. I am sorry that I haven't been up to visit, but I wanted you to feel better so you are able to handle my warped sense of humor that I have been gifted with. I am not a churchgoing man, but I do believe in the Good Lord above and I know that he believes, as I do, that good things happen to good people. I know that he is there with you two to help give you strength in Tom's recovery. I was reading the other entries here in this guest book, and everybody is talking about positive vibes getting sent out to you. As you well know, I am the king of positive vibes, so now I am going to send you some. Here it goes ... umff ... ooooo ... ehhhh ... (Can ya feel them?) ... here's some more ... uhh ... uhh ... *ahhhhhhh*! Wow! Those were some of the most positive vibes I have sent out in a long, long time, and I sure hope they help. Well, time for me to sign off as it still takes me forever to type. I will talk at you soon and I want you to remember, and these are the words of the Big Rude Monster, love ya, babe!

Michael Anderson

Chapter 7

Fairview Riverside Hospital

Thursday, June 5, 2008, 7:12 a.m., CDT—
Chrissie's Journal Entry

Hello,

FYI—I tried to update the Bridge twice yesterday but, as soon as I hit "save," I was denied. So here is the update on Tommy's condition. As the doctor told us yesterday, the clots are life-threatening, which of course I think we all knew. Yesterday morning the nurse ordered an ultrasound on both arms and legs, which showed one clot in his left arm and one in his leg. This led them to put a filter in his groin to stop any clots from his legs going to his lungs. He also had an MRI on his brain and his spine yesterday, along with a battery of other tests so they know what they are dealing with. We will know the results of the MRIs today. They also recalibrated his shunt to make sure everything was working properly and then took an x-ray to make sure it was positioned properly. My poor honey.

After all of this was done and he was all settled last night, at about nine o'clock we were able to see him, two at a time. After all he had been through yesterday, some people actually got the privilege of Tommy opening his eyes to look at and speak to them. The best part is that the nurse (she was awesome) was in the room for this, and then he actually answered her questions! Thank God. He was coughing pretty badly as we were leaving, and that was probably from lying flat for so long for both MRIs.

He is by no means out of the woods yet. They are concerned that at some point, if his breathing becomes too labored, they will have to intubate. We are trying to avoid this because, with his current diminished lung capacity, it may be difficult to get him off of the tube, and then he might have to have a trach tube. So we have to make the decision, if it comes to that, to intubate or do nothing. How do you make that decision? Who am I to make that decision? That was not something we ever talked about. Please pray we won't have to make that decision. And please pray hard for Tommy and send him the most positive of energy.

Thanks to everyone who was there yesterday. It helps to keep me strong during these difficult times, and it reinforces how much Tom means to everyone. I love you all.

Chrissie

Guest Book Entries

Written June 5, 2008, 7:59 a.m.

There is a quote by Babe Ruth that talks about it being hard to beat a person who never gives up.

Tom—I know you won't give up.

I love you.

Nicole Betlach

Written June 5, 2008, 11:07 a.m.

Chrissie,

You and Tom are in my thoughts every day. You are an amazing person, and Tom is so lucky to have you by his side. Everyone on 6A is thinking about you both.

Kelly Ayd

Written June 5, 2008, 12:29 p.m.

Chrissie, I think it's a wonderful way you are communicating to everyone … I think about my friend Tom often and pray for you all! Much love, God bless, and of course, keep the faith!

Dino DiPerna

Written June 5, 2008, 2:08 p.m.

Ving—what the hell, Cha Cha! I am always amazed at the twists and turns life takes us on … you two have one of the most beautiful loves I've ever seen. I've been jealous since you two first found each other.

I know it makes no sense when these difficult things happen to such genuine people … and in that regard I am sorry I can't offer any pearls of wisdom. (We both know how damn smart I am anyway.) I miss you both and love you both, and *please* call if there's anything I can do or if you just want to talk. I'm here for whatever you need, honey.

Love you,

Michelle Notch

Friday, June 6, 2008, 7:08 a.m., CDT— Chrissie's Journal Entry

Hello,

It is very hard to watch Tom and his struggle to breathe. It breaks my heart. He is currently on an oxygen mask that is giving him 100 percent oxygen, and he is keeping his levels between 89 and 100 percent. The nurse said her threshold for putting him on a vent tube is 85 percent or lower. Also, the more he swallows and coughs, the better off he is. This will keep fluids from entering his lungs and causing pneumonia. This is very important because he cannot have anything else in his lungs. In the meantime he is still in ICU and being watched very closely.

We did not hear the results of the MRIs yesterday. We will find out at eleven o'clock today. Also, his platelets dropped again yesterday, and the ICU doc said that it could have something to do with his bone marrow, which could be related to the radiation. We are waiting to hear from the hematologists about that as well.

Man, not one step of this has been easy. Every situation has been extreme, and at this point I am struggling to figure out why. This is the gravest situation he has been in. The nurse at the ICU says he is on the edge and it could go either way. Please pray for Tom to rally and pull through this. Keep praying and sending the positive energy. It is what he needs. Thank you.

Love to all,

Chrissie

Guest Book Entries

Written June 6, 2008, 5:34 a.m.

Tom and Chrissie,

We are writing to show our support during your stressed times. We continue to pray for all your daily struggles and to find a way to keep you strong. Miracles do happen! There is a prayer we say when we are in need. It's the Serenity Prayer: "God grant me the serenity to accept the things I cannot change, the courage to change the things I can and the wisdom to know the difference." Also, praying to St. Anthony has always helped with finding the help we need. Remember that God is always with you. Marlene has been keeping us informed, and we really appreciate that. We will continue to keep you and Tom in our prayers.

Tom and Patty Clayton

Written June 6, 2008, 8:24 a.m.

Chrissie,

I'm thinking about you today. I know how hard it is to watch Tom trying to breathe. I prayed and prayed that a miracle would happen for Tom. I will continue to pray for a miracle! This is such a very, very difficult time for you and all of his family. My heart goes out all.

Love,

Susan L.

Written June 6, 2008, 8:46 a.m.

Chrissie,

Keep it up, girl. Be strong. We're rootin' for you. All our prayers keep coming. Go, Tom! Don't give up now. You've come a long way. Keep the faith!

Victor Zupanc

Written June 6, 2008, 8:50 a.m.

Hi, Chrissie, we're thinking about you and Tom and praying for both of you. We love you both very much!

Barry and Krissy

Written June 6, 2008, 9:24 a.m.

David and I are praying for your entire family through this difficult time. Please, please let us know if there is *anything* we can do for you. (Just remember you might have to repay David with some fudge! JK!) You both are near and dear to our hearts. <3

Love,

Peggy

Written June 6, 2008, 4:54 p.m.

Chrissie, Tom, and all the Vinje Family, Curt and I are praying hard for Tom to come through this. It must be very hard to watch helplessly as your loved one goes through this. Just know that Tom's angels are watching over him and giving him strength to overcome this.

We wish the good things would come a little faster, for everyone's peace of mind. God bless you.

Chris and Curt Saunders

Written June 7, 2008, 10:21 a.m.

Chris,

It breaks my heart to read about what both you and Tom have to go through right now. You are an amazing woman. I know inside it is breaking you apart, but you are such a great inspiration to Tom. I am praying that Tom gets through this quickly and that things turn around. You have both been through so much, and there are *so* many people cheering for you guys! I will continue to pray for Tom to get stronger and to start breathing on his own so he can leave the ICU and get back to his sweetheart! There are many angels looking down on you guys and wrapping their arms around you with positive healing energy.

God's blessings to your whole family,

Kris K.

Written June 7, 2008, 2:21 p.m.

Praying hard for you both …

Robert Notch

Monday, June 9, 2008, 6:33 a.m., CDT— Chrissie's Journal Entry

Good morning,

Tom held his own over the weekend. He is still on the oxygen mask, and his oxygen levels are staying around 94 to 97 percent. This is good. He has pretty much slept all weekend, and they are going down the list as to the reasons why. In the meantime, I remind them that he is still in the after-effects of radiation, and they say while that is true, they are still trying to eliminate other reasons, like infection. I say, go ahead and check everything. The neurology doc said yesterday that this could be how he is (which we know isn't true; we've seen otherwise), or he just needs time to come out of it. *Word*! I can't get upset at that argument anymore because we've seen how he is, and he was just talking less than a week ago. Tommy needs time to heal. The neurology doc also said that he does have pneumonia, which is already being treated.

The results of the MRIs he had last week are extremely encouraging! The tumor has been greatly reduced by the radiation, and the cancer in the spine is gone! Woo-hoo! Now we just have to get him to a point where he can do chemo so we can knock that tumor out.

In other news, all of his blood levels are low. This leads them to the subject of his bone marrow. When they did a blood smear last week, they noticed some abnormal cells. This could be either precancerous cells in the bone marrow or abnormal cells from being so sick. They will be doing a bone marrow biopsy today to determine which it is. They assured me that they would make him as comfortable as possible as it is painful when they stick that needle in his hip to get the marrow. I certainly hope he sleeps through it all.

As far as the blood clots, they keep forming. He now has the three in his lungs, one in his right leg, and one in each arm. I want so badly for this situation to be corrected, but they can't do anything. At least we know the clots in his legs are blocked from going to his heart. We meet with the hematologists today at one o'clock; maybe we can get some answers to our questions on a few things in this regard.

As always, keep Tommy in your prayers and keep the positive energy flowing in his direction. Thank you so much.

Much love to all,

Chrissie

Guest Book Entries

Written June 9, 2008, 7:26 a.m.

Love you.

Wendy Peterson

Written June 9, 2008, 9:41 a.m.

Chrissie and Tom,

We've got you in our thoughts and prayers ... hang in there.

Dianne, Vic, Luisa, and Lydia

Written June 9, 2008, 4:34 p.m.

Okay, Chrissie, I'm back. Been reading your updates, and the MRI results are great news! Now let's focus positive energy and rid Tom of those nasty clots so he can start the chemo and finish off the cancer! I admire your strength. Don't let up. Keep the faith, prayers, and positive vibes keep coming for you and Tom! Rock on!

Tim Hanley

Written June 9, 2008, 8:10 p.m.

We are remembering you guys in our thoughts and prayers each day. Keep your faith in God. He is bigger than any of this and will see you through.

Melinda

(Friend of Tammy Anderson)

Tuesday, June 10, 2008, 6:33 a.m., CDT— Chrissie's Journal Entry

Hello,

Tom was somewhat awake yesterday, which was nice. We got the CD player rolling in his room with a little GB Leighton and Earth, Wind, and Fire. I forgot the Bob Marley CD in the player I brought home from PP. I will be bringing that in today. Otherwise, he is stable at the moment and breathing much more peacefully than he was a week ago. As long as he keeps coughing and they keep suctioning the crud out of his throat, he breathes normally.

They did not do the bone marrow biopsy as planned. The hematologists told us yesterday that he already has an infection he is being treated for, and they did not want to introduce the possibility of another one. They are going to wait a few days and revisit the idea.

We had a visit yesterday from someone on the ICU staff, and I am not quite sure what he was trying to say. He was telling me that Tom has the worst kind of brain tumor, and right now what they were doing for him was "housekeeping" and that I might want to think about what's best for him. What would he want? Not what would I want or the kids (he doesn't even know we don't have any), but what would he want. *(Don't you think I think about that every flipping day!)* So what was he getting at? There is nothing right now that I would do differently, and if he is suggesting that I just let go and let him go when I know he is right there, then he can just %&$@ off! I think you know what I'm trying to say! I need to get clarification today on what that visit was all about and who he was.

In the meantime, the ICU set up a meeting today at 10:00 a.m. with Dr. H, his neurology surgeon. I am more than a little nervous as to what that is about. I hate all these meetings. It ties my stomach up in knots at the anticipation of more bad news. I need some good news for a change, and I want to see my honey get better. I wish we could get rid of those damn clots.

As always, I will let you know tomorrow the news of today. Take care.

Chrissie

Tuesday, June 10, 2008, 11:29 a.m., CDT— Chrissie's Journal Entry

Okay, we just met with Dr. H and Dr. R, and it was not good news. Dr. H told us that Tom has the worst kind of tumor and it has behaved badly, which, of course, we already knew. Along with behaving badly is the issue of its location. The tumor was in such a position that the spinal fluid carried it to other parts of the brain (meaning the ventricles). He also said that because of its location, it was essentially hiding and was left undetected and could not have been found earlier.

That being said, he also said that the radiation did not do enough to shrink the tumor and bring on the rapid changes they should be seeing by now. As far as the chemo goes, he said it would only extend the life of someone (who is functioning well) by about four weeks.

He mentioned alternative drugs (not approved by the FDA, etc.) but said that any of the mediocre ones they had here at the U would not be enough to make a difference. He also said that there were no drugs on the horizon that would cause drastic or dramatic results. He also mentioned "comfort care"—keeping Tom comfortable in the time he has left. This, of course, is something I hate hearing from them because it just can't be true.

What to do next? I'm thinking second opinion from the Mayo Clinic. A second opinion is something we have not yet had, and what better place to do it than at the Mayo? In the meantime the team here at the U is waiting for us to talk it over and get back to them with guidance on how we want to proceed.

I am open to suggestions from anyone who would like to share their thoughts on this current situation.

Love to all,

Chrissie

Guest Book Entries

Written June 10, 2008, 8:20 a.m.

Whoever that ICU rep is that felt compelled to say that *BS* to you does *not* realize who is dealing with in either you or Tom! "Letting go" to him is "giving up" to you, and we all know you are not about to do that. Tom wouldn't want you to do that, and we certainly are not about to do that with all of our prayers, positive thoughts, and energies and support. I think I can speak for every one of us that visits this website that you are doing the only thing you possibly can do for the love of your life by fighting for him every step of the way, and you are doing it with much admiration from all of us.

Tom will get through this because he has you.

These people don't know who they are dealing with. You have God on your side, along with all of us.

I love you!

Beth Timm

Written June 10, 2008, 9:02 a.m.

Oh, Chris!

Some of these so-called medical professionals must have been absent the day they had bedside manner at school. I swear I had the same thing happen to me; I had a doc come in and tell me things that had *never* been discussed. He did not know me; he had never seen me or my family before. Just took a glance at my chart and told me horrific things. When my doc came in, I was in a panic over it. He told me to just tell these doctors to get out of my room, which I did quite often after I figured out I was in control … I am so sorry you had to have an a-hole do that to you. He does not know the strength that is coming from all sides. He does not know Tom or you … I realize that Tom is in ICU for a reason, but he is going to come through this 'cause he has you fighting for him. And as I said before, you look at this picture and see that big smile you know in your heart he is fighting to get through this.

Take care, my dear; hold on to what you know is true. Believe that which is in your heart. And we will all keep praying and sending positive thoughts to you and Tom.

Love you,

Roxie Chudy

Written June 10, 2008, 9:58 a.m.

Oh, girl, I've only met you a couple times and haven't had much time to get to know Tom here at work. The few times we've talked he's always made me smile. I have, however, walked in your shoes a few years ago when *my* Tom was very ill and I alone heard all the scary things the staff will say to a wife. I feel compelled to remind you to trust yourself and never doubt God's fierce love for you both. From what you write daily, Tom is comfortable and you can feel confident that this stage is not just "housekeeping." And the jackass who said that obviously doesn't know that housekeeping is *work*, anyway, ha-ha.

I read your notes every day and want to thank you for updating us all. You are an inspiration in a world where many don't fight to keep a marriage going in sickness and in health and bail at the first sign of problems. Keep putting your healing hands over your honey's body and let your love flow into him. So many people are sending more love to you both. You are daily in my thoughts and prayers.

Deborah Kelly (Receptionist at Jag/Landrover)

Written June 10, 2008, 12:01 p.m.

Chrissie,

You are one brave lady, Chrissie, and I continue to be amazed at your strength. I think you should get a second opinion so you never have to look back and wish you did. The worst thing that could happen is that the doctors would concur and you will know that you did whatever was necessary to look out for Tom, and the best thing is that a new pair of eyes could see something that the others did not.

We are all behind you and love and support you with whatever you decide.

You will know what is best for Tom.

God bless!

Love,

Lynn Robson

Written June 10, 2008, 12:15 p.m.

Chrissie,

There is only one direction that makes sense for you to go—and that is forward. You are one special lady. So many of us have gotten to see just how special since March. You have to go with your gut, your instinct, your intuition. Trust it … and use it. You're not alone.

Jodi

Written June 10, 2008, 12:20 p.m.

Chris,

I would definitely get a second opinion. The folks at the Mayo Clinic are fantastic. I had some things taken care of there. It is such a wonderful environment, and they will treat you and Tom with dignity and respect.

It is heartbreaking that you have to go through this. I hope you know that everyone is cheering you on and truly amazed at the way you keep us all informed and in touch.

Yes, get that second opinion. Mayo is the best. The docs at the U are good also, but a new pair of eyes could give you more answers.

Take care, love you,

Roxie Chudy

Written June 10, 2008, 1:08 p.m.

Chrissie,

I am not sure if I have ever met your husband, Tom. But if he is as half as cool as you ... he must be an *awesome guy*! My thoughts and prayers are with you. You both have such a *huge* support system and are truly blessed with a wonderful, loving family. *Be strong* ... I love you!

Heidi

Bismarck, North Dakota (closer than you can imagine!)

Written June 10, 2008, 1:54 p.m.

Chrissie,

I've started a message to you several times, and I cannot find the words ... Please just know that you and Tom are in our prayers. It is difficult to accept bad things happening to such great people, but please know that God is with you no matter what! We love you both so very much and pray for comfort during this difficult time.

Love you,

Mark and Colleen Storm

Written June 10, 2008, 2:20 p.m.

Chrissie,

Seek out your heart and mind together and go with your gut, but I also think you need a family pow-wow with his mom and siblings before you choose any path. It's a tough road to walk by yourself. I think if you can talk to Tom if he is awake enough, you need him to be a part of the decision. Otherwise you have to speak for him.

Just know that you are not alone, that you have tons of loving arms wrapped around you for good and bad.

Love you both

Julie S.

Written June 10, 2008, 3:06 p.m.

Big Sis,

You have taken on a hell of a lot of challenges in your life and have come out smelling like a rose. So as far as a second opinion goes, I am behind you all the way. They have done a lot of impressive things at the Mayo. The only thing that I would be concerned about is getting him there. I will do anything you want, just say the word, *baby*. So you go ahead and follow your heart, so there are no regrets, and I *will follow you*. My prayers and love to you *both*. Don't worry about what the *docs* say or how they say it. They are in it for what they can do, not how they say it.

I love you more than you can imagine.

Your little brother,

Tony Betlach

Written June 10, 2008, 3:33 p.m.

Dear Chrissie,

I have waited to send you a message, and now I think it is high time. I don't know if you remember me, but I am a friend of the Bishmans. Please know there is *always* hope. I have prayed for you and Tommy. You probably don't know my situation, but I was diagnosed with Stage IV breast cancer last fall. We all know there is no Stage V, right? Well, I *refused* to accept the limitations of Western medicine and decided to explore alternative therapies. Cancer *can be reversed.* I am proof. There is no cancer in my body. The past six months I have been treated at an integrative cancer care center in Chicago, Illinois, called the Block Center. They tell me I have had a "phenomenal" result and that I will live a long life. I assure you, they are not quacks. I've talked to many patients who have had their cancer reversed when they were near the end of their journey. Jacki came with me about six weeks ago, and we told the doctors about Tommy. They would love to hear from you. Their number is 847-328-6632. They have a great website too. *Never* give up. These doctors *never* give up. They will step outside the box of the classic treatment modalities. *God bless you, sweetie.*

Love, light, and prayers to you and Tommy,

Karyn Huemoeller

Written June 10, 2008, 7:27 p.m.

Chrissie,

If you want a second opinion, you and Tom both should get a second opinion. Whatever you choose to do, remember that whatever happens, either way, is out of your hands, both of your hands. You are doing just what you should be doing. You are asking questions, weighing the options, and most of all being an amazing source of strength and support to Tom and an inspiration to anyone who is connected in any way to your circle of love and support.

Heather and Asher

Wednesday, June 11, 2008, 6:49 a.m., CDT— Chrissie's Journal Entry

Good morning,

Here is what I have done so far. Yesterday afternoon I contacted the Mayo and gave them Tom's information. They will contact me in three to four business days and let me know if there is something they can do for him. Also, on the suggestion from Karyn, I did contact the Block Center in Chicago. At the time that I called, one of the doctors was with a patient and they were closing, so they are going to call me back today to get the information about Tommy. I would not be able to live with myself if I did not try to do these things. Our families and I are not ready to give up. We have to do whatever we think is right for him. Thank God for our families and friends because I can't imagine going through this by myself. Thank God again that I don't have to.

In other news, Tommy is off the face mask and back on the nose cannula for oxygen. They have been able to reduce the oxygen levels he is getting, and he is now able to lie on his left side again and breathe easily. His breathing is much better and calmer. Yay! He was awake yesterday morning with his eyes open off and on throughout the day. They are thinking they are going to move him out of ICU today. When I find out what floor he will be on, I will let you know.

At this point I think I need to ask everyone to pray that we make the right decisions for Tommy and also that he accepts any healing that comes his way.

It ain't over till it's over, *and* it ain't over!

Much love and thanks to all,

Chrissie

Guest Book Entries

Written June 11, 2008, 7:05 a.m.

Chrissie

I know I haven't written, but I guess now is the time. I certainly would get a second opinion. If there is anything you need that I can help in any way, I'm here for you. All you have to do is ask. You know I love you guys with all my heart.

Auntie Mar

Marlene Trombley

Written June 11, 2008, 8:46 a.m.

Chrissie,

Our prayers are coming faster and stronger. Keep the faith. Above all, trust yourself. You know Tom better than anyone in the world. *You* have to trust yourself in your decisions. Listen to the second opinions, absolutely. But most of all, listen to yourself. In the end you'll know what's best. Keep strong, Chrissie. And Tom, I hope you're hearing/seeing/feeling all this. It's huge, and it's all for you.

Peace,

Victor Zupanc

Thursday, June 12, 2008, 6:56 a.m., CDT— Chrissie's Journal Entry

Good morning,

Tommy has been moved from the ICU to the eleventh floor. He is in room 1103 in the east building. He is breathing very well with just the nose cannula; his levels are around 96 percent. Nice. He also seems very sleepy. I did get a nod out of him last night though. He also looked directly at me but did not say anything.

Deanna from ICU told me yesterday that he has a type of staph infection (not the bad kind) that they are treating. She said the concern was the presence of the infection while getting the antibiotics he needed prior to the diagnosis. So she switched up his antibiotic yesterday. Hopefully this will take care of it.

I talked to the Block Center yesterday and found that Tom needs to be ambulatory and eating in order to participate being that their treatments involve the proper nutrition. That is currently not possible with the tube feeding and the fact that he is still bedridden. However, she did tell me that I have two other options. The first is a medical review in which I would have to send them his medical records and they would review them to see if they can help him. That would be $150. The second option I have at the moment is to talk to Dr. Block for one hour, and the cost of that is $775. I think for the moment, I will let that ride and will cross that bridge later if the opportunity presents itself.

In the meantime, I am just hoping and praying that I do what is right for him and that he pulls out of this phase of sleepiness that could last in varying degrees for three to six months. This part is very difficult, and the news from Dr. H the other day makes it even more so, especially because they told me a month ago he could be sleepy for a while and then the next minute they are trying to figure out why he is so sleepy. Then they will tell you, "We don't know." What do you do? I was told last week from another neurology doc that it is still a waiting game. That is the direction I am going with it. They *don't* know, so I just have to have blind faith and roll with it.

Bad things happen fast, good things take time, right?

Love to all,

Chrissie

Guest Book Entries

Written June 12, 2008, 8:59 a.m.

Chrissie,

Don't look with your eyes, don't hear with your ears, just keep your heart and head focused on the *one* that can bring the miracle to Tom. He is your strength and your hope. Just allow Him to lead you where you should go to find the help Tom needs. Lean into Him for the comfort you need when your days get long and lonely and you feel like you are hitting your head on a brick wall. It is always, always darkest before the dawn, but *His* light will shine through for you both. I love you and pray for you and Tom continually.

Patty Betlach Russell

Written June 12, 2008, 9:11 a.m.

Hi, Chrissie,

I just heard about Tom from A. J. at Park Place. I will certainly pray for you and Tom. The Mayo Clinic is a wonderful place for help. I will check back often to see how Tom is doing. Take care.

Josh K.

Rochester, Minnesota

Written June 12, 2008, 3:11 p.m.

That's very good, Chrissie. Tommy will *never* stop fighting, but if he does, it means that he has done his job in this world. And it's time for him to take a step back and breathe. I love you guys! God is watching over you two.

Madeline Betlach

Written June 12, 2008, 7:31 p.m.

Dear Chrissie and Tom,

My thoughts and prayers continue to come your way. I'm sad to hear Tom is not making the kind of progress we've been hoping for. It must be so hard to face each day not knowing what to expect and not knowing if Tom will be able to pull through. I'm sure it is harder yet not being able to talk with Tom. You are an incredibly strong woman, Chrissie, and that strength is what keeps Tom going. I'm sure he is very aware of all the love and prayers that are coming his way, and God is watching over all of you through this very difficult journey.

Today I spoke with a very nice man I know. His name is James Taylor, just like the singer. (You can call him Jim.) His wife's name is Winnie. They do healing touch and energy work and have helped many people with their special gifts. Perhaps you and Tom could benefit from their energy as well. I told him what's been going on and sent him a link to your website here so he could understand what you've been going through. He invited you to call.

I know your entire focus is on getting Tom through this. Please remember to take care of yourself as well, Chrissie. And please let us know if there is anything at all we can do to help make it easier.

Peace be with you,

Trish Clancy

Friday, June 13, 2008, 7:24 a.m., CDT— Chrissie's Journal Entry

Hello,

I sat with Tommy all afternoon yesterday, and while he was not opening his eyes, he was alert. I was playing CDs, and when I noticed he was awake, I started talking to him. He was responding by either shaking or nodding his head. I asked him if he wanted me to let him rest or keep talking, and he wanted me to keep talking, so I did. I asked him if he wanted me to print off the guestbook from the CaringBridge so I could read it to him, and he said yes. I will read to him today.

A cool thing happened yesterday while I was in with Tom. I happened to look up and see Dr. R walk by Tom's room to another patient's room. On his way out, he happened to look in our room and saw me sitting there. He backed up and came in to talk for a few minutes. A few minutes turned into about fifteen, and it was really cool. We sat and just talked about everything, and it was not like I was talking to a doctor in an appointment but just having a casual conversation. He asked me if I had thought about what they said the other day, and I told him that I had. I also told him, "No offense, but I am trying to get a second opinion from the Mayo." He said that they don't take offense to second opinions—as a matter of fact, they facilitate them. He also said it would be good for someone with a fresh pair of eyes to look at Tom's case. Additionally, he said that I was doing the right thing. He told me that I was doing more than most families do. (I couldn't believe that!)

I told him that if I took the "comfort care" option, I would feel like I was giving up on Tom, and I was not ready to do that. I told him that I don't feel that I should surrender right now. It doesn't feel right. He asked me why. I said, "I can't tell you; it is just a feeling I have." He then asked me if I would give up at some point, for Tom. I told him when and *if* the time comes, I will let him go. That time is not now. We have a few things to check into before I know that I have done all I can for my husband. As long as I have something to say about it, Tommy will get every opportunity for a recovery that I can give him. It did make me feel good that Dr. R thought I was doing the right thing.

The time has come for me to take a couple of weeks off from work to regroup and get some sleep so that I can gear up for what lies ahead. Be warned that my updates will be coming from home during that time, and they won't happen as early in the morning as they are now. Sorry about that! Maybe I can update from his hospital room. Either way, the timing will be off a little. Take care, everyone, and thank you for your constant thoughts and prayers.

Much love to you all,

Chrissie

Guest Book Entries

Written June 13, 2008, 8:26 a.m.

Chrissie and Tom,

I have yet to sign the guest book and feel it is about time. You know how special both of you are to me, and I would do anything to help make this better for both of you. I just wanted to send the two of you my constant love and support. I am *always* here!

Jessica DuCharme

Written June 13, 2008, 8:29 a.m.

Chrissie,

I read your daily updates with such a heavy heart, not because I believe Tommy can't come out if this but because longtime friends of mine have to deal with such life trials. I have been thinking of you both and praying every day since I first heard of Tommy's diagnosis, and from what I read, so have *many* other people. And there's *so many more* who think of you both daily who don't write. You two are very fortunate in that regard—but you don't have that kind of support by accident, Cha Cha; it's because you guys are two of the *best* friends anyone could ask for.

You are handling the hardest challenges humans can endure with the utmost grace and bravery. I am sure I am not alone when I say I truly don't know that I could keep it together like you have through this, the longest of roads.

Having lost both of my parents very young, I can tell you that you are *absolutely* doing the right thing by getting a second opinion. Your Tommy has *waaayyyy* too much left in him to not explore every option available. He responds to you—that is *huge.*

I am glad to hear you are taking some time off to take care of *you.* That is *so* important.

Please sleep well, honey. You are doing *everything* right. If I can do *anything*, please call. Just because we don't see each other regularly anymore doesn't mean I'm far away.

Strong prayers and positive thoughts your way, *every day* ...

Michelle Notch

Written June 13, 2008, 8:59 a.m.

I check Tom's site every morning. I anxiously await the news, and then I pass it on to Shawn.

I think about Tom several times a day. I pray for him every night. I believe as long as Tom is responding, there is no other decision to make. But then I'm not there *all the time* to see how he is. I feel hope and faith are what gets people through times like these.

Just know that Tom is a blessed man with an irreplaceable laugh. *Stay strong,* Tom and Chrissie!

Angie Lund :-)

Written June 13, 2008, 11:02 a.m.

Hi, Chrissie and Tom,

I am very glad to hear you are taking some time off, Chrissie. I think it will be wonderful for you. I am sure you need the rest, and you certainly deserve a break and some time.

We think about you every day and send you much love and many prayers. We hope you feel the positive energy swarming around you every day, bringing you physical and emotional healing.

It is really neat to read the guest book and look at the very widespread and diverse group of friends and family that you have checking in on you.

Keep carrying the torch, Chrissie. You are an amazing woman. We love and support you.

Thanks for keeping up the journal. It lets us all feel like we are there every day.

Love,

Lynn Robson

Written June 13, 2008, 1:18 p.m.

Chrissie,

Please, dear, just give yourself a little time! You are so very good about writing to all of us, but do take a bit of time for you! Tommy wants you to do so, in order to stay strong for him!

Our daily prayers continue!

Love,

Laura S.

Written June 14, 2008, 1:20 p.m.

Chrissie, it should come as no surprise that you are doing more for your loved one than most. You've been Tom's angel from the start of all this! It's good that the doctor agrees with you. But just follow your feelings; God will guide your decisions! Now take some time, enjoy your break, and get some rest. Don't worry if your timing's off; we can handle it! Prayers and positive vibes continue to flow your way. Be strong—rock on!

Timbo

Tim Hanley

Monday, June 16, 2008, 4:21 p.m., CDT— Chrissie's Journal Entry

Hello, all,

I know this is later than you are used to getting; sorry! Not much change over the weekend. He was only awake for me for a few minutes on Sunday despite Wendy's efforts on Saturday afternoon when she and Keith came to visit. I mean, she was working it! He wanted to wake up; he just couldn't.

I got a call this morning saying that his hemoglobin was lower than it had been, and they wanted to give him a couple units of blood. Normal hemoglobin for a male is 14. Tom's had been around 8 but had dropped to 7.1. Hopefully he will feel better soon.

I also got a call from Patti B. this morning because she wanted to find out if Tom was still at Riverside. During the course of the conversation, she had to throw in there that Dr. T (the radiation doc) said that while the scans look better, due to the history of where the tumor has been, he may not come out of this sleepy state. Yeah, yeah, tell me something you haven't already told me. Cripes. Then, of course, they don't know.

Last night my sister Rachel, Tom's sister Judy, and I met with Don N. He is involved with a product called OPC. It sounds promising but there are issues surrounding the administration, and I need to know more before I make any decisions. I will say, though, that I am finding out more and more that nutrition plays a huge part in preventing and fighting off cancer—*huge*. I will tell you more once I've got it straight in my head. Let's just say I am keeping my options open to many things.

Tom just squeezed Judy's hand! Woo-hoo! On that note; until tomorrow …

Love,

Chrissie

Tuesday, June 17, 2008, 4:34 p.m., CDT— Chrissie's Journal Entry

Good afternoon, everyone,

Here is a bit of good news for all of you. We are going to the Mayo! They called me this afternoon and told me that in his current state we would have to do a facility-to-facility transfer as opposed to outpatient. They told me to have his doctor at Riverside call the Mayo and speak to the medical oncologist on call to facilitate the transfer.

The only thing that bums me out about this is that I may not be here for the transfer. I am going to Boise, Idaho, from Thursday night to Monday afternoon for a family reunion/my aunt and uncle's fiftieth wedding anniversary celebration, which includes them renewing their vows. I talked over my plans with the staff at Riverside, and the social worker said that I need to take care of myself and that I should not change any plans. This has been planned for two years, and Tom and I had originally planned to leave last Saturday in the Suburban with Bailey and go through the Black Hills and up to Montana to visit our friends Dickie and Arleen and then down to

Boise later in the week. I told Tom that trip is postponed and we will do it when he is better.

Tommy seems to slightly wake up enough to squeeze your hand and occasionally nod or shake his head. I really hope they don't transfer until I get back, but we are on the Mayo's time and Tommy's time. We have to do what we have to do. If they move him, I will be featured in Rochester when I get back. I will let you know more as information becomes available.

In the meantime, let's pray that the Mayo can heal our precious Tommy and he can come back to us.

Love to all,

Chrissie

Tuesday, June 17, 2008, 5:18 p.m., CDT—
Chrissie's Journal Entry

Revision,

As I was sending the last update, the doctor came in and told us that she had talked to the Mayo earlier today and they requested his records to review. I thought they had already done that. So, as I was told, they put his scans on a CD and copied his records and sent them to the Mayo for review. I guess we are not a for sure on the Mayo just yet. I will keep you posted.

xoxoxo

Chrissie

Wednesday, June 18, 2008, 7:00 p.m., CDT— Chrissie's Journal Entry

Good evening,

We have not yet heard from the Mayo as they only got Tom's records today. I have a meeting tomorrow at 2:00 p.m. with his doctor, social worker, and care coordinator regarding a back-up plan should he not be accepted to the Mayo while I am gone this weekend. They are again talking about a lower-level nursing facility, but I have some questions about that, specifically, his blood clots (of course) and his infection. Yesterday they told me he was very sick, and now they are talking about a lower-level nursing facility. Which is it! They are all over the damn board constantly about everything. How are you supposed to think?

I got a call this morning from Tom's nurse, Jenny. She told me that he was alert and squeezing her hand and nodding and shaking his head slightly. She had asked him if he wanted her to call me, and he nodded his head yes, so she did. Of course, when I saw the phone number I got all freaked out, and the first thing she said was she wasn't calling to scare me. Woo! I'm glad she said that. I told her to tell him that I love him and that I would see him in the afternoon. Then when we got here, she was saying how he had been at that level of alertness all day. No question. He was squeezing Judy's hand and then my hand super tight tonight, along with a little nodding and shaking of his head. Yay! I took the opportunity to tell him that I was going to Boise tomorrow night and I would be back on Monday afternoon. I also told him I would come straight to the hospital when I got back in town. I got many, many squeezes from him as I was telling him. I think he was telling me it was okay for me to go.

I also told him that Lisa and Mitchell will be watching Bailey while I am gone so he didn't have to worry about her.

I will give you more news after our conference tomorrow. Until then, everyone take care.

Much love to all,

Chrissie

Guest Book Entries

Written June 18, 2008, 10:28 a.m.

Just checking in to say hi; hi! I'm doing my best on giving all of you my very best positive vibes, and I hope they are working. I hope all of you have fun at the family reunion, but how could you not as you're all very fun people to be around? I'm so glad that I have people like you in my life (Big Rude included) because you're all real and caring people and anybody's life has been enhanced by knowing you. I don't know Tom's side of the family that well, but knowing Tom's spirit, I know they must be wonderful people too! Well, time to sign off. I just needed to say what I just said, and I wanted to let you know that it is straight from the heart, and of course, these are the words taken straight from the Rude Monster: "Love ya, babe!"

Michael Anderson

Thursday, June 19, 2008, 4:28 p.m., CDT—
Chrissie's Journal Entry

Good afternoon,

Last night before I left, I happened to look over at Tom, and he was looking right at me, just like he would over the top of his glasses, giving me "the look." It kind of freaked me out a little. I haven't seen his eyes open in a couple of weeks. I said, "Hi, honey!" and then he promptly shut them, only to open them again a few seconds later. It was nice to see his baby blues! He has been somewhat alert today with some kind of smirk on his face. Makes me wonder what he's dreaming about!

We have not yet heard from the Mayo, but they are going to keep him here at Riverside through Tuesday for sure, no matter if the Mayo accepts him or not. They are going to wait until I get back into town before we take the next step, whatever that may be. In my absence, Judy will be updating the CaringBridge, so don't worry about not getting any news. Judy is there for you!

Please keep your positive energy and prayers flowing (as I know you will) for Tommy. I will be checking the Bridge from Boise; you can't get rid of me that easy!

Much love to all,

Chrissie

Guest Book Entries

Written June 19, 2008, 1:41 p.m.

Chrissie and Tom,

I heard from Rolf last week the rough time you two have been having.

If and or when you make it to Rochester, please remember if you need a bed, a backyard to sit in, or a friend to chat with, Diane and I live about a mile from the clinic. We live on a bus line, which means no parking hassles either! Diane is at the clinic in Ped's Oncology and Hematology, so she works with some of the same physicians. She can sometimes get a little extra help as she knows the doctors, and I service the cars so the personal favors come easier.

Send me a note or call me. Give Tom my best, and let him know we are praying and pulling for both of you.

AJ Jedlicka

Written June 19, 2008, 5:41 p.m.

CJMBV,

Travel safe, my love. We are all praying hard for you and wish you peace on your journey. Be well and know that everyone is supporting you.

XXXXOOOO

WHKP

Wendy P.

Written June 19, 2008, 5:55 p.m.

Hi, Chris,

Have a wonderful trip; it will do you good to be surrounded by your family. Tom is being taken care of. He is in good hands. I wish I knew exactly what to do or say at a time like this, but all I know is that you have been in my life forever, and my heart goes out to you and Tom. The love you have for each other is very strong. His looking at you is wonderful; I think he is soaking it up. It is so awesome that you are getting responses from him.

Take care, my friend. Peace and hope are yours. You are in my thoughts and prayers daily …

Love you,

Roxie Chudy

Friday, June 20, 2008, 11:13 a.m., CDT— Judy's Journal Entry

Good morning,

He's waking up! Last night I was at the hospital with my mom, and Laura walked in. She told Tom that she had a dream last night that she had walked into his room, and he was sitting up in his bed and they were talking. Then she said, "That's what I want you to do now!" Then my mom pipes in and says, "Yeah or I'll kick your ass," (Mother!) and Tommy laughed! It was a belly laugh. It was so funny that we all just started laughing. It's funny because my mom doesn't usually talk like that. (*Hmmm,* hanging out at the hospital with Chrissie. Hmmmm …) Oops, hi, Chrissie. Anyway, he smiled a lot and shook his head at my mom's comment, and he shook his head yes and no at our questions. That was the best! He's finally coming out of it. It was so good to see his smile! I can't wait to go up tonight!

Keep the prayers and the positive energy coming; it's working!

Thanks everyone,

Judy Vinje

Guest Book Entries

Written June 20, 2008, 8:40 a.m.

Chrissie,

I just wanted to drop by and say hello! I read CaringBridge every day at work when I get in. I love to hear the good news about Tommy. Also, I believe you are making right choices for your hubby … You're the best woman he could ever have in my eyes. I love ya. :) Have a good and safe trip. *Much love always.*

Cristina Melzer

Saturday, June 21, 2008, 3:41 p.m., CDT— Judy's Journal Entry

Hey, everyone,

Yesterday Tom didn't wake up at all. We played a little Bob Marley for him when we left. Today the doctor came in and she said since she's been working with Tom all week, she sees his improvements with squeezing her hand and moving his feet. He kept taking his oxygen tube out, so they just left it out. He has been doing well without it. Chrissie called while we were up here, so I put the phone to Tom's ear, and you could tell he was listening. His eyes were blinking faster. The nurse just came in and said he is on a medication to help him wake up. We need to find out what that is since they said he is no longer on the Ritalin. On Monday the oncology team is coming up to reevaluate him.

Have a good day,

Judy Vinje

Guest Book Entries

Written June 21, 2008, 4:16 p.m.

Judy,

Thank you for keeping this up for Chrissie. It is good she takes a little time for herself, to reenergize her mind and keep her from getting sick. Tom and Chris are always in my prayers every night before I close my eyes.

Keeping positive thoughts here!

Julie S.

***

While I was in Boise hanging with the family, my dear friend Colleen Storm went to see Tom every day and report back to me in an e-mail about what went on in their visit that day. She would hold his hand (and he would give her hand a squeeze when she grabbed his), talk to him, and pray over him. The best part is, she always felt that he knew what was going on around him, even if he didn't open his eyes; she knew he "got it." How cool is that to have a friend do that for you? I tell ya, I've got some great people in my life!

***

Tuesday, June 24, 2008, 7:43 p.m., CDT— Chrissie's Journal Entry

Greetings, everyone,

I am back from my family weekend in Boise, and it was the best, despite being away from Tommy for three days! It was great to be able to do things with my family and be present for my aunt and uncle's fiftieth wedding anniversary celebration. They had a raffle for Tom at the hall on Saturday night and at the picnic on Sunday to raise money for Tom! A special thanks to Vantz and Nichelle for putting it all together. It meant so very much to me that he means that much to them.

The news about the Mayo is that they think that from the standpoint of neurology and oncology, all is being done that can be done by the doctors here in Minneapolis. I still haven't heard about the oncology consult that he was supposed to have on Monday. No matter. I am exploring other avenues. Those avenues include alternative and spiritual. When you have the two major medical institutions in Minnesota telling you that from a medical standpoint they can do nothing more, you either have to give up and assume they are correct or you need to keep fighting for a better way. I think you know where I am coming from on this subject. Tom is not ready to give up, and neither am I. Game on! As a matter of fact, my cousin Pam has a friend (Evelyn) who is a quantum touch practitioner, and I had a meeting with her on Monday morning before I left Boise. Things are starting to move in a very different direction. I also have a phone consultation on Friday with a doctor I found through my friend Shannon. He is a medical doctor and an alternative healer. Suffice it to say that I will do whatever it takes for my hubby.

Also, tonight is the most activity I have seen from him in weeks. Earlier, when his sister Laura was here, he opened his eyes and *said* hi. Since then, he is moving around, opening his eyes, and answering questions. When I stopped in last night after I got back in town, I got a slight squeeze of the hand, and that was about it. Bring it on, Tommy! Let's go!

I will leave you with a quote delivered by the priest from our niece's confirmation a few weeks ago that was shared by Judy and Laura. It is the perfect way to end this journal update, and I will probably use it again.

The doctors do not have the last say on who lives and who dies.

I couldn't agree more ...

Love to all,

Chrissie

Guest Book Entries

Written June 24, 2008, 10:56 p.m.

Chrissie,

I am like Mikey—I have checked daily. Your spirit has been unnerved, and I know you and *admire* you. I am glad you took some time to be with your family. Your love for Tom has been evident from the day you introduced us (and he liked me!). I completely agree with you regarding alternative measures. Your/our level of spirituality reaches far beyond the comprehension of many others. (Our church walks on Sunday mornings are still an important part of my life.) Keep moving in any direction that you believe will bring the love of your life home! I believe as you do! Like Mikey, it is hard to write here as we both have unique personalities—yet you know our love and that we are pulling for Tom with nothing but positive energy. *I love your undying faith, courage, persistence, and love!*

Terry Jo

Thursday, June 26, 2008, 9:02 a.m., CDT—Chrissie's Journal Entry

Good morning,

Last night Tom was extremely restless. He kept moving all around, taking his sheet off, and then getting cold and wanting it back on. He flipped himself over onto his right side and hung his hand over the railing, grabbing onto his IV stand. He would open his eyes occasionally to see what was going on. My honey is a fighter, that's for sure.

We are very close to going back to Providence Place. He will be there until I can equip the house for home care. At issue are the antibiotics that he will be on for another nine days. The insurance company feels that the hospital has done what they can do and that he can be in a lower-level skilled nursing facility. He is no longer on oxygen or any other IV drug. He is also down to 156 pounds. That translates to fifty-four pounds lost in the last fourteen weeks. A good part of that, of course, is muscle, which we have to get back by doing some range-of-motion exercises.

Please don't stop praying or sending positive energy our way. It is still greatly needed and will be going forward with all we have to face.

Love to you all,

Chrissie

Thursday, June 26, 2008, 1:06 p.m., CDT—
Judy's Journal Entry

Hey, Everyone,

FYI … Chrissie just called and said Tom is being moved to Providence Place today. It's on Thirty-Eighth Street and Twenty-Third Avenue South.

Thanks,

Judy Vinje

Guest Book Entries

Written June 27, 2008, 10:04 a.m.

Dear Chrissie:

I have wanted to send you a message for several weeks, ever since I heard about what you and Tom are going through. Although we have only met once in our adult lives (at our twenty-fifth class reunion), we were early childhood friends who walked to kindergarten together and had an uncommon connection (we both had last names that no one could pronounce—Betlach and Gundlach).

Ever since Roxie told me about Tom, I have been so saddened for you, thinking of you, and praying for you both. Looking at your messages, I can see that yours and Tom's lives are rich in love and friendship

I want you to know that I am praying for Tom's *complete* healing. God can deliver the most magnificent blessings, if we ask and *believe*. And so I join you and your family and friends, in earnest prayer and *belief.*

Please, Chrissie, take time for yourself, to strengthen your spirit. God bless you and Tom.

Launette Figliuzzi

Written June 28, 2008, 1:41 a.m.

Dear Cuz,

It was a delight to be able to see you at my parents' fifty-year anniversary and to just play fun games at the family reunion. Who's the sack race king, huh? And what about that drum circle? Watermelon anyone? What a great reunion. It was nice to see everyone even though it is a stressful time. Being with the family, and having all those prayers go out to Tom and all the Minnesota relatives, was beautiful. We love and miss you all more than ever, and just remember we are all sending our bright white light your way.

Love,

Pam, Chuck, Linzi, Jeremy, and Antonio (last but we all know not least!)

Written June 28, 2008, 10:58 a.m.

Hi, Chrissie!

Just checking in. I'm bummed out. I went right by Providence Place yesterday, and I thought, *Hmm …*

that's where Tom used to be. I missed the update on Thursday, so I didn't know he was there again. Sorry! It did make me say some prayers though, so that was good, and I know exactly where it is now! Glad to hear you enjoyed your time away, and thanks to Judy for the continuing updates! Also, the doctors do not have the final say; anything is possible in the spiritual world! So let the positive vibes flow! Rock on!

Tim Hanley

Chapter 8

Providence Place— for the Last Time

***

I would like to preface this short, but significant, chapter by saying that the *last* thing I wanted to do was bring Tom back to PP after their colossal blunder of not recognizing he was in distress when his blood clots were moving. The only reason I did is because I knew it would not be permanent or for very long. I just needed time to put the plan in motion.

***

Monday, June 30, 2008, 12:47 p.m., CDT— Chrissie's Journal Entry

Hi, everyone,

Sorry it has been a few days, but I have been going nonstop and I now have a few moments. As you know, Tom went back to PP on Thursday. I went to the hospital before Life Link came to transport him, and then I met them at PP when they got there. I have to tell you that when we went up to his room (room 2222), and as I stood there and looked around and saw the sparse side of his room (with no TV; you have to bring in your own in the long-term care department), I just got so depressed and said to myself, *"No!* This is not happening. We have to leave here. It's time to bring Tommy home." Judy had a similar reaction when she got up there that day, as did Laura. It just feels wrong to me for him to be there. So, today I am setting everything in motion for that to happen. I am sure there are things I haven't even thought of that I will need, but here we go … Tommy's coming home.

I have told him every day since he got there that he is coming home, and he squeezes my hand really tight when I tell him. I know he would rather be here with his puppers and his kitty. That way too, we will be free to explore more alternative and spiritual methods for his healing. Some methods have already begun, and he is aware of it. I know some people may think I should go with what the medical people are telling me, and if that is your opinion, that is fine. If that is something that you can live with and that works for you, then that is your decision to make. I, however, do not feel that way with Tommy's situation. I feel that there is something more that can be done, and I have felt that from the beginning and I am not about to stop now. I am not saying that it will be easy, but this is probably going to be the hardest thing that I, or any of our family members and friends, will ever go through. It doesn't feel right for me to stop just because the medical people tell me to. I could not live with that. So I am asking everyone to trust me when I tell you that I *am* doing what is right for Tom, and he is aware and willing to fight for his life. And a hell of a fight it will be.

Tom's mom (Ginny) and I had a meeting with the Fairview Hospice last week just to find out what it was all about, how it works, etc. We found out that when you are on hospice care, you have certain criteria you have to meet to stay within their philosophy of care. Some hospices require that you have a DNR in place; others do not. Tom is a "full code," which means that he will be revived. In his situation, if we were to sign on to hospice and something happens where he needs to be revived, hospice would then sign off. Also, wherever Tom calls home is where hospice will go, in a nursing home or his own home, wherever. So I have some things to think about and work out to bring my baby home where he belongs.

So let's review a few sayings, shall we?

Bad things happen fast; good things take time.

And again, the doctors do not have the last say on who lives and who dies.

Much love to all,

Chrissie

Guest Book Entries

Written June 30, 2008, 2:05 p.m.

Chrissie, I fully support your decision and will be there for you all the way. We all admire your strength and devotion.

Love you both so very much.

Nicole Betlach

Written July 1, 2008, 2:37 p.m.

Just checkin' in on Tommy Boy.

Chrissie, you *are* doing what's right for both Tom and yourself. You can't worry about what other people think about Tom's situation and/or decisions surrounding the same. They are not in your shoes. If they are unable to offer an open mind, then pooey on them.

You go for what you feel is right, Chrissie. As long as Tom is responsive, there is no other decision. I believe you are doing what is right. Hope and faith are very strong factors in some people's lives, and some people just lack that.

Stay strong, Chrissie.

Angie Lund

Written July 1, 2008, 8:50 p.m.

Chrissie,

I have never written in here before, but I just wanted you and everyone else to know that I support you 100 percent. Why would anyone give up when there are other options? We will bring him home because he simply *can't* stay there. I don't believe that there is anything that can be done there that can't be done at home. Actually I believe that more can be done at home. I don't know a lot about spiritual healing, but I'm sure I'm going to learn. *We* won't ever give up. I can't tell you how glad I am that you came into my brother's and our lives. *Rock on, Sister.*

Love,

Laura Vinje

Written July 2, 2008, 8:50 a.m.

Hi, Chris,

Taking Tommy home will do wonders for him. When I was in a similar situation, the care conference docs and social worker lady wanted to send me to a long-term care facility. I told Chris just to shoot me now and get it over with. I would have deteriorated had I had to go there. The decision for me to come home was the best thing. And I believe for Tom it will be the same. You heal better at home; you are more comfortable to be surrounded by your own stuff, your family, and your pets. You have to go with what your gut is telling you … that little twinge is what the right decision is. Go for anything that you believe is possible. I believe that all things are possible and that doctors do *not* have the last say.

Take care of yourself. I believe that you will give Tom what he needs. God does not give us things we cannot handle. There may be a long road in front of us, but He gives us the strength and determination to see it through.

My love and prayers are with you

Roxie Chudy

Thursday, July 3, 2008, 10:34 a.m., CDT—
Chrissie's Journal Entry

Hello, all,

I'm sorry my entries have been so sporadic lately, but I have a lot going on. I am currently off of work until the fourteenth so I can coordinate Tommy's homecoming and get into a routine. That homecoming is next Tuesday at two o'clock in the afternoon! I have signed on to hospice care, which will provide a variety of services, which include:

- skilled nursing visits
- chaplain
- social services
- volunteer
- home health aide visits
- music therapist
- massage therapist

Keep in mind that this is additional care, not primary care. The primary care is coming from family and friends volunteering their time to care for Tom in our home. Everyone who cares for Tom will have to be trained in giving medications, turning him every two to three hours, and other cares. ("Cares" is a buzzword in the medical community that I have picked up on.) As it stands, I do have some gaps during the day, and if there is anyone who is interested in helping us care for Tom, please let me know. They have been telling me that he needs 24-7 care, so our nephew Tony is taking the night shift for a week or two to see what happens at night. It may work out that I can just sleep on the couch next to him or have a baby monitor in our bedroom; Tony will monitor the situation and let me know. (I do know that during the day nurses will go three to four hours without coming into the room; I have to believe it doesn't change much at night.) That would just leave me to have coverage during the day, which would help out immensely so that I can continue to work, which I need to do, of course.

One thing I don't want you to freak out about is the word *hospice*. That word has such a stigma attached to it. It does not mean that I have given up by any stretch of anyone's imagination. It just means better care for Tommy. I feel relieved knowing that a variety of hospice people will be here to show me how it's done in the home so when we get to a point where we can sign off of hospice, I will know what to do. It is a *very* intimidating situation to be in, thinking you can bring someone home and care for their medical needs when I have not been remotely trained in that area. I have always said that it takes special people to work in the medical field and that I was not one of those people. (Okay, maybe only for Tommy.) My opinion has not changed in that regard. Although I do believe I have seen more than I ever cared to in relation to how the medical industry operates, and I don't like it. There are so many things that can go so many different ways without you even knowing about it. This is why when you come across some really awesome nurses, aides, and doctors; you really have to consider yourself lucky. (I am speaking of the nurses on 6A, of course, and a nurse or two over at Riverside specifically.)

I have quite the shopping list that I need to tackle today to get ready for Tom's move home. I will keep you informed as things progress, of course. Everyone have a great Fourth of July weekend!

Much love to all,

Chrissie

Guest Book Entries

> Written July 3, 2008, 1:35 p.m.
>
> Chrissie,
>
> You know in your heart (and in your gut) what you can handle and what is right for the situation you

and Tom are in. We are here to support you in any and every way possible. We love you both so very much, and not only is Tom blessed to have you in his life, but all of us are. It's inspiring to see the drive you have, even with the bumps in the road. *You go, sister!*

Much love and prayers to you both as this new phase of the journey begins!

Karrie Cable

Written July 3, 2008, 8:16 p.m.

Chrissie,

So excited Tom is coming home! I imagine it is overwhelming for you. Savannah and I want to know how we can help. You are awesome, girl!

Here is a note from Savannah: I want you to feel better, Tom. Love, Savannah

Jeanne Galle Franklin

Monday, July 7, 2008, 9:51 p.m., CDT— Chrissie's Journal Entry

Hello, everyone,

I'm sorry, I didn't plan on waiting so long to write again, but I have been feverishly getting ready for Tom to come home for like, the last five days.

Something really cute happened as I was leaving PP on Friday evening. As I stepped out of Tom's room to head to the elevators, there was this cute little Asian lady who said hi to me. As I stopped to talk to her, she told me that her name was Jeanette and that she had a card for Tom. She asked if he was my dad, and I told her, "No, he is my husband." At this point she said that she had not met him yet, so I took her in to meet him. I told her that he might not be awake, but she introduced herself anyway. After she left I opened the card. It was a get-well card. On the inside of the card she wrote on top, "Hi, Tom," and she signed it, "A new friend, Jeanette." On the inside of the card were two dollars and a prayer on a separate sheet of paper. Here is the prayer:

> A prayer for today
>
> Dear God,
>
> So far today, I've done all right,
>
> I haven't gossiped, and I haven't lost my temper.
>
> I haven't been grumpy, nasty, or selfish, and I'm really glad of that!
>
> But in a few minutes, God, I'm going to get out of bed, and from then on, I'm probably going to need a lot of help!
>
> Thank you,
>
> Amen

I, of course, burst into tears. How dang sweet was that? I was just so touched by the fact that she actually gives everyone two dollars and a prayer in a card. And I guess the words hit me too—a get-well card from a new friend. I didn't have the heart to tell her we were leaving on Tuesday. I am going to keep the two dollars and show Tom.

We are set to come home Tuesday at one o'clock. The two o'clock time did not work out for the transport company. No matter, I am ready. Thanks to my dear sister-in-law Judy, who helped me clean the house and the apartment today (so that I could show it on Monday night) to get ready for Tom's homecoming. I am sure there will be a few more things I will need, but we did all that we could today. I will be at PP at noon tomorrow so that I can gather all of his things and make sure everything I have paid for comes home with him, including his medications. I certainly don't need to pay for those twice! Also, thank you to my brother-in-law Gary for figuring out our electrical circuits so that we will not be blowing circuits with all these air conditioners running once we plug in the bed and food pump. And of course, thank you to my mother-in-law for making the curtain panels that will be going up halfway on our living room windows so Tom gets the privacy he needs. I must also give thanks to my wonderful neighbors, Larry and John and Bill, for helping me with the air conditioners, blinds (and the Ikea trip—thanks, Larry!) and other miscellaneous tasks I had going at this house over the weekend. I certainly could not have done any of it and be as far along at this point if it weren't for all of you, so thank you!

So, tomorrow is the big day! I am so excited for Tom to be here in his own environment! I cannot wait to see how he reacts over the next few days. The animals will have an adjustment period, but I am sure it won't be for long! Bud will be sitting on his chest, nose to nose with him almost immediately. Wacky cat! Bailey has seen him occasionally but not at home. I hope she doesn't expect him to get up and take her for a walk, as much as I wish he could; lots of changes coming on. It is time for the next phase.

Wish us luck in our in-home care for Tom. It is the best thing for him, and I know he is happy to be finally coming home. As I have told a few people, please do not hesitate to come and visit Tom at home. I support visitors 100 percent, as I know it will help him immensely. We will have people here 24–7, and please do not worry about the time of day. If you find a time that will work for you to visit and you are not sure, just call the house and let us know. I am sure it will be fine. If you are not sure, let me say it again: please feel free to visit Tom whenever you can!

He loves the visits, and it will be *very good* for him.

I will let you know tomorrow how everything went as I am sure you will want to know. Please continue to keep us in your prayers, and keep those positive thoughts coming! It ain't over till it's over, *and* it ain't over!

Much love to all,

Chrissie

Our wedding day, September 18, 1999

The wedding party

The guys of the wedding party

The Betlach family at our wedding

The Vinje family at our wedding

Tom in a bathtub at the farm

Tom, Chrissie & Bailey

Tommy & his Mommy

Tom skydiving on his 40th Birthday

Tom waving good-bye

Chapter 9

He's Home!

He's home!

After sixteen weeks to the day, Tommy came home around 1:30 this afternoon. It went well except they couldn't get the gurney through our front or back doors so they had to lift him in his sheet and carry him in to his bed waiting for him in the living room. I am *so* relieved to have him home. No more worrying about him in the dang nursing home! We had about eight people here learning how to care for him from our hospice nurse, Judy. She will be back in the morning to go over everything again because it is a bit overwhelming. My mom told me that she thought she had already seen an improvement in him. He was already more alert and interactive than he was in the hospital or nursing home. He was saying a few words to my sister Beth and raising his eyebrows at her. He was opening his eyes so he could get a good look at Bailey, but she was backing away. You can't force that girl to do anything! That's all right—she had already come up to her daddy and licked his hands right when he got home and later, his feet. Bud is still not sure what is going on, but I am sure it won't take him long to figure out his daddy is back! Tom really wanted me to go find him, but as soon as I realized he went outside, I thought I would just wait for him to meander back. He is a cat, after all; everything is done on his schedule, dontchaknow!

Carl W. is a coworker of Tom's. His sister Abbey and her husband, Ben, are Christian missionaries in Belize. They have been involved in healings and are currently in the area. They are coming to pray over Tom tomorrow night. God bless them for coming over. I cannot wait to meet them.

Tom has had a really busy day, and I hope he gets some rest tonight. Our nephew Tony is here to care for him overnight, and I can honestly say he will be under the best care he has had in a while.

Thank you to everyone for your continued love, support, and prayers. They mean so very much.

Love to all,

Chrissie

Guest Book Entries

Written July 8, 2008, 8:41 a.m.

Love you, CJMBV. I'll be with you all day today hugging you.

XXXOOO

Wendy P.

Written July 8, 2008, 9:42 a.m.

It's time! I know I sound like a broken record, but we are here to support you in any way you need!

Tyler is extra happy that Tom is coming home. After last week when he visited Tom by himself, he can't wait to just walk across the alley!

Love and all the best wishes to you both!

Karrie, Ian, and Tyler

Written July 8, 2008, 11:09 p.m.

I agree with Mom. Tom had his eyes wide open quite a bit. I was even telling a story about our cabin from the weekend, and Tom was looking at me and listening to the story. I can tell that him being home is going to do wonders for him, and I am so happy for him that he is finally there!

Beth Timm

Written July 11, 2008, 4:12 p.m.

Hellooooo!

How's everybody! I'm glad to hear that Tom is home. I think it will make a big difference being in his own surroundings. I suppose getting him in his garage is out of the question because, as you may already know, a man's garage is the ultimate castle of castles and I know how much he loves his garage. *(Just kidding!)* Ah, on second thought, I'm not! *Get that man in his garage!*

Now I'm rambling as usual, and I guess I do that a lot (at least that's what my sister always says to me!). *But anyway*, I'm glad for both of you that he is home, and I hope it eases a lot of the stress that you have been going through. I will talk at you soon, and as always, and I'm quoting the words of the Big Rude Monster, and I'm sure you already know what I am going to say but I'm going to say it to you anyway—love ya, babe!

Mike Anderson

Written July 12, 2008, 9:46 a.m.

This is my first time writing, so bear with me! My typing and spelling skills are definitely lacking!

I've known Tommy for roughly ten years. I loved him the first time I met him. Funny, sincere, obnoxious, territorial (inside joke), and full of life!

Since March, even through all the tubes, machines, and sterile settings, I still see Tommy. Funny—he made fun of me the first time I visited him in the ICU. Obnoxious—he tried to unbuckle his honey's belt buckle right there in the hospital in front of his *mother*! He didn't care. Territorial—you know he wanted to be in *his* home with *his* loved ones. Lastly, full of life—Tommy is full of life. Nothing more needs to be said about that.

I'm so glad he has a loving wife, family, and friends like he does. That's what makes his life so full!

All my thoughts and prayers are with him!

xoxo

Jackie Thomas

Written July 12, 2008, 11:54 p.m.

Hello, Chris and Tom,

I just wanted to let you know that I have been thinking about you a lot since Tuesday and hope that everything is going well at home. You are in my thoughts and prayers! It must be a *great* feeling to be in your own home again, Tom! Take care, and keep on smiling!

Love,

Kris K.

Monday, July 21, 2008, 7:53 a.m., CDT—
Chrissie's Journal Entry

Good morning, everyone,

Sorry about the lapse in communication, but it has been busier at the house than I anticipated. I swear to you, every day I said to myself, "I will update the CaringBridge tonight" (or whenever), and when that time came, I didn't have the time! Holy Hannah! Hopefully I will get back on track now. There is never a lack of anything to report, that is for sure. Instead of giving you a play by play, I will give you a brief (maybe) synopsis of the last two weeks.

Obviously, this has been a *huge* learning experience for all of us who are caring for Tom. I have to admit, I was scared to death to bring him home and think that I could care for him in the way that he needs. I have not been trained in the medical profession; I work in an office in a car dealer, for God's sake! How intimidating is that! We are learning by trial and error though. I am trying to follow my intuition on certain things to make sure that we do what is best for him.

The first couple of days went fairly well. It was Thursday, the tenth at 5:30 p.m. that began a twenty-six-hour session of Tom throwing up every three to five hours. This was the day I started him on the homeopathic remedies. There were three different drops and a capsule that he was to be given. One of the drops was to be given three times a day while the others were five times a day. I only got to the second round of drops when he started getting sick. I quickly knew that was not working and we needed to move on. Unfortunately, he was sick until Friday night at 7:30. Following that, he was sick once (sometimes twice a day) until last Wednesday. Tom's hospice nurse, Judy, called the doctor and told him that she had pulled some undigested food out of his stomach. From this phone call, the doctor said that his digestive system was shutting down and I had to make a decision whether or not to keep feeding him. Excuse me! Isn't it funny how you can diagnose over the phone like that and that becomes the course of action going forward?

At our sign-up meeting for hospice, I was told to let the nurse know about anything else I gave him other than his prescribed medications. When I showed Judy what I had given him, she pretty much blew me off. She did not even consider that these remedies were involved. Now, I have taken homeopathic remedies in the past, and I can tell you that they are very powerful. (There is even a remedy that Tom takes when he gets anxious; it makes him sleepy so he can get past that feeling.) Here is where my intuition kicks in. I *know* Tom's digestive system is not shutting down. Everything else is working as normal. So, we pick ourselves up, brush ourselves off, quit the homeopathic remedies, and move on.

Now, as I mentioned weeks ago, we had explored the possibility of OPCs with Don N. Don and his wife, Christina, came over a week ago Sunday to pray over Tom and to bring some OPCs to try. OPCs are antioxidants for the blood and have been proven to cure cancers and a myriad of other diseases. (Look them up on the Internet if you are curious. They are also good for well people to take to stay well and relieve *many* physical issues, such as allergies.) Tom is currently taking two OPCs, a multivitamin and enzymes for his digestive system. They are in powder form, and you mix them with water. We put them directly in Tom's G-tube at various times throughout the day. (We started them last Monday night, and by trial and error, because he was still getting sick, we have decided that instead of giving them to him all at once, we will stagger them throughout the day.) Through the suggestion of our dear friend Karrie, we are giving Tom SmartWater instead of tap water in the OPCs and for all of his hydration. (SmartWater is just water with electrolytes.) A bonehead move that I made was giving him aloe for his digestive system that was supposed to be refrigerated after it was open, and I forgot to do that. I stopped that one on Wednesday (the last time he got sick), and he did not get sick again until Sunday morning. I had gotten some new aloe on Friday night and decided to try it one more time. I can't tell you why, but I had a feeling that he would get sick from this again even though it was refrigerated properly. I told Judy I was going to give him the aloe last on Saturday night, so that if he got sick after that, I would know what it was. Well, it happened. He got sick on Sunday morning, and I stopped the aloe. He has not been sick since. He has been on continuous feeding since Wednesday (except for four hours yesterday). A week ago when he was getting sick so much, he was shaking pretty badly from lack of food. I have noticed that he is more alert and seems to feel better. He is not nodding off so much and is responding to everyone really well for long periods of time. I guess what I am trying to say is that, if I took the doctor's telephone diagnosis to heart and then in turn stopped his tube feeding, I would essentially be killing my husband. I have a huge problem with that!

One more item I have to mention is this. I have to take Tom's blood sugars every day and give him insulin. (This is due to the tube feedings and the steroid he is on for brain swelling). When his blood sugars started going up, I told his nurse Judy that I was giving him the OPCs. Once again, she blew me off and said that his sugars were elevated due to the continuous tube feeding. Sure, so when I looked at the OPCs, the first ingredients were glucose and fructose. Okay, whatever you say. Apparently, I know nothing. Funny how they discount these things I was supposed to be telling them. Maybe they just don't want to deal with it. That's fine—I'll deal with it.

Basically, Tom is doing well under our care, and I have to say thank you to everyone who is volunteering to contribute to Tom's care; a special thank you to our nephew Tony. If it were not for him, it would not be possible for Tom to be at home. Tony is currently doing overnights and volunteers to sleep during the day at our house in the event that he is needed when I am not there. What a guy! You don't find that many twenty-two-year-olds with that type of dedication to their uncle. And he is great with Tom. I honestly cannot say enough about Tony; words don't describe him. Tom and I are both very lucky to have everyone in our lives. Who knows where we would be without every single person. We thank you all, and we love you.

Let us all remember:

Bad things happen fast; good things take time ...

And: The doctors do not have the last say on who lives and who dies ...

Word!

Much love to all,

Chrissie

Guest Book Entries

Written July 21, 2008, 9:38 a.m.

Word is right, Chrissie Vinje! We talked about this last night; Tony is amazing! For those of us who are around every day and see how much he cares about his uncle, it is truly wonderful. There are not many twenty-two-year-olds who can or will show the amount of dedication, love, and kindness that pours out of Tony while he is working with Tom.

I also have to say I have seen you almost every day since this all began in March, and you have been incredibly strong in some very difficult moments. These past two weeks since Tom has been home have been a bit of a roller coaster. I am hoping things will calm down and a routine will settle in. Just remember you too are amazing! Tom is still with you (and us) because of your watchful eye, love, and dedication to him.

Love to both of you!

Karrie, Ian, and Ty

Written July 21, 2008, 11:56 a.m.

Chrissie honey, I'm not sure if you have done this or may have forgotten in all the commotion. But in our last conversation, we talked about that maybe you should make an appointment to talk with Tom's family practice doc and make him the "gatekeeper" in Tom's care. That will keep hospice, specialists, and everyone concerned honest in Tom's care, and you also would have a doc to have as your *go-to guy*.

With all my love,

Baby Brother

Tony Betlach

Written July 21, 2008, 11:58 a.m.

Prayers continue for you and Tom. You are never far from my thoughts. May God continue to give you the grace, strength, and peace you both need.

Melinda

Written July 12, 2008, 11:54 p.m.

Hello Chris and Tom,

I just wanted to let you know that I have been thinking about you a lot since Tuesday and hope everything is going well at home. You are in my thoughts and prayers! It must be a *great* feeling to be in your own home again, Tom! Take care, and keep on smiling!

Love,

Kris K.

Tuesday, July 22, 2008, 8:38 a.m., CDT— Chrissie's Journal Entry

Good morning,

It is my second day back to work after a five-week break, and everything went well at home yesterday. Tom's mom, Ginny, comes over at 6:30 every morning so Tony can sleep, and I have different people during the day until I return from work. Yesterday, my mom, Sherrill, and my aunt Marlene were there along with Ginny. They only had to wake Tony twice! If you are not a big strapping young man like Tony, you need two to three people to care for

Tom because he needs to be moved and given medications, etc. It turned out to be a pretty good day. It certainly helps if Tom is not getting sick. I think we have that under control now.

Last night, my niece Nicole (she and her daughter Alexis are currently living in our apartment upstairs) came home and read the sports page to him. When she told him that they had the milk carton boat races over the weekend, he looked at her and said, "Oh, they did?" This is funny because Tom likes to mess with all of us. He knows that we all want to see him open his eyes and talk to us, and that is why he doesn't do it. It is his form of entertainment. Earlier in the evening when my sister Beth walked into the room, she saw Tom's eyes were open. She was trying not to make a big deal out of it, so she said hello to our mom and Aunt Marlene and then said hi to Tom. He immediately shut his eyes and did not respond. Beth then proceeded to call him an a**hole. See what we have to put up with! Mr. Stubborn!

There was something I planned on mentioning yesterday, and then it got away from me. One of the Buds, Davey Fischer, passed away last week. He was a neighborhood buddy, and Tom had known him since childhood. He was forty-six years old. He had been sick for quite some time. A few weeks after Tom went into the hospital, Davey sent Tom a get-well card while Davey himself was in the Mayo Clinic. We didn't know he was in the hospital until well after Tom was a patient himself. When we went to see Davey over a week ago now, the first words out of his mouth were, "How's Tommy?" He did not want people to see him sick and did not want to dwell on his illness; he was always concerned about other people. I have not told Tom of his passing, although it would not surprise me if he knew just by listening to everyone talk around the house. I just knew he would be crushed, and I did not want him to stress about something he couldn't do anything about being as he could not attend the funeral. And a tough funeral that was. Davey will be greatly missed. Here's to you, Davey! We miss you already!

Much love to all,

Chrissie

Guest Book Entries

Written July 22, 2008, 11:27 a.m.

Hey, Chrissie, good to hear from you again! It's wonderful that friends and family are rallying around you and Tommy. It's a big adjustment, but it's times like these when you realize just how much you mean to one another. I honor your fighting spirits. Keep it up! You know what's best. The prayers and positive energy keep coming! Rock on!

Tim Hanley

Written July 22, 2008, 12:01 p.m.

Might I add that after I called him an ***hole that I could see muscles in his face tense up as he was trying to hold back a smile! He was so busted, and he knew it! Anyway, I like the new picture. (Beth is referring to the CaringBridge profile picture.) It was time for the Christmas one to come down!

Beth Timm

Thursday, July 24, 2008, 7:39 a.m., CDT— Chrissie's Journal Entry

Hello, all,

Tommy is holding his own and is beginning to get more active. Tony reported to me that Tuesday night, as he was watching TV, he saw movement out of the corner of his eye. He looked over at Tom and saw him grabbing the left rail of the bed, pulling himself up to look at something. (We have learned not to make a big deal out of these things because he will just stop and be unresponsive.)

Then last night, Karrie came over with some pictures she had printed off on eight-by-ten paper so that Tom could see them easily. By telling him to open his eyes and look at the big fish that her son, Tyler, had caught, she got him to open his eyes to look at all six or seven of the pictures she had brought over. Just then, our niece M'Kenzie walked in looking all old with her newly straightened hair-do. I told Tom to open his eyes to look at her and see how old she looked, and he did! Very nice. Later on, before I went to bed, Tony and I were tending to him and noticed that he had his hospital gown halfway off. Tony asked him if he wanted to lose the whole thing completely, and he nodded yes. (It might have been a different story had the AC been on.) So he slept like that all night and had no intention of putting it back on when I left this morning. Too funny.

I still have other methods in the works to try and heal my honey. How can I not? I purchased some detoxifying foot sheets. You put them on the bottom of the feet, and they pull the toxins out of your body. It sounds like a good plan—antioxidants (OPCs) in, toxins out. I just got them last night and have not tried them yet. He does seem to feel better, which is why, I think, he is more active. I am also thinking of acupuncture and energy healing. And of course, there are always the healing powers of the Lord. I do believe he is working his magic on Tom as we speak. I do know that Tom has accepted the Lord into his heart, and that is an awesome thing. I think it would be appropriate to ask that everyone pray that a divine healing take place so that we can have Tommy back. He will be a changed person, without a doubt. I know that everyone is continuing to pray for Tom, and I thank you. Also, keep that positive energy coming. There will never be a time when we won't need both of these things.

Much love to all,

Chrissie

Guest Book Entries

Written July 24, 2008, 10:31 a.m.

Tom and Chrissie, my arms and prayers are around the both of you. The miracle of Tom and Chrissie started some time ago. It's just easier to see now. Love you.

Robert Notch

Written July 24, 2008, 11:55 a.m.

Hey,

Just wanted to stop by and say hi! I just got off the phone with Ty a few minutes ago, and he was just about to give Tom his meds. I am so happy that he is feeling better and opening his eyes again! It makes a big impact on the whole entire family and friends. :) Also I just love Tom's sense of humor. He keeps it with him at all times. My son and I prayed last night before we went to bed and we asked for a blessing for Tommy! We love you both. Have a good day.

Always,

Cristina Melzer

Monday, July 28, 2008, 7:52 a.m., CDT— Chrissie's Journal Entry

Good morning,

I just want to start out by saying that I would like to take this time to thank everyone for their continued support, prayers, and caring. I also want to give a special thank you to everyone who gives of their time to help care for Tom and offer their support by coming over and calling to see if there is anything they can do. It all means *so* very much because I could not remotely do this alone. While there may be a few moments for Tom that before may have been unimaginable, I know that when it really comes down to it, what matters is that he is being cared for by people who love him and it is being done in the privacy of his own home. That is priceless, and it means the world to both of us.

I cannot even begin to know what he is going through. All I can do is take care of him the best that I can. Since he cannot tell me everything that he needs or how he is feeling, I have to constantly ask him if he is okay, if he is comfortable, if he feels okay, etc. I have now started to pick up on some of his gestures that let us know if what we are doing is being done properly or if something needs to be adjusted. It is all a learning process. I think a lot of us will come away from this experience having learned more than we ever thought we could learn in a lifetime. I believe I am there already because you always think, *This kind of thing doesn't happen to me.* And then it does.

As far as Tom goes, he is doing pretty well. He is certainly more alert and opening his eyes more. He also likes to mess with us, of course. He has had a lot of people coming to see him, and while he does not always respond when people are there, I know it is not because he doesn't want to; it is just that he can't at that moment. Timing is everything. One thing I have noticed in the last week or so is something that Tom has stopped doing. In the hospital, and at home in the beginning, he would nod off. You would be talking to him, or not, and all of a sudden you would see his head drop to the side and drop like he just fell asleep, and then you couldn't wake him for anything. He hasn't done that now in well over a week, maybe two. Rock on, honey!

I have started removing the toxins from Tom's body by using foot pads that draw them out at night. I am also doubling the amount of OPCs that he is getting. It is a good regimen; antioxidants in and toxins out. Who wouldn't feel better? As we work to make him feel better, feel free to send *lots* of positive energy his way. I know I do not have to tell you to keep sending prayers his way because you haven't stopped doing it since the beginning. You guys rock!

Much love to all,

Chrissie

Guest Book Entries

Written July 28, 2008, 2:27 p.m.

Chrissie,

Thank you for all your information. I'm sure you know that there are a lot of prayers going around from people like myself who don't sign in frequently, and we will continue to do so. You are truly a wonderful person … Much love to Tom and you and all who care.

God bless,

Dino DiPerna

Tuesday, July 29, 2008, 7:43 a.m., CDT— Chrissie's Journal Entry

Morning, all,

Tom has been home three weeks today, and I must say, things are going pretty well. A few months ago I could not have imagined that he would be at home in this way. It seems a little surreal, yet we are making it work. Yesterday after I got home from work, my mom and aunt Marlene were telling us about how they were cracking up trying to give Tom his meds earlier in the day. It was the blind leading the blind, but they got 'r done! I was making comments to Tom about it, and he just shook his head with a smirk on his face. I can totally relate because it's like that for me sometimes still. I just tell him, "Sorry, honey, I'm just a rookie. I have no formal training!" Oh hell, it's still better care than he was getting at other places, for sure, and with a little humor thrown in. He just shakes his head at us, and *that* is nothing new, trust me.

Overall, Tom is doing well despite the occasional episodes of throwing up, which does not happen every day. We just try to figure out if there was something different that we did and if so how can we do it differently, things like that. In the meantime, it is apparent he is becoming more aware of his discomfort at times and the things going on around him. Last Friday night, my friend Jackie stayed overnight with her dog, Cedar. Cedar got up on Tom's bed and snuggled with him for about ten minutes. Tom was petting him and scratching him nonstop the entire time Cedar was with him. I wish Bailey would jump up there like that, but she is a little skittish about the bed itself. She hates it when we move it up and down. She is hypersensitive to noises; it's enough to drive you batty. She does, however, go over to him and lick his hand and lets him pet her. Maybe she'll get a little braver. I think it would really help if Tom were to talk to her like he used to. Time will tell.

For today I am going to leave you with words from a card that Jackie gave me last Friday: "I don't believe in miracles, I rely on them."

Once again, *word*!

Much love to all,

Chrissie

Guest Book Entries

Written July 29, 2008, 8:43 a.m.

VING,

I read every entry you make and follow Tom's progress, and I don't think it's occurred to you—you and everyone who's helped—*are* Tom's miracle! There was a reason why that doctor said, "You're doing a lot more than others would." *You are*, silly goose!

I am so glad to hear Tom is making progress—and you're right, he's receiving far better care than he otherwise would have. It's not always the schooling or the knowledge of the care that's important; it's the pure love behind it that's obviously making your Tommy better.

You go, Cha Cha. I am in awe of you and your strength and dedication. I will continue my thoughts and prayers for you both!

Take care,

Michelle Notch

Wednesday, July 30, 2008, 11:56 a.m., CDT—
Chrissie's Journal Entry

Greetings, everyone,

Just a short note to let you know that Tom is hanging in there. He got a little sick this morning, but I think that was due to the foot pads that are pulling the toxins out of his body. He did not get sick yesterday. Tom's hospice nurse, Judy, is a little confused as to why he is sick some days and not others. Well, maybe if she listened to me when I try to tell her the things I am doing for him, she might understand. This would be a much better attitude to take than to assume the doctor gave a correct diagnosis over the phone. But again, I have to remember that it is not their fault. They are doing what they know how to do. It is what they do every day. Having never been in the medical field, I don't see it as black and white as they do. I think there is more out there to heal people than what the doctors can give. And let me tell you, as time goes on, I hear from more and more people that this is true. So I will be carrying on as I have been.

I heard from our friend Kent this morning, and he is in contact with an old neighborhood friend of the Buds who would like to come over and pray for Tom. He also has been involved in a prayer group where people have been healed and declared cancer free. Kent wanted to know when they could come over, and I said, "You tell me when you can come." My schedule is open for anyone who wants to come and pray for my husband. Bring it on!

Until tomorrow … Keep the faith!

Much love,

Chrissie

Guest Book Entries

Written July 30, 2008, 2:06 p.m.

My dad always used to say, "When the going gets tough, the tough get going." You two fit that adage.

Take time to be still and know a higher power is taking care of you even though sometimes you gotta wonder, "Where the hell is He now?"

We are keeping you both in our thoughts and prayers.

Dianne, Victor, Luisa, and Lydia

Written July 30, 2008, 8:07 p.m.

Hi, Chrissie and Tom,

It's great to know Tom is home with family and to have such a support group. You are both very blessed. I keep up on the journal entries, and I will try soon to come over for a visit and see ya both.

Well, always in my prayers; keep the faith and a positive attitude. "It's a good thing." Hmmmm, who always says that …

Lots of hugs!

Julie S.

Thursday, July 31, 2008, 7:58 a.m., CDT— Chrissie's Journal Entry

Hello, all,

There is not much to tell today, other than Tom has not been sick since yesterday morning. I totally dig it when he maintains like that. It says to me that he is okay and we are doing something right. His left leg was a little more swollen than it was yesterday, which I do not like. It has been a week since his legs have been swollen. I was wondering if constipation has anything to do with that, because it was about the time that he became constipated that his legs swelled. In addition to laxatives, we are hoping that some range-of-motion exercises will help with that.

I have a gentleman coming over this evening who is a certified healing touch practitioner. His name is Jim Taylor. He is coming to see both Tom and me. It will be interesting to see what happens. As always, I will keep you posted.

Keep the positive energy and prayers coming. They are working. Keep the faith!

Much love to all,

Chrissie

Tuesday, August 5, 2008, 7:41 a.m., CDT— Chrissie's Journal Entry

Greetings, everyone,

Well I must say that last Thursday night with Jim Taylor was pretty cool. Jim works with people's auras. He said that Tom's was short. It stopped midway down his body. It should be all the way around our bodies and go out about a foot or two. Jim went to work on reminding it where it was supposed to be. He also worked on getting rid of the residual radiation in his body, and on opening up the chakras on the upper part of Tom's body. He did all of this without touching him. Even at that, the work was so intense that Tom opened his eyes twice to see what was going on. Jim also works with healing stones. He went to his bag and pulled out kyanite. What is cool about that is when I was in Boise, my cousin Pam (who also works with healing stones) told me that I needed kyanite for Tom, so we went shopping and I bought a piece for Tom. It has been in his pillow since the day he came home. When Jim found out that I already had some kyanite, he asked me how I knew about it. He also had said earlier that Tom's aura was out about two inches, which was better than he expected. After finding out about the kyanite I had been using, he said that was why his aura was better than he anticipated. (Pretty cool, huh, Pam? Thanks, Cuz!)

Since Jim has been over, Tom's feet have warmed up, (they had been a little colder after swelling up), and best of all, he is becoming more awake! Yesterday, when I got home from work, my mom and aunt Marlene told me that Tom was awake earlier in the day and watching TV for about ten minutes. Then, later in the evening, for a period of about two to three hours, whenever we walked into the room, he had his eyes open. He actually wanted his glasses on so he could watch the Twins game. At one point, I was telling him that our "precious" Bailey had dug a trench to lie in alongside our neighbor's house. His eyes had been open the whole time but, this time, he turned his head and eyes over toward me and looked at me while I was talking to him! He did it again a little while later when I was talking about something else! Sweet! It looks like signs of things to come …

Last Thursday night I ran into an old friend of mine that I used to work with at Jay Kline Chevrolet, Tracy W. (Beth and I call her TLW). She asked me how married life was treating me, and of course, I told her about Tom. I also told her about the CaringBridge and that I was doing different things to try to heal him. I then told her what Abby and Ben told me the last time they were over. They said that when they come over to pray for Tom, they don't hope for a miracle; they *expect* one. (I totally dig that!) Tracy then replied with a line that I told her I was putting in print on the Bridge. She said, "You have to keep on living until you die!" You know damn right! And as far as I am concerned, Tom is still living! The doctors can think what they want (or what they know to be true), and I can do whatever it takes to prove them wrong. That is my purpose in life—to heal my husband and prove that medical miracles do happen, and they happen to people like you and me. I know that everyone who knows and loves Tom would want nothing less. So, thanks, TLW, for that quote. It gives me renewed energy on a goal I have been working toward for exactly five months today.

I also want to let everyone know that I am doing exactly what Casey Kasem said to do years ago. It is a quote worth repeating: "Keep your feet on the ground, and keep reaching for the stars."

Indeed!

Much love to all,

Chrissie

Guest Book Entries

Written August 5, 2008, 8:29 p.m.

Chrissie,

I wanted to share a possible alternative care possibility with you, if you are interested. My dear friend Kimberly has a brother in-law who is a Lakota medicine man. I shared Tom's journey with her today (as you and Tom continue to be in Asher and my thoughts and prayers), and she wanted to extend an invitation to you to call her or her sister and see if they may be able to help Tom. My friend Kimberly can give you more information on their altar, which is in Iowa, or you can call Mindy and Lester O. directly or you can call me too. We will continue to keep you and Tom in our prayers.

Peace,

Heather and Asher

Written August 5, 2008, 9:20 p.m.

Chrissie,

Over the past several months as I read your updates, I have been in awe of your strength, courage, and perseverance. You have taken this challenge head-on and have been a great inspiration and a never-ending source of energy. Now that I am in the situation of caregiver for my critically ill mother, I see you as a role model. Thank you for all that you are doing for Tom and for giving me courage to face my own battle. I hope to get over and see you both soon.

Love,

Jeanne Galle Franklin

(Former neighbor)

Chapter 10

Back to 6A

**Wednesday, August 6, 2008, 12:54 p.m., CDT—
Chrissie's Journal Entry**

Hello, everyone,

I wanted to share the events of the morning with you. I got a call at work this morning saying that Tom was having a seizure. We called hospice to let them know, and they told us to give him some medication to calm him down. After I got home and saw what was happening, I told Ginny to call 911.

Long story short, we are back at the U of M Hospital (not Riverside) in the ICU—back where we were in the beginning. As of this moment, he has been intubated to control his breathing. His oxygen level is fine, but he was breathing at a rate of fifty breaths per minute, which is double what normal is. They did a CT scan and did not see anything, so they will be doing an MRI. They have also taken a chest x-ray to look for pneumonia and started antibiotics as a prevention for pneumonia or bladder infection.

Tonight, we were having a prayer group come to the house to pray for Tom. I am hoping they will be willing to come here instead. Please send some more prayers and positive energy our way so Tommy can feel it …

I will update as more information becomes available.

Much love to all,

Chrissie

Wednesday, August 6, 2008, 6:55 p.m., CDT— Chrissie's Journal Entry

Good evening, everyone,

So far what we have learned is that they are still trying to figure out why he had a seizure. The doctor said that one possible reason would be due to bleeding on the brain (and something else, but I forgot what), but that was ruled out by the CT scan on his brain … Good. Another reason could be due to respiratory issues, but as I said before, his oxygen levels are fine; he was just breathing too rapidly. The other reason could be that his blood sugar was 59 when he got here this morning. When I checked it before I left for work, his blood sugar was 105, and I gave him the 15 units I was supposed to give him. So the next step is the MRI. That may happen tomorrow, or it may happen on Friday. This is due to the dyes they use for the CT on his lungs and the MRI. You cannot do them within forty-eight hours of each other unless, because they are two different dyes, they are compatible (or something like that …).

This brings up the subject of his lungs. The CT scan on his lungs showed that there are no new clots and the old ones are resolving! Woo-hoo! Rock on! And I would not be surprised if the clots are gone (or resolving) in his arms due to the OPCs. I say this because his arms are no longer swollen like they were when he had the clots. Time will tell …

Also, the prayer group will be here at seven thirty tonight to pray for Tom. I spoke with Todd this evening, and he said that since he found out about Tom, he feels very strongly that God is calling him to come pray for him. And as I think I told you before, he has been involved in a healing where a man had cancer throughout his whole body and had no hope of survival. After being prayed for, he went to the Mayo and was declared cancer free. *That* is what I am talking about! Let's go!

Much love to all,

Chrissie

Guest Book Entries

Written August 6, 2008, 6:49 p.m.

Chrissie,

Sorry to hear about Tom. You're doing an awesome job of caring for him, and your dedication is amazing! All prayers and positive energy are around you and Tommy tonight. Keep the fire burnin'. Rock on!

Tim Hanley

Thursday, August 7, 2008, 1:57 p.m., CDT— Chrissie's Journal Entry

Greetings,

Here is an update on Tom's condition. The results of the MRI showed that there was no significant change in the size of the tumor, so this was not the cause of the seizure. Their "guess" as to the cause is what I had mentioned yesterday about the sodium and glucose levels, along with the little bit of fluid on the brain.

The issue at hand right now is the vent tube and taking Tom off of it. They want to be clear on my intentions as far as the full code/ DNR issue. They are asking me *again* what I would like to do even though it is clearly in print. They are talking to me like I don't understand what is going on when, in fact, it is them who do not understand what is going on. They will understand soon enough. For whatever reason I am being driven to do what I am doing, and the things they are asking of me do not feel right to me. I could not live with myself if I did the things they are asking of me, plain and simple. So I have to stand my ground against them (and in their mind, their better judgment) and do what I feel is right, right now. I am truly tired of this crossroad and hope that I do not have to face it too many more times.

So as it stands, he will be given more antiseizure medication that will make him more tired (at first)—great. And once he gets off the tube, he should be able to go back home. That's where we are at. Also, Jim Taylor will be making a return visit this evening, this time to Tom's hospital room. I think he is really needed here tonight.

As always, I will keep you posted.

Much love to all,

Chrissie

Guest Book Entries

Written August 7, 2008, 10:11 p.m.

Hi, Chrissie,

I can only imagine how frustrated you are by the medical "professionals" you have to interact with on a daily basis! They should know by now that you are not one to give up, especially since you and Tom have come this far in beating the odds! They clearly do not understand the level of faith we all have that Tom can recover.

Keep your head up, and continue to follow your heart. It is by the grace of God, your love, and the love of Tom's family that he is still here today and continues to put up the good fight!

All of you are in my prayers!

Trish Clancy

Written August 8, 2008, 9:01 a.m.

All I can say is you go, girl! Don't let them push you around. They have no clue who they are dealing with ... we do!

Love ya,

Kim Peterson

Saturday, August 9, 2008, 3:04 p.m., CDT— Chrissie's Journal Entry

Happy birthday, Tommy!

Yes, it's true. The "blessed holiday" is upon us. (That's how Tom always refers to his birthday.) He is forty-six years old today. I am sure neither of us ever expected he would be spending any of his birthdays in this way. But the present we got today from his nurse was that the vent tube came out, and he is breathing at 100 percent oxygen on his own. He does still, however, have an oxygen mask on at this point as they try to clear his throat of all the mucus that collected. You go, Tommy!

Lisa, Nicki, and I were in his room earlier singing "Happy Birthday" to him. We then read him the birthday cards he received, and one of them was a musical card with the *Star Wars* theme. I gave him a couple of little things I found in the coffee shop downstairs that I have sitting in his room. When I asked him if he liked them, he said yes ... Let's hope he wasn't jackin' with me!

Yesterday, Wendy, her mom, Sharon, and I went to the Enchanted Rock Garden on Sixty-Fifth and Lyndale in Richfield to look for some healing stones. Jim Taylor told me I should get lepidolite, which aids in transition among other things. While we were there, Mary, an employee of the Enchanted Rock Garden, was helping us pick out stones and such. After a while we started telling her how we were led to her store—Tom's illness, of course. Once she found that we were dealing with a cancerous tumor, she looked up what stones were for cancer and tumors, and I bought a couple. She also lit a candle for Tom and placed it in the rock candle holder she had behind the counter. Before she did that, she had me speak the intention of the candle, and I said, "Heal my husband's whole body, and bring him back to us." She also pulled up the meaning of yesterday's date of August 8, 2008. In the meaning of the date were the words *healing* and *breath*. We told her about Tom's CaringBridge website, and then she hugged all of us before we left. It was an awesome experience; thank you, Mary. We'll be back to see you.

Yesterday afternoon ended up being a rough one, dealing with the hospital *again* about Tom's code status. The doctor I was talking to said that the people here at the hospital were confused about his status because he had come in from hospice care. They thought he had been a DNR for hospice and that I changed it when we got here. That is not the case. Here is what I told her: "Tom has been a full code since he was at Riverside in June. I did not change anything." I also told her, "Not every hospice requires a DNR. As a matter fact, we are with Fairview Hospice, which is your hospice program, and they do not require a DNR. You can be a full code in their program." (She did not know that … really!) *"Right now*, this is the right thing to do. If I even think about changing that, something happens to me inside and I know it is not the right decision at this time. *If* I have to make that decision at some other time, I will know it is the right time when it happens. So for right now, please pass along to the doctors that I do understand what is happening with him. I am not in denial, and for right now, this is the correct decision. Also, tell them I want that vent tube *out*! He is not dependent on it, and I want it out before he is. We came in here for a seizure, and now we are dealing with a frickin' ventilator issue."

I had a headache after that one. But needless to say, the vent tube is out, and so far in the last five months, his code status has not come into play except for the fact that they keep asking me about it. Give me a break, man.

On the lighter side of things, today is my husband's birthday, and next year on August 9, 2009, I want us to look back on this one and thank our lucky stars that he is still with us and that while he will still be recovering, we are together and life will be going on as planned. So, if you get a chance, raise a glass and toast Thomas Lyle Vinje today, on the blessed holiday.

Here's to Tommy! Happy birthday, honey!

Much love to all,

Chrissie

Guest Book Entries

Written August 9, 2008, 10:25 a.m.

Hi, Chris,

Take to heart that you know you are doing what is best for Tom. The medical profession seems to forget sometimes that there is another force beyond their fingers. He will be healed. God will grant a miracle; you have to ask and expect it. Believe it will happen. You keep fighting for Tom and yourself. You are amazing.

I am sending positive energy and my prayers to you guys.

Love ya,

Roxie Chudy

Written August 9, 2008, 4:17 p.m.

Happy birthday, Tommy; I just wanted to thank you both for the present of love and courage that we all receive from the both of you every day. My arms and prayers are around you both.

Robert Notch

Written August 9, 2008, 10:07 p.m.

Happy birthday, Tom! Here's to many more. You're an inspiration. Our thoughts and prayers are with you daily. Keep it up, dude!

Victor Zupanc

Written August 9, 2008, 10:30 p.m.

Dear Chrissie,

My family and I continue our prayers!

Happy birthday, Tom!

Love,

Laura S.

Sunday, August 10, 2008, 1:34 p.m., CDT— Chrissie's Journal Entry

Hello, everyone,

A very cool thing happened yesterday after I updated. I walked into Tom's room, and they had removed the oxygen mask! And as of right now, it has stayed off! His oxygen level today is staying right around 94 percent. Yesterday it hovered around 96 to 98 percent. They get concerned if it drops below 92percent.

Another cool thing is the rate of his tube feeding. Right after we got him home a month ago, after he got so sick, we were instructed by hospice to drop the rate he was receiving his food to 25 ml per hour. I had started to up that a little bit when he got sick again, and then I left it at 25 ml. Well, here in the hospital their goal was 45 ml. That is where it has been for at least twenty-four hours, and that's what we will start at when he comes home. I will then test to see if I can up it even more, especially to the 50 ml that it was at PP when he came home.

Tom's legs and right arm are *extremely* swollen at the moment. They finally wrapped his legs last night to move some of the fluid up his body. I am concerned about the swelling and the fact that his urine output is minimal. I do not yet know what the cause is. That will be something I will have to find out about tomorrow when all the docs come back from their weekend. My guess is that he will be released to the floor sometime tomorrow as he really does not need to be in the ICU any longer. They generally don't do too much moving around like that on the weekends. They just wait for Monday. Let's just pray that his kidneys are fine and the swelling will go down.

Everyone enjoy the rest of your weekend with this beautiful weather we've been having ...

Much love to all,

Chrissie

Guest Book Entries

Written August 10, 2008, 10:21 a.m.

Another miracle has happened for Tom and Chrissie. It was when Tom was able to breathe on his own. After he was admitted to the hospital last week, I never imagined that would happen. The next miracle that needs to happen is for Tom's kidneys to work on their own. When Cheri and I were at the house when Jim made his first visit, a miracle happened there in that Tom's eyes were not only open, but his pupils were in the natural position. Whenever I saw his eyes open, his pupils were way at the corner of his eye, barely visible. That really blew my mind. Cheri assisted Jim with the "force of energy." She really felt it coming from her feet up through her body and through her hands going over Tom's body to Jim. She said afterward her fingers were tingling. We sincerely hope that miracles will continue to happen for Tom. We hope that he doesn't continue to lose weight. We hope that the seizure medicine will not make him sleep any more than he did before. We hope for a complete miracle!

Susan L.

Written August 10, 2008, 9:42 p.m.

CJ-MBV,

It was pretty powerful being with you these last few days.

I can't stop thinking about the way I felt that night—connected to Tom and Jim and how Tom looked me directly in the eye. Something is happening.

Stay strong, love. I'm always here for you. Something changed in me all those years ago and made me different. This is changing us now. Always believe …

XXXXOOOO

Wendy P.

Written August 10, 2008, 9:47 p.m.

Chrissie,

Having spent the past week at U of M Hospital with my mom, four days of which were in ICU (she moved out just as Tom was moving in—I think they had the same nurse), I have only begun to experience what you have been experiencing for months. As I have said before, *you* are what is giving me strength during this period of time with my mom. I took a break from visiting Mom on Thursday and spent some time with Tom. I hope he felt the positive energy I was trying to send his way. On Friday, I took another break from mom and spent a good period of time in the meditation room, offering up prayers of strength and courage for both of you.

I've thought a lot about Tom recently and about his birthday. I can vividly remember the evening of his fortieth birthday, hearing all about the sky-diving trip. Here's to you, good buddy, and may there be many more to come!

Love to you,

Your former neighbor,

Jeanne Galle Franklin

Monday, August 11, 2008, 4:52 p.m., CDT—
Chrissie's Journal Entry

Greetings, all,

Tom is going back to 6A very shortly. We will be out of ICU! Sweetness! I have a meeting at nine thirty tomorrow morning with hospice to sign back up so we can get Tom back home. My guess is that he will be home on Wednesday or Thursday at the latest.

He is still off of the oxygen and tolerating his food at rate of 45 ml per hour. If there was anything positive we could get from this current hospital visit, that would be it. I am still not completely sure what caused the seizure. I have heard there are some theories, but I have yet to be told a definitive reason. The results of the EEG showed no seizure activity. What that means is there was no seizure activity at the time of the EEG. It does not measure past seizure activity. So I really don't know a whole lot more than that. I am hoping to be able to talk to a doctor on 6A before we go home so that I can get some answers. The doctors seem so elusive in the ICU.

That is all I know for now. We are moving to 6A! Gotta go!

Much love to all,

Chrissie

***

As an aside, I want to mention that I went with Tom and was present when they performed the EEG. I was having a really hard time seeing him with so many electrodes stuck to his head and face. As the tests were progressing, the technician performing the tests sensed that I was having a hard time and asked me if I was okay. I just told her that it had been such a long road already, and

I felt so badly that Tom had to be put through all of this while not being able to speak up for himself. She assured me the tests were okay and that he was fine. Of course, I knew this, but it was difficult nonetheless.

***

Guest Book Entries

> Written August 11, 2008, 1:22 p.m.
>
> Sorry I missed Tom's birthday over the weekend, but I wanted to send belated wishes, Hope it was great! By the way the log sounded this morning it was a good weekend. You and Tom continue to surprise us, which I pray to God never ends! Rock on!
>
> Tim Hanley

Tuesday, August 12, 2008, 11:09 a.m., CDT— Chrissie's Journal Entry

Good morning,

Well, Tom is back on 6A, room 2. I had a meeting with hospice just now to sign him back up so we can go home, but we are not sure now when that will be. His legs have been swelling up more and more since he was in the ICU, and now it is moving up his body to his stomach. (His right arm is also swollen.) He just got back from having an ultrasound to find out what is going on. I have not talked to a doctor yet (imagine that), but I would expect that there will be some testing done on his kidneys. Pray that this will resolve itself so we can get him back home. We are losing very precious OPC time. And he is not the only one taking them now; a bunch of us have started to take OPCs, and now we can know how much better he is feeling because of them.

Please continue to send prayers and positive energy his way so that we can get back home sooner than later. I will update more today if I get some information.

Much love to all,

Chrissie

Tuesday, August 12, 2008, 2:18 p.m., CDT— Chrissie's Journal Entry

Hello,

I am now informed and have news to tell you. They found out from the ultrasound this morning that Tom's legs are swollen for two reasons.

1. They are full of blood clots.
2. Malnutrition

So the plan of attack is as follows. He is now able to take a blood thinner, and if you remember back in June when the others were discovered, he was not able to do that because it was too close to the ending of the radiation and his platelets were too low. (I did find out last week that his platelets have doubled since June.) Also, we will be feeding him with a supplement that has more protein and at a higher rate. The writing on the wall on this factor is plain as day for me. The hospice doctor thought his digestive system was shutting down, so they slowed down the feeding to 25 ml per hour. When we tried to up it, we were told to leave it at 25 ml. Hmmm, I guess that was incorrect information, huh! Like I said before, how can you make such an important diagnosis over the damn phone! Crimony!

The other news is that we are going home tomorrow. The equipment will be delivered in the morning, and we should have Tom home sometime tomorrow afternoon. The one thing that will be more difficult for us is that his legs are extremely heavy right now due to the swelling, so it will be harder for us to move him around. It will take some time for the blood thinners and nutrition to work their magic.

And oh yeah, I almost forgot to tell you the most important news … His kidneys are perfectly fine! I was kind of worried about that. I have also gotten some range-of-motion exercise handouts so we can start that as soon as possible to keep his joints and muscles flexible. We will have to be gentler with his legs right now due to the clots. There will have to be minimal movement.

Thanks everyone for your prayers and positive energy. Tommy and I are most appreciative of all of them.

Much love to all,

Chrissie

Guest Book Entries

Written August 12, 2008, 2:38 p.m.

Trust your gut! You probably know more than most of the people working on his case!

Thinking of ya,

Irene and Dave Peterson

Written August 12, 2008, 3:48 p.m.

OMG, WTF, unbelievable! I just can't believe those
people. We are so being jacked with, and why is it
that I noticed his legs but the doctors and the nurses
noticed nothing? Said nothing! Uuggh!

Judy Vinje

Chapter 11

Home Again

**Thursday, August 14, 2008, 10:29 p.m., CDT—
Chrissie's Journal Entry**

Hello, everyone,

The last couple of days have been a little overwhelming for me. Tom came home on Wednesday around 3:00 p.m., and it all just kind of hit me. I felt really overwhelmed by the increased medication he is on (from three to seven meds) and also by the extra care he needs due to his *extreme* swelling. I have never seen anything like it. So we have to be very careful in everything we do. I won't get in to the particulars, but it's really kind of stressful to deal with. It's okay, though; it will get better. The good news, as far as I am concerned, is that they are not completely sure why he had a seizure. I was expecting to hear that it was due to the tumor, but I didn't hear that once. When Dr. H walked into his room on Tuesday morning, he asked me if I had any questions and I said, "What caused the seizure?" He said, "We don't know. It could be due to the small fluid on his brain, the low sodium levels, and the low glucose levels, or any one of those on their own could have caused it." So maybe it happened so we could find out about the blood clots and malnutrition. That is my thinking. Either way, we know how to proceed and correct. The good news is he can now take the blood thinner to dissipate the dang clots. Thank God.

I put Tom's oxygen back on last night because it was a little warm in the house until the AC kicked in and he seemed a little labored. I asked him if it felt better, and he said yes. It is still on now. I plan to test him over the weekend and ask him to see what he prefers. I now have an oximeter so I can test his oxygen levels to see where he is at. I also got some information from, of course, Elizabeth on 6A about what to look for when someone is not breathing right. That is also forefront in my mind. Thanks, Elizabeth. I need some handy hints! I also want to thank Monica for coming down to help with Tom before we left the hospital. I know she keeps up on Tom's progress along with so many of you. You know, it really is a testimony to who Tom is. Even though his nurses did not know him before he got sick, I think it is just so amazing that they still want to know what is going on with him. It means so very much, and I thank each and every one of you. He is an awesome dude, and you will get to see that someday. Thank you so much!

Much love to all,

Chrissie

Guest Book Entries

Written August 15, 2008, 7:56 a.m.

A "little overwhelming"? You kill me! They may have increased his meds, but *you* are his best "med."

We love you …

Mrs. Kreps

Wendy P.

Monday, August 18, 2008, 8:00 a.m., CDT— Chrissie's Journal Entry

Hello,

We got through the first weekend back at home. Tommy is so swollen that I can no longer lift him with another woman. I need to have a guy in the mix to be able to lift, move, and help us do what has to be done. The good news is that he is now starting to output his urine at a much higher rate, and some of the swelling is starting to go down. I have seen that it kind of shifts from day to day because for a day or two his left foot looked better, and now it is puffy again. His stomach has been stretched to the max, and now I can pinch an inch to give him his blood thinner shot. Before we left the hospital on Wednesday, I asked how long it would take for the swelling to go down, and I was told it would be weeks. That works because the way they were talking I thought it could be months. The swelling has created a whole new set of problems in ways you don't want to know about. I feel so bad for my honey it makes me want to cry. Some days, man …

I'm kind of—no wait, I *am* having a problem with the hospice doctor. I am fairly certain he has a God complex. I was exposed to the scope of his arrogance on Friday afternoon when he came to visit Tom for the second time ever. While I understand what his job is, I am afraid for the people he has come in contact with who take his word as gospel. It is because of him that Tom was malnourished, and when he came to the house on Friday, he mentioned dropping Tom's food rate down from what the hospital had ordered. I can *guarantee* you that I will not ever follow that order again, and when it comes to anything he tells me to do, I will be double checking it with the good folks at the U of M Hospital.

We had continuous care coverage with hospice nurses for the first forty-eight hours that Tom was home. Lydia was the nurse who was there from eight till four on Thursday and Friday. When the doctor was there and I was asking him about when to give Tom insulin (the hospital discontinued it due to the reduction of the steroid he is getting), he said he wouldn't give him any unless his blood sugar reached 250! (Lydia even thought that was a little weird.) Let me tell you that in the hospital, he gets insulin if his blood sugar is 120 or over. Trust me when I tell you that I *will* call the hospital if his blood sugar goes over 150. I do not need to sit and watch my husband suffer at the hands of "Dr. Kevorkian" any more than he already has.

The last thing I will tell you about "Dr. K" is that when he asked me what I thought about Tom's hospital visit, I told him that they did not know what caused the seizure. He told me it was the tumor. I told him that was not what *his* doctor told me. He said, and I quote, "That is what *I* am telling you!" (Excuse me! When did you become a fricking neurosurgeon, dude!) What the hell! Hmmmm, let me see, do I trust Dr. H, the *chief* of neuro surgery at the University of Minnesota, or a hospice doctor (whom I found out on Friday has experience with chemical dependency)? Geez, what to do, what to do! As you can see, he thoroughly pissed me off. You know, it's hard enough to deal with all of this, let alone deal with a-holes like him, seriously.

On the up side, since yesterday afternoon, Tommy is opening his eyes more again and watching TV like he was right before the seizure. I believe he was awake and looking around most of the night. Yesterday he was watching me move around the room and followed with his eyes when I was talking to him. I haven't seen that in a while. He would also watch me while I gave him his OPCs and other meds. I just explained what I was doing and what I was giving him.

Please continue your prayers and positive energy while we are on this leg of our journey. It will be twenty-two weeks tomorrow, and I miss my hubby terribly. We expect that this miracle will happen sooner than later. It has to.

Remember: bad things happen fast, good things take time ...

(The doctor who told me that quote has moved on from the U to another hospital in his residency. I must say that I missed him during this last hospital stay. Thanks, Dr. R. Hope to see you again.)

Much love to all,

Chrissie

Guest Book Entries

Written August 18, 2008, 9:57 a.m.

Hang in there, Chrissie! We're sending positive thoughts and healing prayers your way.

Dianne

Tuesday, August 19, 2008, 7:43 a.m., CDT— Chrissie's Journal Entry

Good morning!

Well, I think it is safe to say that Tommy is starting to come out of the radiation sleep he has been in for the last three months. He is opening his eyes more and more, and yesterday, when my mom was telling him what time the Twins were on that night, she told him it was on at, "Seven" and he repeated, "Seven." Also, last night

I walked into the living room with our niece Alexis and saw that his eyes were open and he was watching the game. I went over to him and held his hand, and then I went and got his glasses and put them on him. As he was looking at me, I just kept saying, "I love you, I love you," and he got this great big smile on his face as he kept looking at me. He kept smiling for a while, and then I called Alexis over to see Uncle Tommy. As she came over, Tommy was watching her and looking at her. When I said, "Isn't she just the cutest?" he just shook his head in disbelief like, "Yeah, she's dang cute!" I started telling him about the fact that Alexis considers Tony her "best friend." She had come outside saying, "Best friend, best friend. I just took a bath, and I dumped out all the soap!" Yep, Alexis and Tony are tight. As I was telling him all the Alexis and Tony stories, he started to chuckle. Then Tom's brother Gary came into the room and saw that he was awake, so I got up to let him sit next to Tom and finish watching the game.

A few minutes later Judy walked in, but Tom had shut his eyes. As Judy was about to leave, she started to tell Gary and Tom that the church next to their mom's house (Epiphany) was closing on Saturday and that they were having a mass and a catered meal afterward. As soon as Judy mentioned the name of the church, he opened his eyes and listened to the story, shaking his head. He really does like to hear about all the things that are going on. He seems to respond well to that. This is why I keep the news on for him, along with shows like *60 Minutes*. I also put on his favorite comedies, but I think we need to start jamming out on tunes again, so maybe it's time for a little Bob Marley again. I also want to put on KFAN for him. He likes listening to Dan Barriero. I need to put a note on the radio so whoever is at the house at four o'clock can put it on for him. I was doing that before the seizure, but now it is time to resume. He is actually back to where he was right before the seizure when he wanted to wear his glasses all day.

I *really* needed that last night. I had kind of an off day, as you noticed from my entry yesterday. It just kind of carried on for the rest of the day and was just getting worse. I was extremely crabby by the time I got home from work. That totally broke my mood in the best possible way. Thanks, honey! Hopefully I will be able to keep making entries like this the more he wakes up. He just needs to not be so stubborn and throw us a frickin' bone once in a while! Good luck to us!

Thank you all so much for your constant prayers, positive energy, and support. I know I have said it before, but I *really* couldn't do what I am doing without all of them from all of you.

Much love to all,

Chrissie

Guest Book Entries

Written August 19, 2008, 8:37 a.m.

It was amazing to see him smile the way he did last night. It truly is a gift. It is such a pleasure to be there every day with the both of you. We love you both very much.

Nic and Lex

Written August 19, 2008, 9:33 a.m.

I agree, Chrissie, news is good, and it's great to hear Tommy laugh. But music is the universal language of the soul, and it's "high" time he and Bob "Mon" get reacquainted. So let the jammin' begin. Rock on!

Tim Hanley

Wednesday, August 20, 2008, 8:07 a.m., CDT—
Chrissie's Journal Entry

Greetings,

Tommy was not as forthcoming yesterday as he was on Monday. He was awake last night but not really answering any questions and looking away from me instead of at me. It was like he was mad. Who wouldn't be? It could be that he is becoming more aware and he is angry. I don't blame him for a minute. I feel the same.

One thing that really touched me yesterday was that I received a card from Tom's family doctor. (What's funny about this is that my brother, Tony, has been telling me that I should contact him to discuss Tom so I have a doctor to go to. After we left the TCU, I have kept wondering who his doctor is. I was especially confused after we left PP. Who do I call if I need a doctor? We all know what doctor I am *not* going to call.) The card said that he was very sad and sorry about Tom. He also said he has been receiving reports from the U of M and knows what we are going through. Additionally, he said that he knows about his illness and if he can help in any way that I am to call him. Then he gave me his number. I was absolutely astounded by that. I almost started crying. I guess I never expected a doctor to reach out like that. He must really like Tom. So I guess he did my work for me. I now have Dr. D at my disposal, as well as the doctors from the U. This is more than I had before his last hospital stay, and it is most comforting to know I have some medical support even though Tom is at home. I say this, even though I know and so do you, that they do not have the last say on who lives and who dies.

Much love to all,

Chrissie

Guest Book Entries

Written August 20, 2008, 11:54 a.m.

Chrissie, I am glad they got a hold of you. Know you can use him as a *gatekeeper* for all his meds, for refills, and to keep an eye on Dr. Kevorkian and all the other doctors that have anything to do with Tom, including the hospice nurses. Also let him know about all the homeopathic stuff too. He can take a lot of weight off your shoulders, once he knows the route you are taking with Tom—like that whole staying *alive* thing. He may even have some fresh ideas on everything. *Hey, I love you like a sister.*

Tony Betlach

Written August 20, 2008, 6:59 p.m.

Hi, Chrissie,

Thank you for keeping up this journal. I am so proud of you! Your fierce love and protection of Tom shines through! You are strong and amazing!

Keep your faith … follow your heart … and *believe*! Good things are happening!

Launette Figliuzzi

Written August 20, 2008, 9:06 p.m.

Hi, Chrissie,

I just want you to know that my boys have been saying special prayers for your Tommy since we first heard about his condition from Rach. We are all pulling for him, and if there's anything we can do for you and for Tommy, please don't hesitate to ask.

We love you,

Amy Loughrey

Thursday, August 21, 2008, 7:59 a.m., CDT— Chrissie's Journal Entry

Hello,

Not too much to tell you today except that Tommy's swelling *is* visibly going down. Thank God! It is a slow process, but he is definitely looking better and I hope feeling better. We are doing our very best to heal his skin and prevent any further breakdown in his skin due to the swelling. He is also looking good because Tony shaved him yesterday before the home health aide (HHA) came to bathe him. Nice job, Tone! Tony likes to shave him before the HHA comes to bathe him so that he can clean up all the stray beard hairs that fall.

After receiving the card from Tom's doctor the other day, I put a call in to him yesterday afternoon. He called me back around five o'clock, and we discussed Tom's situation. Come to find out that he knows Dr. Kevorkian and thinks he is a good doctor. I told him I wasn't of that opinion. As it turns out, Dr. D is in the Allina Health System (we are in Fairview), so he is not able to be Tom's doctor as we cannot bring him into the clinic. Also, it is not practical to think that he would be able make a house call. He did tell me that I can call him if I need advice, which, I think, is huge. It is exactly what I need. It gives me some sense of peace knowing Tom's doctor, someone who knows Tom, is a phone call away.

I've been in kind of a funk for a couple of days this week, and I am hoping that I can shake it. I need an attitude adjustment. I did have a major one the other night when I had Tom's undivided attention, but something is going on and I don't know what. I am feeling kind of crabby (okay, bitchy), and I am trying to hold it at bay. I suppose a meltdown is on the way, and I just have to let it come and see what happens. Weird.

Anyway, everyone have a great weekend and have fun at the fair. If anything major happens, I will be sure to let y'all know about it. (See, even when I think I don't have anything to say I manage to come up with something!)

Much love to all,

Chrissie

Guest Book Entries

Written August 21, 2008, 8:45 a.m.

Chris,

You have been put through five months of a living hell to not only watch Tom go through what he is going through but to deal with what you are going through as well. Beyond just having a tumor, he has had many serious complications arise on top of that, and you have had to make some huge, important decisions on his behalf, all the time not knowing what he would do. This has all been happening to you, and all the while you have to stay on top of regular life like paying the bills and taking care of your pets. You have been superhumanly positive and upbeat during all of this, and I don't think there is a person out there who is going to fault you for cracking a little bit under such enormously stressful circumstances. You and Tom have been fighting for his life for months on end, and you are allowed to feel that pain and frustration that you are going through. I love you!

Beth Timm

Written August 21, 2008, 9:23 a.m.

Chrissie,

I can't begin to imagine all you are going through, but you have got to be one the strongest, most tenacious women I have ever known. Your positive outlook and willingness to do whatever it takes for Tom truly is an inspiration to all. Tom is very lucky to have you by his side fighting for him every step of the way. Your determination and persistence in seeking as many answers as possible will be the reason that Tom will come back around. As you have quoted so many times, "Doctors don't have a say in who lives and who dies." It is those who put their trust in God's hands and continue to encourage and fight for their loved ones. Tom will pull through this because he has you to come back to! Hang in there, and we are praying for you both!

Jeanine Hay

Written August 22, 2008, 4:29 p.m.

Hey, Chris,

I honestly don't know what to say except I am thinking about you and Tom constantly. I will ask the ladies at church to put you both on the prayer chain. I can't imagine going through all that you are. If you need anything, let me know.

Love ya,

Vicki Johnson

Written August 23, 2008, 11:43 a.m.

Hi, Chris,

With everything going on in your life the past few months, you deserve to "lose it" once in a while. You have gone through more stress than most people encounter in their entire lives. You deserve an award for being the most dedicated wife in the whole world! Tom is so lucky to have you in his life. Your positive attitude and energy are such a strong testament to your love and your faith. I am so glad to hear that Tom is doing so much better. I will continue to pray for you and Tom and send positive energy to you and your whole family!

Love,

Kris K.

Monday, August 25, 2008, 7:56 a.m., CDT—
Chrissie's Journal Entry

Good morning,

Tom has his eyes open a lot more now. He will follow me around the room as I come and go getting stuff done around the house. He spoke a few words to Nicki again the other night. She seems to be the one he talks to ... What's up with that! Oh hell, I'm just glad he does it! Judy came in on Saturday night and showed Tom some memorabilia she picked up for him from the church that had their last service yesterday. He was very attentive looking at everything she got him. He loves that kind of stuff.

I feel bad for my honey because he keeps getting these hiccups. This happened the first time he was home too. He had them for a week or so, off and on, and we gave him the medication to help get rid of them and they eventually did. Now he has them again. Hopefully they will go away soon. They seemed pretty hard this morning, like it probably hurt. We'll keep at it until they go away.

I had to leave yesterday for a couple of hours to visit my brother Tony, who was admitted to Abbott for heart/lung issues. He wasn't feeling well, and Maddie told him that he was pure white. When he went in to look in the mirror, he saw that she was right and told her to call 911. They brought him to the Cambridge hospital, which then transferred him to Abbott. They did a CT scan on his lungs at Cambridge and ruled out a blood clot in his lung. The doctor at Abbott was going to double check that because his oxygen level is *really* low. Without the oxygen mask on his levels are in the 80s, and when he lies down it drops to 75. As we know, they don't like it to be below 92. They did an echo on his heart yesterday when Nicki and I were there, and they planned on doing an angiogram and another, more intensive, scan on his lungs. While it sounds like a lung issue to them, they are approaching it as a heart/lung issue. Please pray for Tony that they find and correct the problems he is having.

I have just one question. Can 2008 be over yet? This has got to be one of the worst years *ever*. There has been *so* much death and tragedy this year that it just needs to end. Let's go. The year 2009 *has* to be better. I'm ready. I don't even care that winter is coming again; let's just move on. I'm done, and I know most everybody I know is on board with me.

As I just found out this moment, the right side of Tony's heart is enlarged, and they will probably be moving him up to ICU today because he is on a PAP machine. Please pray for him.

Bring it on, 2009.

Much love to all,

Chrissie

Tuesday, August 26, 2008, 8:35 a.m., CDT— Chrissie's Journal Entry

Hello, all,

I feel so bad for Tommy having these fricking hiccups. They get so violent at times that he throws up. We are doing everything we can to get him through this. They completely wipe him out. One minute he is awake and wanting to watch the Twins game, and then the hiccups start. When they finally end, he falls asleep. It's just not right. He has had them off and on for a week now. This did happen when he was home before, and he got through them. Let's just pray they end soon.

Of course, it would be a lot easier to get him through this deal if the medication would be properly ordered and delivered. Damn! The hospice nurse was supposed to pick up his medications and bring them with her yesterday, but the pharmacy was not open when she was there so they were going to deliver them instead. That was fine, but he needed them for his dose at 6:30 and it was 5:50 and no medications. They did come in time, but guess what medication was not there? That's right; the hiccup medication. Holy Hannah. (This happened *right* after she left.) So I called hospice. They said they would have the prescription delivered this morning. After I got that handled, I noticed we were down to two cans of food. So I called them back. Our nurse was supposed to order the food on Friday, and it had not yet arrived. They said it should be there today by ten o'clock. If not, we need to call back. They then told me it takes three days to ship it UPS. *Good to know* … If I had known that earlier, I would have had her order it earlier. What we ended up doing was slowing down his food to 45 ml per hour so it would hopefully last until the shipment arrived. Cripes!

I must say, I like our current nurse but she tends to drop the ball in big ways that our first nurse did not. Judy was always *on* those medications and supplies. We did not have to worry about a thing. Now I have to watch everything very closely. Thanks—I don't have enough to do already.

My brother Tony is having an angiogram today, and then they will go from there. They need to rule out any problems with his heart before they move to the lungs. His oxygen levels dropped to the 50s yesterday and to 65 quite a few times. They need to figure this out fast.

With everything that is going on this year, I thought I would share a couple of quotes that I found yesterday that I think we all need. They are as follows.

"You can get through anything if you stay put in today."

"Everything can change in the blink of an eye. But don't worry; God never blinks."

Much love to all,

Chrissie

Guest Book Entries

Written August 26, 2008, 9:18 a.m.

Chrissie,

I just wanted to tell you how proud we all are of you and the amazing job you are doing caring for Tom. It is very frustrating to have to keep up on all the medical terms and try to make sense of it all on top of normal life.

I am sure you could write a book on how to be a care advocate after all your experiences. Keep up the tireless efforts (like you would do anything else) and know that we all keep up with your journey in healing Tom daily.

We will keep you in our prayers!

Love,

Lynn Robson

Written August 26, 2008, 9:42 a.m.

Oh, Chrissie,

The struggles that you and Tommy are going through just rip me apart. And now that your brother Tony has some issues, I can't help but wonder how much more can the good Lord dish out without some ray of light. But it appears that you have some sunshine every now and then. And I would assume that it comes when you really need it to keep going.

Remember when I located Tom just by his laugh a few years ago on St Patty's Day? Well, I was at the state fair the other day and swear I heard that laugh. I did do a turn around, but I immediately realized that it could not be our Tom. But it sure brought a smile to my face and heart. Maybe that was my little ray of sunshine! You are both in my thoughts and prayers constantly. Keep the faith, hope, and love around you. It can only make you stronger.

Much love to you and Tommy.

Lory Ruggles

Wednesday, August 27, 2008, 7:34 a.m., CDT— Chrissie's Journal Entry

Good morning,

Not too much change in Tommy today. The dang hiccups are persistent, but we are diligent in giving him his medication to rid him of them. I just feel so bad every time he gets them. I just want to take them and all of this away from him and make him well again. I need him back.

I don't mean to sound like such a downer, but I guess I've been having a streak of emotions lately. I think I need to feel it for a little while so I can come back stronger and grab the bull by the horns and get my hubby back. That is the only thing that makes sense to me at this point. It is what I need to focus on so that I can function. Just wait; I am a work in progress.

In other news, my brother Tony had his angiogram yesterday, and it was very good. His heart is stronger than it was in 2003, which is not bad for a forty-five-year-old man who smokes and has a couple stents in his heart. We will find out today what the next step is in the discovery of his mystery illness.

I know I haven't said this in quite a while, but I want you to know how much I treasure your entries in the guest book and the personal e-mails I receive off of the website. It means everything to me, and I look forward to them every day. Some days, they are what keep me going by giving me the boost that I need to know that *what* I am doing is exactly what I *should* be doing. Thank you for that. Like I said before, I wouldn't have the strength to keep going without the support of all of you.

Much love to all of you,

Chrissie

Guest Book Entries

Written August 27, 2008, 8:43 a.m.

Chrissie and Tom,

I just wanted to say thank you for being such huge role models in my life. You guys have taught me, along with everyone reading this, the power of love, strength, and admiration. You are showing us that with love and hope, we can conquer and rise above life's challenges. I have always respected and admired the two of you— but with every passing day, the admiration just grows more and more. Chris, you're doing one hell of a job. I only hope that I have half of your strength one day. Thank you for everything you are doing.

I love you.

Nicole Betlach

Thursday, August 28, 2008, 8:57 a.m., CDT— Chrissie's Journal Entry

Hello, everyone,

Tom's swelling continues to go down. Woo-hoo! It seems to be taking a while, but at least we are moving in the right direction. The hiccups seem to be happening for a shorter amount of time, so we are still working on that. I did notice yesterday that after I cleaned out his mouth and gave him his mouthwash that the hiccups stopped. Maybe we have a new strategy …

I took Drae to school last night for his open house. Drae had initially planned on playing soccer for Washburn. (Tom played soccer for Washburn when he went there.) Then Drae broke his arm and could not play but, he got the all clear from the doctor on Tuesday and was able to sign up again last night. Yay! He told Tom last night that he will be playing soccer for Washburn like he did. We told him he had to get well so he could go watch Drae play. Trust me, there is no way Tom would miss one of those games.

It sounds like my brother has strep pneumonia. He will be going home on Friday with oxygen for a few days until his breathing returns to normal. At least we know his heart is good!

Thank you to everyone for your continued thoughts, prayers, and positive energy. Thanks also to those who found time to pray for Tony as well.

Everyone have a safe and happy Labor Day weekend!

Much love,

Chrissie

Guest Book Entries

Written August 28, 2008, 11:19 a.m.

Thank God! You sound sooo much better today! Can't wait to hug you. See you both soon ...

XXXXOOOO

Mrs. Kreps

Wendy P.

Written September 1, 2008, 9:51 p.m.

Dear Tom and Chrissie,

I hope you guys are doing well. We all miss you at the Tailgate. I miss your smiling faces. I hoped you guys would sit in my section. You two always made my night. I never really knew your correct names except that you were the Bacardi diet couple! You guys are so cute. Miss you a lot and hope to see you soon! Be strong! Our prayers are with you!

Sincerely,

Tanya Newell

(Tailgate)

Wednesday, September 3, 2008, 7:42 a.m., CDT—Chrissie's Journal Entry

Good morning,

Tommy is doing a little better a far as the hiccups go. As I was waking up on the couch near him on Sunday morning listening to him hiccup, I was trying to figure out what I could do to help him. Peanut butter is what he usually uses to get rid of them, but that is too scary to use right now. So my mind kept going back to sips of water. The next time he hiccupped, I poured a Dixie cup of SmartWater and had him drink it. They stopped right away. I couldn't believe it! They do come back, so every time he hiccups, he drinks some water and they go away for a while. At least I figured out a way so that he doesn't have to be hiccupping for an hour or two or more. *And* as I have found, the water is good for his mouth. It loosened up a bunch of mucous that had collected on the roof of his mouth that I could not see, and I was able to clean his mouth out over the course of a couple of days. Now I have added frequent sips of water (hiccups or not) to Tom's daily routine so we can keep his mouth clean and moisturized more than we were with just swabbing. Live and learn, man. Maybe he can start eating a little bit going forward; something to explore, for sure. In the meantime, I am taking satisfaction in the fact that he is getting some real sleep now because he is not hiccupping. I know this because he was snoring on Sunday and Monday. That is something I have not heard in a while.

We get more and more excited for Tommy as his swelling continues to go down. We feel so much better watching his body return to normal. The worst areas are his ankles and feet. His legs are still somewhat big, but we can see the definition coming back in his calves. Woo-hoo! Also, we have just about successfully healed all the irritation, rashes, and blisters caused by the extreme swelling. He is looking (and I hope, feeling) *much* better. That was a helluva thing—just brutal.

We are taking the best care of Tommy that we can by making sure he is comfortable, pain free, has perfect skin, and that his hygiene is as he would have it, so that when his miracle comes, he will be in the best possible shape he can be. I saw another quote the other day. It simply says: "Believe in miracles. We do."

Much love to all,

Chrissie

Guest Book Entries

Written September 3, 2008, 9:13 a.m.

"Believe in miracles. We do." Wonderful words to live by! We are continuing to keep you and your families in our prayers. My parents are battling cancer, and I find your entries great inspiration. Take care, and please call if there is *anything* we can do!

Peggy

Written September 3, 2008, 10:31 a.m.

The will of God will never take you where the grace of God will not protect you.

Judy Vinje

Written September 6, 2008, 12:50 p.m.

Hey, babe, just thinking of you and Tom and thought I'd drop a note. Give Tom a hi from me when you get this, okay?

How're you holding up? You're in our prayers every day. Keep on keeping on, and we'll see you soon!

Barry and Krissy

Monday, September 8, 2008, 7:26 a.m., CDT—Chrissie's Journal Entry

Good morning,

Tommy has had his eyes open quite a bit the last few days. I fully anticipate him to have his eyes open much more once we rid him of these damn hiccups. We did get him a higher dosage of his hiccup medication on Friday, but I am thinking we need to up it once again. It seems to be fine for a while, and then he has a round that just won't quit. It sucks to hear those damn hiccups (while wanting to make it stop), but I'm sure it is much worse for him. He was just shaking his head this morning. At one point this weekend I noticed as I walked over to him that he was holding his breath to make them stop.

Tommy had a few visitors this weekend that made him smile … and shake his head! Steve C. and Kent P. were over, as were Lisa B. and Mark and Colleen S. Everyone got to see him with his eyes open. Colleen and Mark were praying for Tom, and the words that Mark was saying were totally awesome! They took time out on their anniversary to come see us, and a few days before Colleen dropped off a blanket that her Mom, Rita, had made for Tom. It is the Minnesota Twins on one side and … guess who on the other! SpongeBob, of course! Very nice! That would be Tom to a tee!

Lisa sells products for Market America (which is the only place through which you can buy OPCs), and through a meeting she had on Saturday before she came over, she found out about another, more concentrated, if you will, antioxidant. Yesterday she spoke to a man whose doctor had written him off due to his cancer and had taken this new supplement. He said that his doctor is now excited about his blood tests and that he is beating his cancer after receiving a death sentence. Lisa is having this overnighted to her so we can start Tommy on them right away, in addition to the OPCs he is already receiving. I also need to obtain all of his records so that his blood draws can be studied in relation to the OPCs. I have to get on that; we will see how many hoops I have to jump through to get this done! I could tell you stories …

Keep the faith!

Much love to all,

Chrissie

Wednesday, September 10, 2008, 8:23 a.m., CDT—Chrissie's Journal Entry

Morning, all,

We are still battling the dang hiccups. Yesterday I talked to Bridgette (our nurse), and she told us to give him the maximum dosage of his current medication, and if that doesn't work, we move on to something else. Tony said it seemed to help overnight as he didn't have to give him sips of water overnight to stop them. They would only last about a minute or two. Rock on. I can't wait to get past this.

I received a call yesterday from Dr. H's office. He wants to see him for a check-up. I just find that interesting and somewhat comforting that Dr. H wants to check up on him. It is just weird that when we went home before (from PP), I didn't know what doctor, if any, I was supposed to go to. Now that he was released from the hospital, it is a whole different ball game. I like this better.

For the last six months I have had to deal with a *lot* of financial matters, up to and including automatic payments set up on the Internet with our bank accounts, power-of-attorneys, dealing with credit card companies and utility companies, the insurance companies, etc. There is also the matter of Tom's code status and the fact that he would never talk about death, dying, or code status because he hated those topics. I just would like to give everyone a bit of advice. When it comes to the issue of code status, get an advance directive. Get it in writing. If you don't have anything in writing yet, do it soon. In the meantime tell your partner what your wishes are in terms of "Do Not Resuscitate," "Do Not Intubate," etc., so that they are not faced with having to make the types of decisions I have had to make and be constantly questioned about it.

If you are like Tom and me (although this has obviously changed now), where only one person takes care of the household bills (the house was his when I moved in, and he just kept taking care of all that stuff) and has their own bills that are set up for automatic payments either through your bank or that particular company … educate yourself. If you can, have both names on the accounts, and make sure both of you know how everything is being paid. In the event, God forbid, that something like this should happen to you, it will help you in the long run. I have been battling a credit card company to stop taking money out of our account when we don't owe them anything. They said, "Tom set up the account, and he is the one who has to stop it." Bite me. In order to straighten this out, I had to file and obtain a certified copy of our power-of-attorney and send them a letter telling them to stop the automatic payment, and, as you may have guessed, I am closing that account.

It is a little harder in our situation because Tom cannot tell me everything that is out there and what his passwords are, etc. I have had to go about everything the hard way, and I have had a few surprises along the way and not necessarily good ones. I guess I am just trying to say, you never know what God will bring to your life. So regarding finances and your personal wishes, in the event that something bad should happen to you, communication is of utmost importance. I have gotten a handle on just about everything, I hope, but I would not be surprised if there was another situation waiting in the wings. Cover all your bases; it will be much easier later if you are faced with a situation similar to mine. This is probably something I should have addressed earlier, but I have had a few battles in the last week or so and it has been quite frustrating, so I thought now would be a good time to bring it up.

Take care.

Much love to all,

Chrissie

Guest Book Entries

Written September 14, 2008, 10:59 p.m.

Hi, Chris,

Ooh, you are so on the money with the advice. You know we went through the very same difficulties when I was in the hospital and my Chris had to go through the same situation.

Boy, Tom sure has endured it all.

Stay strong, keep the faith, and know you are in my thoughts and prayers always.

Take care,

Roxie Chudy

Monday, September 15, 2008, 7:49 a.m., CDT— Chrissie's Journal Entry

Good morning,

Well, this weekend, Tom was the most awake I have seen him in months! On Friday night, Gary and Judy were over singing nonsense songs to him and he got the biggest smiles on his face, and then he gave Judy the ol' eyebrow raise! Of course, it's hard not to laugh when Gary is over there going "One More Time!" That is when Tom started smiling. Then, on Saturday, he was awake most of the day. I was talking to him all day long as he was looking at me and listening to me. I had him smiling from ear to ear when I told him that when his miracle comes, his claims of his birthday being the "blessed holiday" would then be true. We wouldn't be able to deny it! We were wrong; he was right! I tell you, it would have been hard to wipe that smile off of his face. He had it for quite a while. (Tony and I actually had that conversation earlier in the summer, and I brought it up again to Tom when Tony was in the room and we got that smile back!)

On the other side of the coin, we got some different medication for his hiccups on Friday. It seemed to work at first, but then on Friday and Saturday nights I was up with him every ten to twenty minutes giving him sips of water so the damn things would stop. We are at a point now, as of yesterday and this morning, where he is extremely tense over these things. He is clenching his jaw and hands, and he has an angry look on his face. They are just so violent, and they come and go without warning. He was awake all day and all night Saturday battling them. I will be calling his nurse today to let her know that we need to try something else. I got a call from our friend Julie at Jaguar telling me that medicinal marijuana works for the hiccups. I asked Bridgette if we could get some, and she said that Dr. Kevorkian said that it was not FDA approved, so it is not an option. Whatever, I think that is something I should verify. I know I have to do something because he has tears in his eyes most of the day now. I just want to make them stop!

I need to be recharged, I think. I have been taking a break from everything trying to figure out what my next move will be. I need some direction. I am waiting for my next epiphany. While I have an idea, I need to know how to go about it. I have been praying for a sign. Let's hope I get one soon.

Much love to all,

Chrissie

Guest Book Entries

Written September 15, 2008, 8:53 a.m.

Hey, Chrissie,

If you can't get your hands on "medicinal" marijuana, would street MJ do the trick? That should be pretty easy to get your hands on.

Hang in there,

Dianne

Written September 15, 2008, 10:04 a.m.

Dear Chris,

When Mike's grandfather was dying and his organs were shutting down, he had the hiccups. I forget what organ caused it. Maybe some tests should be run on his liver, kidneys, or something else to see if all his organs are working properly. (I am not implying he is dying! Please don't think that. I am just wondering if the doctors aren't overlooking something.)

Still praying.

Your cousin,

Shari

Tuesday, September 16, 2008, 9:36 a.m., CDT— Chrissie's Journal Entry

Greetings, all,

Well, Dr. K paid a visit yesterday and said that he was going to figure out what to give Tom next for the hiccups. Bridgette will be there this afternoon, so hopefully she will be bringing whatever that is with her. In the meantime, I did some checking on the Marinol (the medicinal Mary Jane) and found out from one of my doctors that it is, in fact, on the formulary. He told me that doctors frequently use drugs that are not FDA approved, but they work. Pitocin (used to induce labor) is one of them. He would have written me a script for the Marinol, but he has never needed to prescribe it, so it would not have been a good idea. That's cool, but I certainly appreciate the thought! Now, at least, I have something to combat him with if I have to ask about it again. We will see what Dr. K comes up with this time.

In funnier news, Tom is starting to really mess with us when we clean his mouth. He did this to my sister, Beth, weeks ago, and now he is doing it to all of us. When we are cleaning his teeth and mouth out with the dental swabs, he is starting to clamp down on them and not let go for as long as twenty to thirty minutes. On Sunday night, he held the swab between his teeth on his right side, so I took the other swab and started on the left side. He grabbed that one with his mouth and held them both in and would not let go. He had two sticks hanging out of his mouth in two different directions. I was just cracking up, and he was not budging. I ran downstairs to get Tony so he could see what we were up against. He started cracking up, and then Tom let him remove the swabs. He did it again last night to Judy. Judy threatened to get their momma over there, and he let them go. Can you say stubborn? Are you feeling our pain! LOL! This morning now, his momma was cleaning his mouth, and he did it to her. (I guess we can't use her as a threat anymore.) She and Tony could not get him to release them, so I tried. I finally gave up and left him there like that for a good ten minutes. He was definitely in control. After a while, I went back to him and decided to give him a smooch. After that, he finally let go enough to pull it out. Way to go, honey. I think those things were in his mouth for over thirty minutes.

As it turns out, we cannot give Tom the new OPC that we wanted. It specifically says on the label that you should not take the supplement if you are on Coumadin, which is a blood thinner. So, until he is off of the blood thinners, he will not be able to take the Resveratrol, so I am. We will see what happens.

Thank you so much for keeping up the prayers and positive energy. We are still very much in need of them.

Much love to all,

Chrissie

Wednesday, September 17, 2008, 7:36 a.m., CDT— Chrissie's Journal Entry

Hello,

The hiccups persist. I found out yesterday from Bridgette that Dr. K has prescribed another medication. I was told that this is a nerve medication. I am not sure what that means, and I don't really know how I feel about it. I will be doing some web surfing before I give it to him. I also will be calling Tom's family doctor and asking him about the Marinol. Maybe he has a different view on it than the arrogant Dr. K. I have a question for you. If this man is running a hospice, wouldn't there be a large number of his patients with cancer? Isn't Marinol commonly used for people with cancer, specifically for nausea and other side effects of chemo and radiation? You cannot tell me that as a hospice doctor he has never prescribed it, and if he hasn't, then it is my opinion that he likes to see people suffer. I can't help but shake the feeling that this man has a severe God complex and brings about situations that don't need to be. I need to find out if he is the only doctor at Fairview Hospice. If he is, I may have to search for another one. That can be scary though too. We are already used to the people, like the home health aide, the nurse, the music therapist, and the masseuse. It will be something I have to think about if this guy gets in my face too much.

On Monday my mom brought over a couple of drawings for Tom that were left at her house. We think they are from Maddie. One of them says, "Family loves Uncle Tom" and my favorite: "Uncle Tom Rox!"

Word.

Much love to all,

Chrissie

Thursday, September 18, 2008, 7:45 a.m., CDT— Chrissie's Journal Entry

Morning, everyone,

Tommy and I have been married nine years today! After I got up this morning, I checked on him and told him it was our anniversary. He was kinda sorta awake, and his eyes looked droopy. I was kind of freaked out thinking the new medication was doing this to him, but later as I walked in the room, Tony was telling him it was his anniversary today and his eyes were wide open and he had a big smile on his face. That's what I'm talking about! I was able to tell him happy anniversary and give him a few smooches when he was more awake. Very nice.

I called Tommy's doctor yesterday to talk to him about the Marinol and found that he is out of the office for the rest of the week. I will see how this weekend goes with the new medication. If this does not work, I will be calling him back next week to see what his thoughts are. I would so love to get past this hiccup thing, as I'm sure Tommy would also. Dang!

Our friend and former coworker, Nick, was over to visit with Nicki and me last night, and as we were talking about today being mine and Tommy's anniversary, he said something that Nicki and I both thought I should put on the Bridge this morning. And because today is our anniversary, it seems rather fitting. He said, "He will live with you or die without you."

Happy anniversary, honey! I love you!

Much love to everyone!

Chrissie

Guest Book Entries

Written September 18, 2008, 8:53 a.m.

Happy anniversary, Chris and Tom!

What Nick said is very beautiful and also so very true … cheers to that!

Love you both!

Beth Timm

Written September 18, 2008, 9:11 a.m.

Congrats and cheers to you both!

I knew your anniversary was close to ours. We celebrated ours last Sunday.

Have a wonderful day … so glad that Tom acknowledged you with his eyes—the windows to the soul.

Hugs, prayers, and love,

Roxie Chudy

Written September 18, 2008, 9:20 a.m.

Happy anniversary to you!

You two were meant to be together with the strong love that is between you. You were meant to be brought together and live as husband and wife in this world. You two can teach so many other people about love. It is also my sister-in-law's anniversary (same year too). It is sad to think that both she and Tom are both fighting so hard for their lives right now; but both of you are strong and have the *best* spouses in the whole world. I hope you can take some time to look at pictures and talk about your beautiful wedding day! You have modeled and shown everyone through this website the strength of your love.

Have a great day!

Love,

Kris K.

Written September 18, 2008, 9:27 a.m.

Oooooooohh, *happy anniversary* to you *both*!

I feel that I need to add one more thing, dear; you are truly an inspiration. :) If there's any day that I'm just feeling in the dumps, one quick thought of how strong you are and how much courage you have to do what you gotta do— I don't feel down. I feel inspired, so thank you, Chrissie. I'm sure you're touching the hearts of many. :)

Nine years—*woohoooo*!

Hannah Strahota

Written September 18, 2008, 9:32 a.m.

Remembering that super-fun wedding day and looking at all the pictures and memories sounds like a great thing to do tonight. We are all blessed to have you in our lives. I hope everyone takes today to hug the one they love.

XXXOOO. We love you.

Thank you for being you.

Wendy and Keith

Written September 18, 2008, 10:26 a.m.

Happy anniversary, Uncle Tom and Auntie Chrissie! I love you guys very much.

See you tonight.

Nicole Betlach

Written September 18, 2008, 10:39 a.m.

Tom and Chrissie,

Happy anniversary! A match made in heaven! I love you both so much!

Judy Vinje

Written September 18, 2008, 11:55 a.m.

Congratulations to you both! Such great love and strength! I was not at that party nine years ago, but I have been at quite a few since and can just imagine the fun!

Kudos to you, Chrissie. You are a great inspiration of what we will do for someone we love—all it takes!

Candace McCown

Monday, September 22, 2008, 8:37 a.m., CDT—
Chrissie's Journal Entry

Greetings all,

As you probably suspected, the hiccups are still a problem. We worked out a plan with Bridgette and Dr. K with three different meds to see what would work, and while they are not constant, they are still present. Bridgette told me on Friday that it is not that Dr. K did not want to prescribe Marinol; he thought there were more effective drugs that we could try. I will give him the benefit of the doubt on that one, barely. I did tell Bridgette that if Dr. K would not prescribe them that I was going to try calling Dr. H to see if he would. All I want to do is see if the Marinol would work. Some of the other meds we are trying are drugging him up, and I don't want to do that. Tommy would not want that. He is the kind of guy that whenever his back went out, *if* he filled the prescription for pain meds that he was given, he *might* take them. If he did, it was only one or two, so I know he does not want to be like this. The drug that they gave us last week for the hiccups, Gabapentin, I will not give him. He looked totally and completely drugged and out of it, and I told Bridgette I was *not* giving it to him. I had a bad feeling about the drug from the first time she mentioned it, and when I saw what it did to him, I could not continue with it.

I know everyone is probably tired of hearing about the hiccups and the drugs, but that is the reality of our situation. It is all-consuming and quite frankly, we are all over them. I can't imagine what Tommy is feeling.

I wish I had some exciting news to tell you. It seems like it is time for just such a thing. Please pray that at some point *real* soon I will be able to do that. Once again, I would like to thank you all for your love, support, and prayers. They continue to sustain me and all of us who care for Tom on a daily basis. It feels like we are all in this together. I personally thank God for all of you. I would *never* be able to do this alone. So again, thank you and God bless you.

Much love to all,

Chrissie

Tuesday, September 23, 2008, 7:46 a.m., CDT—Chrissie's Journal Entry

Hello,

As it turns out, Dr. H's nurse practitioner will not prescribe Marinol for Tom because she says it is in the same family as the chlorpromazine that he is getting now. And she says that I need to work with the hospice doctor. Hmmm, I think I have been trying to do that. Anyway, Tom has an appointment to see Dr. H on the eighth. If this is still an issue, you can bet your sweet bippy that I will be asking him for it. Other than that, Dr. K called the house yesterday and said that trying to get rid of these hiccups is all trial and error. There is no pat formula that works. That's fine, let's just not wait weeks in between the "trials." In the meantime, it just sucks to watch and listen to him during a bout of hiccups. He has let us know that he doesn't always want to drink water to stop them by clenching his mouth shut or holding the water in his mouth while we beg him to swallow because we all know it works. We'll just keep trying, I guess. There's not much more we can do.

I think this is a good time to remind myself of the old saying: bad things happen fast, good things take time.

Bring it!

Much love to all,

Chrissie

Guest Book Entries

Written September 23, 2008, 8:16 a.m.

Ving—if I *have* a sweet bippy, feel free to bet it if it helps your Tommy! While the hiccups seem like such a boat anchor right now, it is still so great to hear how well he is doing otherwise. That's all because of you, Cha Cha, because *you* are Tom's miracle. I cannot imagine what you must be going through on a daily basis, but rest assured, God picked the right angel for Tom, and that is you.

Maybe when you need a break, you could put on a little Stray Cats and dance like only a Betlach gal can ...

I pray every day, Chrissie. Take care. You are the *best*.

Michelle Notch

Written September 23, 2008, 8:36 a.m.

Bippy? I forgot I even had a bippy ... well, now that I've found it again, I'm betting on it too!

Chrissie, you *are* Tom's angel! Keep your eyes upward. He's right there beside you.

Love to you both, and our prayers and positive energy will *never* stop flowing for you guys.

PS: You betcha those Betlach girls can dance! It's in our genes.

Patty Betlach Russell

Written September 23, 2008, 6:32 p.m.

Hey, Chrissie,

I have been thinking about you, and happy belated anniversary! You are correct, good things take time, so hang in there. You are an inspiration to all of us … I love you both with all my heart. Give Tommy a kiss, and Barry and I will pop over this weekend to visit. Love you.

Krissy

Thursday, September 25, 2008, 7:41 a.m., CDT— Chrissie's Journal Entry

Good morning,

Yesterday was a bad day in the Vinje household. Tommy vomited a few times yesterday morning from the violent hiccups he was having. They were brutal. The good news is it stopped after 10:30 a.m., and he was able to keep down his food and meds. Later on in the day the violent hiccups came back, but he did not get sick. Dr. K prescribed a different medication yesterday called metoclopramide. We gave him one dose, and after looking it up on the Internet, I called home and told them to stop. The side effects include:

- seizure (excuse me!)
- swelling and fluid retention (are you fricking kidding me!)
- masklike appearance of the face (WTF!)
- tremors or restless muscle movements in your eyes, tongue, jaw, or neck
- fever, stiff muscles, confusion, sweating, fast or uneven heartbeats, rapid breathing
- depressed mood, thoughts of suicide or hurting yourself

- hallucinations, anxiety, agitation, jittery feeling, trouble staying still
- jaundice

Less serious side effects may include:

- feeling restless, drowsy, tired or dizzy
- headache, sleep problems
- nausea, diarrhea
- urinating more than usual

Now tell me, why would anyone even take this drug? Not only that, but I am expected to give this to my husband who cannot tell me what it is doing to him. Give me a fricking break! One of the side effects landed him in the hospital six weeks ago, and another one we are still trying to recover from. I don't get it. I know we are trying to get rid of the hiccups, but do you see a pattern here? This guy would rather give Tom these harsh drugs that could land him back in the hospital than try the Marinol that I have asked for. And what the *hell* does "masklike appearance of the face" mean! Holy balls!

Here's the thing. My sister Theresa found a product (it is a dietary supplement) on the Internet called Hiccups Away. The website will tell you that it is meant for people with normal hiccups, not necessarily for sick people, but it *has* worked on sick people. It is there in the testimonials. Needless to say, I ordered some; it should be at our house today. I would rather try that than the crap he is trying to shove down Tom's throat. Man. I just can't wait to get rid of these things. It is painful to have to watch and listen to him. I can't imagine what he is going through. It's a bad deal all the way around. We are doing what we can to not overmedicate him. As soon as these hiccups are gone, all those meds go away, done.

Please pray for the hiccups to finally leave his body. We can use all the help we can get!

Much love to all,

Chrissie

Guest Book Entries

Written September 25, 2008, 8:25 a.m.

Chrissie,

My friend from California is sending me Marinol strips (her mom just finished chemo) in the mail. Marinol is much easier to get in California, and she still has a prescription. They should be here today or tomorrow. I will bring them down if you want to try them. If you do, and they work, they also come in lollipop form.

Heather

Written September 26, 2008, 7:30 p.m.

Hi, Chrissie,

This is Lisa. I am Kent's cousin. I read your updates daily and am so amazed at what a strong woman you are. I truly believe you are doing right by Tom. You are doing everything I think anyone in your shoes would do.

I was talking to one of my customers a few months ago, before Tom came home. She deals with helping people rid themselves of poisons in the body. Her success rate is outstanding! I was telling her about Tom, and she said she would love to talk to you and see if she could help you in any way. Long story short, she came in again today. I told her Tom was home and all the things you were doing for him, and she would really like to talk to you. If it may be something you are interested in checking out, please call me and I can give you her phone number.

All my prayers are with you every day. Stay strong!

Lisa Farness

Tuesday, September 30, 2008, 7:56 a.m., CDT— Chrissie's Journal Entry

Hello, all,

As you might have guessed, Tommy is still hiccupping. The Hiccups Away that I bought through the Internet worked immediately, but as they have been doing, they came back sometime later. For the most part, they seemed to have diminished in severity and length, but they persist nonetheless.

Since this past weekend, Tommy has started to throw up once or twice a day. We know when it is coming because he coughs for a while before it happens. I don't know the cause. I can guess, but I don't like what comes to mind. We have his appointment with Dr. H next Wednesday (October 8), so maybe I can get some answers at that time.

Last Friday, the hospice nurse, Nancy (filling in while Bridgette is on vacation), and a social worker, Mary Beth, came to the house for a joint visit. We got to talking, and I ended up asking them if it was possible to change doctors. I told them about my experiences with Dr. K and that if changing was not an option then I would just deal with it. Mary Beth told me that she would check into my options and let me know. They both said that maybe Dr. K was not a good fit for us. No question. I guess there is another doctor who is very part-time, so he might not be an option. If it turns out that I cannot get another doctor, then they will schedule Dr. K's visits when Bridgette is there so there will be another medical person in the room and I won't be left twisting in the wind listening to his BS.

I am a little overwhelmed this morning. I wasn't going to mention this, but I could barely sleep last night and because of the way I feel right now, I have to. Our friend Karrie ran into a gal named Shellie, who is a soul reader. Basically what she does is communicate telepathically with a person's soul, subconscious, and conscious mind, what have you. She says there are many parts to us and messages can come from all of them, even to the point that you don't know where it is coming from. She was over for almost two hours last night and got some pretty powerful messages from Tom. I am not able at this point in time to share them as, like I said, I am overwhelmed. This is where one minute at a time, one day at a time comes in. Way too painful. But at the end, she did say, "I am open to miracles. I welcome them." As do I. Her saying that made me feel better. I think it is time to remind you of the card my friend Jackie gave me this summer. This saying was on the card with a magnet attached to it that is currently on my fridge: "I don't believe in miracles; I rely on them."

That is exactly what we need to do. Rely away. Let's go.

Much love to all,

Chrissie

Guest Book Entries

Written September 30, 2008, 7:53 p.m.

Hey, Chrissie,

I love you ... let me know when you want to chat. I am here.

Hugs,

Krissy

Written October 1, 2008, 8:10 p.m.

Dear Chrissie,

Just continue to be strong! I, as well as my family, pray for you daily and know that you are making the right decisions! Take care of yourself, and I look forward to seeing you!

Love and prayers,

Laura S.

Thursday, October 2, 2008, 8:02 a.m., CDT— Chrissie's Journal Entry

Morning, everyone,

Those fricking hiccups. They were probably the worst this morning that I have heard, and Tony told me they had been going on since 2:30 a.m. On Monday the hospice nurse was over and told Tony that the Metoclopramide (or Reglan) would probably be the thing that helps him stop the hiccups and the vomiting. (If you remember, this is the drug I bitched about last week.) She told Tony that those side effects happened in less than 1 percent of the people who took it. I decided to try it but, if I see something I don't like, I will stop it. As of right now, I am not seeing any improvements. I don't know—it is just so frustrating, and it breaks my heart to see him like this. He doesn't deserve any of this. I am struggling to understand it all, and I'm not coming up with anything that makes sense. I sometimes still can't believe this is really happening and that we are actually at this place. Some days it really does not seem real, and other days it just comes slamming home. If I could take this all away from him I would do it in a heartbeat. Actually, I think that's what I have been trying to do … now that I think about it. If we are at the "good things take time" part, I am thinking, *Dang, how much time!*

I know I may be wavering now, but I will come back full force. This week has thrown me for a loop. I am gearing up for what comes next. Stay with me! I guess I have been allowing myself to think negatively this week, which is something I have been avoiding, and it is kicking my ass. That is why I was not doing it. I need to think positive to keep my strength and endure. Don't worry, it will be fine. I will not stop fighting for my honey any time soon because he is *my* miracle. And that is what I have been telling him lately.

For now, the constant prayers and positive energy continue to flow, and that is an awesome thing. I know Tommy feels it. Thank you all for making that happen.

Much love to all,

Chrissie

Guest Book Entries

Written October 2, 2008, 1:21 a.m.

Hello, Tom and Chrissie,

I really admire you and your courage and strength, and my prayers are with you. Don't give up hope.

Rese Patton

Written October 2, 2008, 9:07 a.m.

Hang in there, Chrissie. We are still holding you in our thoughts and prayers. Try to take time to breathe deep and be still.

Best wishes,

Dianne, Victor, Lydia, and Luisa

Written October 2, 2008, 9:15 a.m.

You are a miracle, sweetie. Hang in there. We all love you both so much.

Wendy P.

Written October 2, 2008, 2:15 p.m.

Hi, Chris,

Kathie (Birklid) Stanville here—Kris, Sarah, and Susie's mom.

My heart is breaking for you after reading this morning's entry! Whatever you do, please don't beat yourself up for having an occasional "down" day. You have been a rock, and there's no doubt in my mind that Tom feels your love and dedication through this horrible ordeal. As hard as this has all been on Tom, no one would argue that it's been a dreadful strain on you too. You deserve to fall apart now and then and ask for a little help for yourself. It takes nothing from your ongoing strength (it may even foster it) and all you have to offer Tom. My thoughts (and a ton of admiration) are with you!

Kathie Stanville

Written October 5, 2008, 1:44 p.m.

Hey, Uncle Tom and Auntie Chrissie!

Just wanted to stop by and let you both know I pray and think about you all the time. *Love you!* And everything will be A-okay!

Love always and forever your one and only flower girl,

Michelle Vinje

Monday, October 6, 2008, 8:08 a.m., CDT— Chrissie's Journal Entry

Good morning,

Nothing much changed over the weekend despite trying two new medications. The hiccups continue to come and go. Sometimes they are harsh, other times, not. This weekend I noticed that he is trying to sleep while hiccupping instead of being awake for it all. He has to catch up on all the sleep he's losing somehow, because let me tell you, when they stop, he *sleeps*. He starts breathing really heavy, and sometimes you will hear a snore or two. That's when I know he has got some good sleep rolling. Maybe Dr. H will have some suggestions on Wednesday when we see him.

Today I am at a loss for anything else to say. I feel kind of blocked, weird. Anyway, let's see what this week brings. I am hoping for good things, as always! And as always, I will let you know what happens, as it happens.

Much love to all,

Chrissie

Tuesday, October 7, 2008, 6:50 a.m., CDT—
Chrissie's Journal Entry

Hello, all,

For the first time in a *long* time, the hiccups have subsided. He has gone from 7:00 a.m. yesterday morning without hiccupping, except for maybe a couple here and there. Woo-hoo! I don't know if it is this new drug or the fact that we are trying a different route. That route would be trying to keep his stomach less full so it doesn't push against his diaphragm. We have to stop his food for four hours a day due to medication, so we just hold it a little longer. It is still trial and error at this point, so we will see what happens. All I know is that he slept all day yesterday and all last evening. I haven't found out for sure if he slept most of the night, but I wouldn't be surprised. That came just in time for him to be more ready to make the trip to the doctor tomorrow morning. Let's hope it is the beginning of a new trend. Tommy also has to get a bath, a shave, and his nails clipped before we go tomorrow. My baby has to be looking good!

I will have more news for you tomorrow after Tommy's appointment with Dr. H. I have to admit, I am a little nervous about it. He has not had good news for me since March 18, and I don't expect he is about to start; but as we know, there are bigger things at work here than the medical side of things. If you pay attention, you can feel it. It is truly amazing, and I have all of you to thank for it. It has been quite the experience so far.

Let's do a little Casey Kasem once again: "Keep your feet on the ground, and keep reaching for the stars."

That's all we can do …

Much love to all,

Chrissie

Guest Book Entries

Written October 7, 2008, 7:18 a.m.

Chrissie,

Hang in there! Dave and I, and Olivia, Quinn, and Lewis, are always sending positive prayers to both you and Tommy. We love him, and we want *both* of you to have continued strength and love and support.

All our love,

The Martin Family

Chapter 12

A Trip to the Doctor

Thursday, October 9, 2008, 8:21 a.m., CDT—
Chrissie's Journal Entry

Good morning,

Our trip to the doctor yesterday was pretty uneventful. It was as I thought it would be, just a quick follow-up on his hospital stay. There were no tests run or anything like that. Dr. H just checked the setting on Tom's shunt and asked if we had any questions. He also asked how he has been, as far as functionality. I know I don't talk much about that, and many of you are probably not aware of his current limitations. I did tell the doc that he has not spoken in almost a month. There were some changes after his hospital stay in August where, due to the swelling, he has not been moving around like he was. He has been squeezing pretty well with his right hand (which is his weak side) but in the last week I have noticed that has stopped, and I suspect that something similar might be happening with his left hand. He has not been shaking his head yes or no for us lately either.

I guess I don't talk about these things because, yes, I am trying to think that it is not really happening. Denial, sure, why not? But it in *no* way means that I have given up hope. I will never give up on Tommy, and neither should anyone else. I am still trying like hell to keep my positive attitude because, as I have said before, I won't be able to function and keep it all going if I don't. I just thought that you all should know where he is at.

Dr. H said yesterday, "We can't predict the future." Now, you can take that one of two ways, and I know what way he meant it. He was not saying, he was just saying. I know what he was telling me without telling me, but he has never given me a timeline and I prefer it that way. I want to sit in my own little world and keep praying for the miracle that is my husband. My greatest joy in life would be for Tommy and me to walk into Dr. H's office together so that he could order an MRI and see that that blasted tumor is gone and never coming back. Never say never. Do not give up on hope, prayers, positive energy, and miracles. Blind faith, baby! Let's get my precious Tommy back!

Bad things happen fast; good things take time.

Much love to all,

Chrissie

***

I would like to insert here a shocking reality. I did not put this on the CaringBridge at the time because I didn't think it was appropriate. The round trip cost of getting Tom to his doctor's appointment was $900. Yep, just to bring him in and have the doctor say, "We can't predict the future." Yes indeed, $900 for the ambulance-like vehicle with oxygen to take him four miles away. No wonder people go into debt due to medical bills.

***

Guest Book Entries

Written October 9, 2008, 10:21 a.m.

Chrissie,

Denial? No. Hopeful? Yes. Only one person has the last say on who lives and who dies. As we have learned on this journey, *miracles* happen all the time, and we should expect them! We are here to give Tom the best care possible, and that is exactly what we are doing. Everyone can have an opinion, but that's all it is, an opinion. You're doing what is best for Tom, and that is all that matters. You are taking such good care of him! I'm so proud to have you as my sister-in-law; you are the strongest, most caring, most loving person I know. I look up to you!

Judy Vinje

Written October 9, 2008, 10:39 a.m.

Chrissie,

Your feisty spirit, determination, and unfaltering love are remarkable. You go, girl! You are simply amazing …

Dianne, Victor, Lydia, and Luisa

Written October 10, 2008, 12:05 p.m.

Hi, just wanted to drop by let you know I'm thinking of you guys and praying that everybody will be all right. Keep your head up, and don't stop believing in the miracle.

Rese Patton

Tuesday, October 14, 2008, 7:40 a.m., CDT— Chrissie's Journal Entry

Good morning,

Well, it has been one week and the hiccups are still gone. Thank God! There are times when he will hiccup a few times here and there, and if it stays that way, we'll take it.

Tommy is currently congested. This is a condition that started on Friday night. I called hospice over the weekend, and they told us to give him a couple drops of atropine every couple of hours. Atropine allegedly dries up secretions. (In the beginning they give you some meds to have around in the event that you need them. Atropine eye drops is one of them.) I am not sure whether it is working or not, but he does sound better than he did this weekend. His chest was rattling pretty good there for a while. The good news is that Bridgette comes today; maybe she can ease our minds a little and tell us that it is just congestion and not pneumonia. I guess there always has to be *one* other thing going on just to keep us on our toes.

I would like to say, once again, how fortunate Tommy and I are to have so many awesome people in our lives—everyone from family members to friends, coworkers, and neighbors. There is an awesome energy working. I am constantly aware of it. You can feel it without much effort. It's almost like you could reach out and touch it. It is that close. I see it when I look into Tommy's eyes, and I feel it when I am around him. I just want it to become so strong that it picks him up, bestows a miracle upon him, and then puts him back down, whole once again and ready to carry on with his new life. Because when that miracle happens, he will be a changed man. He has been through so much, and he is still here. God knows what he has experienced while teetering between both worlds. I just wish he could verbalize it. Soon, very soon.

Much love to all,

Chrissie

Wednesday, October 15, 2008, 7:34 a.m., CDT— Chrissie's Journal Entry

Morning,

Still no hiccups! Rock on! Although, it seems as if my poor honey has a cold. This is his first cold since he has been home, so he had a good run as far as that goes. I was waiting for Bridgette to check his chest yesterday when she came so I could rest a little easier, but of course, she forgot her stethoscope. Great, perfect. By the sound of it though, she seemed to think it was not pneumonia. (We have a book that the people from hospice are supposed to write in when they visit, and this is what she wrote.) She will be back on Friday morning with her stethoscope, so we will get a better answer at that time.

At the moment, all else is going as best it can. We just have to take time to recognize how our prayers are getting answered in little bits or sometimes, bigger bits. A bigger bit would, of course, be the hiccups stopping. Thank you, God. I was speaking to one of the hospice nurses last night on the phone, and she asked about the hiccups. When I told her they were gone, she said, "Praise the Lord!" While this particular nurse is not one of my favorites, I truly appreciated her sincerity in that statement because I knew she meant it. Then it got me to thinking about taking time along the way to notice the little miracles happening all the time. Even with everything going on and being so busy at home and at work, I need to take more time to do things like this before it gets away from me. Stop and smell the roses, if you will. Some days are harder than others to do that, but the point is to do it.

Have a great day everyone.

Much Love,

Chrissie

Guest Book Entries

Written October 15, 2008, 8:14 a.m.

Hi, Chris,

So glad to hear that the hiccups have subsided. Hallelujah!!

Up and down days are to be expected. You are facing the toughest journey, and you will have down days. It is not a reflection on who you are or what you are doing; it is that you are just human and sometimes feel as if you should be doing more.

You are doing what you need to be doing—loving Tom through this, advocating for him, being there … You truly amaze me.

I am thinking of you guys every day and sending positive waves of energy to you.

Take care, stay well,

Roxie Chudy

Thursday, October 16, 2008, 7:43 a.m., CDT— Chrissie's Journal Entry

Good morning, all,

Yesterday was a pretty cool day with Tommy. I talked to Laura in the afternoon, and she said he had been responding all day with her and Beth. Laura said when she walked into the room she asked Tom, "Aren't you glad I'm here?" Then he shook his head no! Nice guy—LOL. Yesterday he was doing a lot of head shaking and nodding as well as hand squeezing. (It was awesome; it made me feel so good.) After I got home, I was telling Laura how Alexis was saying that Eric, Tony's brother, was her best friend as well as Tony and that Tony was not having it. I turned around to look at Tommy, and he had a huge smile on his face listening to the story. He was also moving his hands around a bit. Another little miracle …

Tommy's cold does not appear to be as bad at the moment; we will see how he is tomorrow when Bridgette checks him out. In the meantime, we seem to be in a holding pattern, just waiting for, oh, I don't know, a miracle or something. Bring it on; we're more than ready. Tommy has suffered enough. I want to hear his voice, see him smile and say, "What now!" his infamous phrase, among many others! (Some of which should not be in print here on the Bridge, to be sure …)

We do not believe in miracles; we rely on them …

Much love to all,

Chrissie

Guest Book Entries

Written October 16, 2008, 9:29 a.m.

Chrissie,

You just made my day! Go Tommy, it's your birthday. LOL.

Judy Vinje

Written October 16, 2008, 1:37 p.m.

Hey, Chrissie,

That is good news. It just makes the heart warm thinking about it! God bless. Have a wonderful day. Love ya!

Cristina Melzer

Written October 18, 2008, 3:04 p.m.

Dear Chris,

I have been reading your journal entries and wish I had done this when Bob was ill. It's like mental therapy! It's good to share your emotions during this difficult time, and it's okay to even share the "off" days with us. Then we know how to pray for you. Please know that you and Tom are in my thoughts and prayers always.

Love,

Ramona Froberg

Monday, October 20, 2008, 7:54 a.m., CDT— Chrissie's Journal Entry

Morning, all,

It seems as if the hiccups might be starting to make a return appearance. He had been having them here and there very briefly, but yesterday I noticed it more often, and then overnight they became more violent again, although they are still brief. Let's hope it stays that way.

Tommy's looking dang good this morning! Tony gave him a good shave before the home health aide (Albert) came to bathe him. Lookin' good, baby!

Tommy had lots of company over the weekend. Thanks everyone for coming over to see him and show your support. It means more than you know. I also want to take a few moments to thank our friend and neighbor, Candace, for continuing to take our precious little girl to the dog park with her and Whitney. The other day I saw the funniest damn thing on my way home from work. As I was taking a left to go home, there was Candace's car at the end of our alley with Bailey riding shotgun and Whitney in the back. It has to be this way because Whitney does not allow Bailey in the backseat with her, so she sits in front with Candace. It just cracks me up to see Bailers in her car looking straight ahead as they cruise down the alley. I am just happy that she has the opportunity to go to the dog park, as that is something I don't really have the time for. Thanks Candace and Whitney (the most tolerant of Great Danes!).

Much love to all,

Chrissie

Guest Book Entries

Written October 20, 2008, 8:54 a.m.

Hello, all!

It is our pleasure and most fun to take Bailey to the dog park with us. It just warms my heart to see that beautiful girl, Bailey, jump in the air, tail flying high, and watch her bring me a *huge* piece of tree for me to throw! Of course, Tom would just break it apart and throw a part of it, but I tell her it is *too* big, and she goes to find something I can throw. Yeah, we get smiles as we are driving to and from the park. My car looks pretty full! No problem, Chrissie. Bailey is always welcome to play with us!

Candace McCown

Wednesday, October 22, 2008, 7:43 a.m., CDT— Chrissie's Journal Entry

Good morning,

Tommy is hanging in there. After I got home last night, I just sat next to him for a while looking into his eyes and talking to him. It is just wrong on every level that this is even happening, and what makes it so much worse is the fact that he can't talk back and tell me what is going on with him. It has been a guessing game since practically the beginning. Sure, in the beginning, he was commenting here and there, and then all the other incidents happened; the fluid on the brain, the brain swelling, and then the fricking tumor growing. All of these things prohibited his communication and sent him into a deep sleep. It's not bad enough that he has the blasted tumor (the worst of the worst due to its aggressiveness), but it has to be near the sleep part of his brain with all these other complications. So here we are seven months later still guessing and hoping we are doing what is best for him and all the while, never knowing for sure. I am pretty confident with my intuition. I think it has served me well the last seven months. I am just praying that it continues, but there is a part of me that still wonders if what I am doing is right and if he is okay with it all.

I just miss him so much it hurts, and like I told our friend Kimmy, I burst into tears every time I think it, write it, or speak it. It is instant water works thinking about how much I miss him. I have been thinking about saying that here on the Bridge for a while, but I couldn't bring myself to do it. God knows what possessed me to do it today. Maybe I just needed to get it out. It doesn't matter how many people know. It is the damn truth and most assuredly the most painful part of what I am going through at the moment. There it is. Now I should put my face back on and get on with the day—day by day, minute by minute. Such is my life.

Much love to all,

Chrissie

Guest Book Entries

Written October 22, 2008, 8:22 a.m.

Chris, never second guess what you are to write on the CaringBridge. All who read it are people who *care*. We all are amazed by you. I always hope to read the truth.

Love you much,

Nicole Betlach

Written October 22, 2008, 8:55 a.m.

Chrissie, I wish there was something I could say to take away the hurt and pain you are feeling. My parents are going through a number of health problems recently, and they just want their old life back. It goes without saying you must be feeling the exact same way. I'm just in awe of your strength. What comes to mind is the "Footprints in the Sand" poem. Where would we be without faith! Give that hubby of yours a big ol' hug from us. Always in our prayers; take care, Chrissie.

Peggy

Written October 22, 2008, 8:58 a.m.

Oh, and on a lighter note, I wanted to say I got such a chuckle out of Bailey sitting in the front seat of the car. What a funny visual, thanks for sharing! Pets are the greatest. :-)

Peggy

Written October 22, 2008, 10:03 a.m.

Chrissie,

No words can describe it. Tears are the only emotion that can truly describe what you are going through and we are going through. My tears are flowing as I write this. God put all of us in this position for a reason. Like Nicki, said don't second guess what to write on the Bridge. This is your journal, your diary, your testimony of the love you have for my brother.

You are doing everything right, Chrissie, because you do it with love.

Much love back to you, Chrissie!

Judy Vinje

Written October 22, 2008, 8:14 p.m.

Chrissie,

Like I emailed you this morning, I just wish there was something I could do to make the hurt stop. Just know that Barry and I think about you and Tom every day and we pray for both of you every day. We love you both so much.

Krissy

Thursday, October 23, 2008, 7:44 a.m., CDT— Chrissie's Journal Entry

Good morning,

Now I know why I didn't tell you about missing Tom before yesterday. It is because I knew what it would do to me, and it did. I just knew it was going to be an invitation to weep all day and feel all that raw emotion. Mission accomplished. I guess it was the right time. But really, is there ever a good time to put yourself through that! Thanks everyone for your love and support. Without it, I would be lost and most likely a basket case.

Tommy's left eye has been weepy and mildly irritated the last few weeks. He has had some mucous in there that I try to get out when I can. I have been thinking that maybe he was developing fall allergies along with his spring allergies, so I had ordered him some Allegra through hospice. It seemed to work for a while, but not so much right now. The most it did was take the red out. You know when your eye is really irritated and it becomes gelatinous? That's how his has been lately, but last night, as I was sitting next to him, I noticed that practically the whole white part of his eye was swollen and gelatinous. So, I called hospice and talked to the nurse. Nothing was done other than she was going to leave a message for Bridgette today, but she said that sometimes glaucoma (doubtful) or intracranial pressure could cause that, or they don't know. (Kind of a standard answer, I've noticed.) The ironic thing is that I have been asking Bridgette about his eye for a couple of weeks, and she keeps saying that she was going to talk to Dr. K to see what he wants to do … I'm still waiting. Maybe now that I called in, we can get an answer. It is always something—something else to worry about and manage. All these little things just make your stomach drop and your heart hurt because it's just one more thing he has to deal with as well. Shit, for a man who never spent a day in the hospital before all of this, he was certainly handed one of the worst possible situations out there. He got it with both barrels. My poor honey. My heart hurts for him every day. But we will get through it. This too, shall pass, like the hiccups (knock on wood).

Thank you for keeping the prayers and positive energy going. Just because he doesn't have another huge complication right now doesn't mean they aren't needed. They are needed regardless. I know I don't have to tell you that; you guys are awesome at keeping it going. Thank you *so, so* much for your continued love and support.

Much love to all,

Chrissie

Guest Book Entries

Written October 23, 2008, 8:51 a.m.

Chrissie,

Although it is so painfully hard to "let it all go" like you did yesterday, please remember that during your difficult times, your soul needs an occasional "bath." ("Cleansing" sounds so cliché.)

When you feel saturated in the "what nows," try to think about your journey as happening one day at a time because that's how it's happening. (Oops, a cliché dammit!) You can only deal with what's in front of you. The rest is God's job. Deep breath in through the nose, out through the mouth, eyes closed. Repeat. (Seriously, it helps!) Leave the big stuff up to him. You do what *you* can control.

There isn't a word invented to demonstrate my admiration. If someone asked me to describe you to them, I don't think I could run out of good things to say. You don't have this many friends by mistake, Chrissie. I sincerely hope you look in the mirror every day, and even when things are tough, I hope you whisper, "Dammit—I *am* fabulous!" 'Cause you *are*, on more levels than I can count.

I pray every day. Take care, you.

Michelle Notch

Written October 23, 2008, 10:38 a.m.

Chrissie,

I know how hard you try to be strong, and God knows you are a lot stronger than most of us. You need to allow yourself to cry and mourn the Tom you miss so much. He is still there, but right now not in the capacity that you were so used to … along with the rest of us.

Stay strong and cry; it is good for you! You need that.

Kim Peterson

Written October 24, 2008, 3:32 p.m.

Hello, Chrissie,

It is so great when I read all these letters and support you receive from family and friends. "Footprints in the Sand," that is one of my favorite ones, and seeing all the love people show you and all the prayers proves that you are not walking this alone. You are a really strong and supportive woman (which some people don't have and maybe never will) by getting as far as you have come and continue to try to achieve the goal you are trying to achieve—Tom being well again. God has given you and Tom a challenge that you both have lived up to 110 percent to the best of your ability. It's even hard to put in words right now the strength and courage you have both displayed. As I have been in this situation with family/friends more than once, my advice would be never give up the hope and prayers and feed off the love and support you have received. And go with it. You are going to have bad days, and rightfully so, very understandable, but when you have those days, try to the best of your ability to think about the good times you have had with Tom and all the love and support you have from your family and friends. Another way is change of pace, whether it's going out or whatever could take your mind off the mainstream that you are doing now. (I know very hard to do, but it helps.) But no matter what life has to go on. This goes for the family and friends also. Think about it—is Tom a sad, unhappy person? Always think about what he would do or say. Would he want you all to be sad?

On that note, my prayers and thoughts are with you, present and future; forever in my thoughts.

Peace and love always,

Rese Patton

PS: This document has been pimped out with spell checker.

Written October 25, 2008, 4:40 p.m.

Hi, Chris,

Well, today was the Anoka Halloween parade. I was looking for your family and you. Then I saw Beth and talked to her. I am so sad I haven't been in contact with you. If there is anything I can do, please call me.

Your old friend,

Donna Muehlbauer

***

I did not post this on the CaringBridge, but you will find references to it later. I am just going to let loose with the events of the next couple of days in the best way that I can.

Saturday, October 25, 2008, was a *beautiful* October day. It was sunny and seventy degrees. I know because I had the windows open at the house enjoying the sunshine and mild temperature while my family was at the Anoka Halloween parade. (Anoka, Minnesota, is *the* Halloween Capital of the World, you know. I was born and raised there!) Usually Nicki and my sister Jessica would be over on Saturday helping me with Tom, but on this day I was at home alone with my love tending to him. His chest was rattling, so I called Karrie to tell her about it. She ran across the alley with a nebulizer for Tom to try in order to clear his airways. I think it did help a little bit.

During this time I also noticed that Tom's fingers were turning blue. Now, I knew that fingers turning blue meant that he was losing oxygen, and coupled with the congestion, I knew that meant he was dying. Normally in this situation I would call 911 to help out with the situation. But this time, I did not call 911. I called hospice and had them come out. The nurse told me that meant he was dying.

Almost automatically I said, "No it doesn't!"

Then she said, "Okay, it doesn't."

Then I said, "Don't patronize me. I know what it means."

She alluded to the fact that it would not be long. Being that Shellie had been out three weeks before, and I was now aware of Tom's wishes. I just let him be. He had already been through enough. As it turned out, he never woke up again after the nebulizer. The other thing that occurred to me was that his eyes were gelatinous, which was more than likely due to intracranial pressure. I knew what was happening.

On Sunday morning at 6:30 a.m., Ginny came over, and we gave Tom his meds. I went to bed at 7:00 a.m. to get a few hours of rest. I sprang upright when I heard Ginny calling me at about eight o'clock. She was yelling, "Chrissie, he's not breathing!"

I bolted out of bed to find Tom ashen in color and not breathing. I immediately called 911, and they were there within minutes. I called Karrie, Larry, and Tony right away to let them know what was happening. Larry and Tony were there quickly (Karrie had her son's confirmation that morning), and we stood in the kitchen while the paramedics were working on him. I simply could not watch what they were doing. I felt so bad for Tom. They pulled him off of his hospital bed and on to the floor and were implementing some experimental revival method that (I guess I had given permission for it, although I don't remember when) involved putting a needle in his shin. While we stood in the kitchen, Bailey was standing in the doorway watching. I will never forget it.

After a little bit, they came into the kitchen to tell us that they had started his heart again. I said, "You did?" I couldn't believe it. I also knew the probability of brain damage was great. They asked me where I wanted him to go, and I said the University of Minnesota Hospital.

During this time many phone calls were made, and everyone from the Vinje family, the Betlach family, the Buds, and the general managers at both of our stores were notified of what was happening. While everyone took off for the hospital, Ginny and I waited at my house for my sister Beth to come over and ride down with us. Her husband, Bob, had run over to their church to pull her out of Mass to be with us.

When we arrived, Judy came up to me to tell me that the doctor told them he was brain dead, which I already suspected. I ran back into the emergency room to find Tom. As soon as I laid eyes on him, I knew my husband was no longer in the body that had betrayed him so badly. I knew he was hanging out above watching the flurry of activity. There were people on top of him making sure he was still breathing and people all around doing various other functions in this regard as he was a full code. When I asked them what was going on, they proceeded to tell me the scientifics of what they were doing.

Then I said, "No. *What* is going on?" They told me to talk to the doctor. They called in the doctor, and he started the scientifics once again. So I asked, "Is he brain dead?"

He replied, "Yes."

Then I said, "*Stop*. Please stop."

The doctor asked, "Are you his power of attorney?"

And I replied, "Yes. Please stop. It's time. But please keep him on a vent until some people can get here."

As it turned out, pretty much all of my family—my mom, my siblings, and their spouses—the Vinje family, and some friends were in that emergency room. Here we were seven months later in the midst of a repeat performance of his initial brain surgery, where once again we had more than thirty people in attendance for our precious Tommy. I had people calling asking to wait until they got there to unplug that vent, but it got to a point where I didn't think it was right to wait any longer. Part of me is not sure that having everyone in the room was even the right thing to do, but with everything we had all been through and knowing it was not just my loss, I allowed it, right or wrong.

While we were waiting for family members to arrive, the chaplain came in to deliver last rites. She seemed truly touched by the amount of people who were there for Tom. (We took up two rooms. Thank God no one was in the adjoining room.) As a matter of fact, the entire emergency room staff was amazed by all of us who were there. Our nurse, Kelly, from 6A was notified that we were there, and she came down. During this time, I also told Drae that nothing was going to change. I told him that I would fulfill the promise that Tom and I had made to him, and he would stay with me through high school.

After a bit, I told them it was time. The ventilator wasn't even halfway off when Tom's body stopped breathing, confirming what I already knew. He was gone. He was pronounced at 12:12 p.m. on October 26, 2008. Everyone broke down. Soon a few of his nieces arrived and began their grieving. His niece Tija took a picture of the eagle tattoo on his arm, and everyone began to filter out and go back to my house. I couldn't leave—not yet. I stayed in his room a while as I knew this would be the last time I saw him as himself. The next time I see him would be in the funeral home. This was really it. While I was so happy for him that his suffering was over, I knew mine was really just beginning. The hope of my miracle was gone, but Tom had finally received his.

I did not want to leave the hospital while Tom was lying in the emergency room all alone, so while we were waiting for them to take him away, Judy and I went up to 6A to let Kelly know that Tom was gone. We were there for a bit talking to her, and when we got back to the ER, Ginny and my mom were still there waiting with Tom for us to get back. I didn't leave until they took his body out of that room. What … the … fuck! The whole concept is still hard to grasp at times.

Upon leaving the hospital, everyone went back to my house and picked up food along the way. There were about fifty people at my house that afternoon as people who were not at the hospital came by. We called hospice, and they came that evening to pick up most of their equipment. It would be a few days and a phone call before the remaining equipment was retrieved. The hospice nurses who came told us that we could donate some of our supplies to Doctors without Borders. The supplies would be taken overseas to areas in need. Of course we gladly did that. I was so happy that some of the items could be used to help others. Also, hospice comes out immediately to get that tube-feeding equipment right effing now because it is so expensive. But really, what else would you use it for? Just sayin'.

Over the next few days, people were over helping with the picture boards, the video, and everything else that needed to be done. During this time, Ginny brought up the idea of giving up her plot in the cemetery next to her husband and her oldest son, David, for Tom. We decided to move forward with that plan. To compensate she will be cremated and buried on top of her husband, Lyle, in a plot that I was able to pay for since hers had been paid for long ago. As I said, I hadn't planned for Tom's death, so all of this was last minute and worked out for the best. He is with his father, brother, grandparents, and uncle. He is in good company indeed.

Chapter 13

Good-Bye, My Love ...

Monday, October 27, 2008, 3:01 a.m., CDT—
Chrissie's Journal Entry

Good-bye, my love ...

All weekend I have been thinking how much I had to tell you on Monday morning, and not once did it occur to me that it would be what I am about to tell you. My beloved, beautiful husband passed away on Sunday afternoon October 26, 2008 at 12:12 p.m. It happened fast. I will tell you the details in a day or two, but I wanted to put this out there before too many people commented. I have not remotely thought about funeral arrangements because, in my mind, that was not happening, but it did. We did not get the miracle we had expected, but it is what it is. In the last few weeks I knew (but did not tell you) that he had gone past what he could recover from. I wanted to keep hope alive! After all, he is my honey, my love—the man I thought would be mine for eternity. That was not to be in this life, but Tommy and I were connected long before we met through other situations or family members who knew each other before we could connect the dots … I will miss him forever. This is *so* not real yet, and if you think this is the last Bridge entry, you would be wrong. I will have *much* to say in the coming weeks … if you care to listen. For now, suffice it to say, the love of my life has made his transition. He is free (which is what I told him today), and he will forever be the most fun, kindest, thoughtful, and yes, most stubborn person I will ever know. I love you, baby, forever … You are free. Come see us all very soon … We'll be waiting …

Sleep well, my sweet.

Love,

Your baby

Monday, October 27, 2008, 11:20 p.m., CDT—
Chrissie's Journal Entry

Hello, all,

I am sincerely and forever grateful to all who volunteered their time and energy to care for Tommy during the time he was at home. Tommy could not have been home without you. I am also most grateful for everyone who helped out around our house in other ways these last seven months in ways like shoveling snow, mowing our lawn, putting in and taking out our air conditioners, cleaning the bathroom, etc. I feel most honored that we have been worthy of your help and kindness. We love you all.

Much love to all,

Chrissie

Guest Book Entries

Written October 26, 2008, 7:41 p.m.

Chrissie,

I'm so sorry. Tom will be greatly missed by all.

Love,

Peggy

Written October 27, 2008, 5:06 a.m.

Hi, Chrissie … many, many, many hugs for you and the family. I am deeply saddened by Tommy's passing. He put up a good fight, and all your strength is what kept him going.

I am truly sorry I never got the chance to come visit. I have always kept you both in my prayers every night. God will lift him gently on to the clouds and into his arms, and you and Tommy will be reconnected in the afterlife.

God bless Tommy and you both. He could not have had a better partner in life.

Please let me know if there is anything I can do when you have made the plans.

Julie S.

Written October 27, 2008, 7:12 a.m.

Hey, Chrissie,

Even though I saw you on Sunday, I just wanna say something. Tom Vinje was one of my favorite uncles. He was funny, he always picked on you in the strangest ways, and most of all he had lots of love to give. Tom was one of *the biggest* parts of the family, and that's not a secret. This week is going to be a long, heartfelt week and scary (not in a bad way). Just the scary feeling of him not being there is enough. Tom will visit you in your dreams even when you don't see him. Tommy loves you a *whole* bunch; never forget that, Chris. I love you so very much, and Dad and I are here for you.

See ya soon,

Maddie Betlach

Xoxoxo

Written October 27, 2008, 7:49 a.m.

Hi, Chrissie,

I am so sorry to hear about Tommy. I know how much you loved each other. I have never seen two people more in love and more meant to be together. Tom is in a better place, and you should have peace of mind knowing you cared for him, never gave up hope for him, and loved him more than he could have ever wished for. You are both two of the kindest, funniest, and most loving people

Alyssa and I have ever had the honor to know. We miss you both.

Take care of yourself. We love you!

Lylis C. and Alyssa S.

Written October 27, 2008, 8:13 a.m.

Chrissie,

All my thoughts and prayers are with you at this difficult time.

Dana Duffy

Written October 27, 2008, 8:24 a.m.

Chrissie,

All my love and support for you and your family right now. You and Tom are and will be together forever. You are amazing.

Peace and love,

Heather and Asher

Written October 27, 2008, 8:52 a.m.

Chrissie,

I think that even those of us who didn't really know Tom very well could say that he would be proud of the tenacity you showed in taking care of him.

What is there to say? We are so sorry for your loss and your family's loss. I'm not sure if you knew this, but Dave was married before. When he lost his first wife, Becky, he got a piece of advice that he still holds close: feel the feelings, but don't feed them. Don't be afraid to scream and yell!

We're thinking about you!

Irene Peterson

Written October 27, 2008, 9:10 a.m.

Dear, Dear Tommy,

Inserted here was the writing entitled "In Our Hearts"

We love you, Tommy and Chrissie!

Lisa Berry

Written October 27, 2008, 9:29 a.m.

Chrissie,

My heart is breaking for you and your families.

I checked this site daily and always admired your courage and strength. You took such good care of Tom and gave him everything you had. But I knew you would because that is the kind of caring, loving person you are.

I wish I could be there to put my arms around you but I cannot, so I am sending you hugs and kisses long distance. Rely on your friends and family right now to help you with the next few days. Know that I am there with you.

Hugs and kisses,

Staci Burke

Written October 27, 2008, 9:33 a.m.

Chris,

I do not have any words of wisdom today. The only thing I can say is that I am so sorry for your loss. You have wonderful memories of your life with Tom. As always I send my love and hugs to you.

Take care,

Roxie Chudy

Written October 27, 2008, 10:24 a.m.

Hello, Chrissie,

I just wanted to tell you how special Tom was to me and the other staff on 6A. Kelly actually let me know personally of Tom's passing last night. I am deeply saddened by his passing. You are an amazing woman, and Tom was lucky to have you and the rest of your family and friends so involved with his care. Even though I never knew the Tom that you all knew, there was something special about him, way back in April when we first had the pleasure of caring for him. I have followed the CaringBridge since then, and through your journal entries, you allowed us to come along on your journey with you. We will greatly miss Tom on 6A, and he will never be forgotten. Even though he couldn't communicate with us and show us the "real" Tom, he will be greatly missed. I wish nothing but the best to you and your family at this time. Thank you for letting me be a part of this journey. It truly was my pleasure.

Monica Lang

Written October 27, 2008, 10:38 a.m.

You are in our thoughts and prayers. Tommy gave a good long fight, and he will be missed.

Kit and Marie Bolton

Written October 27, 2008, 10:50 a.m.

My thoughts are with you, Chrissie. I know this is very difficult and will not seem real for a very long time. But you have been so strong up to this point that I know that strength will remain with you. I'm confident Tom is in a much better place now, and I'm sure he is happy and laughing again. Love and prayers are with you.

Angie Warner

Written October 27, 2008, 11:11 a.m.

I just wanted to send a note. I met Tom during his stay at Fairview Transitional Care. I was one of the many therapists that worked with him during his stay. He touched so many of us, and we have been following his journey via CaringBridge since. I know I speak for everyone at Fairview TCU when I say we are so sorry for your loss. We will keep you and your family in our thoughts and prayers!

Stephanie P.

Written October 27, 2008, 11:22 a.m.

What is there to say, other than Kent and I love both of you very much, and that will never change? Needless to say, we are both pretty shaken up, especially Kent with the year he has had losing both parents and another bud, Davey. You know we will both be there for you for whatever you need us for. You will be a Bud forever!

Love ya, sistah!

Kim and Kent Peterson

Written October 27, 2008, 1:40 p.m.

Chrissie,

I am so sorry.

When we met I told you how happy I was that Tom had finally met the woman of his dreams. Your love for him is so evident by your words and actions—that love will last forever.

God's peace, Tommy.

Julie Ordner

Written October 27, 2008, 2:40 p.m.

Chrissie,

We are so deeply sorry for your loss. Our thoughts and prayers continue to be with you through this very difficult time.

With sympathy,

Dianne, Victor, Luisa, and Lydia

Written October 27, 2008, 3:30 p.m.

May the peace that comes from the memories of love shared comfort you now and in the days ahead. Lots of love to you and your family.

Love,

Bonnie Versboncoeur (Judy's coworker)

Written October 27, 2008, 3:57 p.m.

Chrissie,

I know how it feels to lose someone very close to you! I lost my mother in June of 2001, and she was my best friend. It's been seven years, and I still have a very hard time. I know she is in a better place, and she's not suffering anymore! I also know now she is with me and my family every moment just like Tom is with you! Love you lots.

Cristina Melzer

Written October 27, 2008, 4:01 p.m.

Chrissie,

Tom was and is a vibrant man who was quick to love and always so loving and open with his many, many friends. You know how many lives he touched, and your incredible strength and unquestioning devotion during this trial has touched and humbled us all. We will carry Tom with us forever; he will never be truly gone. Please, please let us know if you need any of that strength back, a shoulder to lean on, or simply some time for yourself.

Love,

Barry and Krissy

Written October 27, 2008, 4:03 p.m.

Chrissie,

I am so sorry for your loss. I have been following your website and praying for you and Tom since I met you at the Enchanted Rock Garden. You are a wonderful woman. I feel blessed to have met you.

Mary John

Written October 27, 2008, 4:13 p.m.

Oh, Chrissie,

My heart just bleeds for you. Tommy was such a wonderful joy to be around. And that laugh! It will be remembered by all of us. I don't profess to know the good Lord's plan, but for sure he brings us all closer together in the times when we need each other.

I wish for you (and all you Vinjes) a peaceful, good night's sleep.

Lory Ruggles

Written October 27, 2008, 6:21 p.m.

Chrissie,

I am sorry for your loss. I will keep you in mind and prayers in your time of sorrow. If you need anything, just call. I could sing you a tune, maybe start a singalong. You're such a great person. I met Tom only a couple of times, but the greatest of you two together was out of this world. He is with you forever. The loss of a loved one is always so hard. Someday you will reunite and he will welcome you with open arms. In the meanwhile live life to the fullest and be your crazy and wild self. Oh, do you know anything else? I'll talk to my dad, and they can kick back and have a beer and watch over us.

You're the best, Chrissie. Stay strong, and if you need anything just call.

I love you

Julie and Alexis

Written October 27, 2008, 11:09 p.m.

Chris,

Ever since I found out about your dear Tommy, I haven't been able to get you out of my mind. All day I have been trying to come up with the right words to put on this website. I know that just to have the support from all your friends and family is what you need. No fancy words are needed. I believe that Tom smiled as he went to be with God, knowing that his wife gave him the perfect gift—knowing that you did absolutely *everything* in your power to give Tom opportunities to get better. Tom knows that you fought tooth and nail the past several months to try to bring him back, and he will forever be grateful for that. You are such an amazing person, Chris! I know that I cannot possibly conceive what you are going through. I do know, however, that Tom had the *best* wife in the entire world. I am so sorry for your loss. You and Tom found each other and found the best in each other. You were both miracles to each other, and that is so evident in all of the journal entries you have posted here. You are an inspiration to so many and have been such a strong person through this horrific ordeal you have had to deal with at a much-too-early age.

I thought of how your character was developed through everything you did for Tom, knowing at the end that you know in your heart you did everything you could humanly do for Tom while he was here.

I know I haven't seen you for such a long time, and I don't know why I feel the need to write so much, but I guess it has just affected me more than I thought it would. My heart is heavy, and I wish there was more I could do than offer these words to you.

I wish you peace, love, guidance, and understanding.

Love,

Kris K.

Written October 28, 2008, 8:24 a.m.

Chrissie,

I am at a loss to say anything that anyone else has already said. Maybe just that in following your journey since March, I have seen (for the very first time, I might add), total, unwavering, unconditional love between two people. It makes me think of all the things over the years that I quit—mostly because they inconvenienced my life.

You have shown me that unconditional love really does exist. I prayed every day for a different outcome for you and Tommy, as did everyone. And I don't claim to know why God does what he does. But I *do* know it's for a reason.

I am truly very sorry for your loss. Tommy was a great man and I'm sure a kick-ass husband, to say the least.

I continue to pray as you start yet another journey to find peace and strength. You are a hell of a woman, Chrissie. I am very blessed to know you.

If there is *anything* I can do, please let me know. Thank you for the life lesson you had no idea you were teaching.

Michelle Notch

Written October 28, 2008, 9:48 a.m.

Chrissie, when I think Tom, I will have an everlasting image of his memorable smile and his unmistakable giggle. I *always* enjoyed seeing him, and he truly did brighten the room when he entered it. My other everlasting memory will be you! I feel blessed to know you, and I am happy that Tom had you holding him when he left us … God bless.

Dino DiPerna

Written October 28, 2008, 2:24 p.m.

Dear Chrissie,

You don't know me, but my husband and brother-in-law worked with Tom at Jaguar. Philip and I have been praying for Tom, and you, since this ordeal began, and I've read all of your journal entries along the way. You are an amazing woman, and my heart has been heavy for you. I am so sorry for the loss of your best friend, Tom.

I applaud you for your energy in maintaining hope. The Bible tells us to have faith like a child; in other words, always believe, do not doubt. You were right to maintain hope—to never give up. While God allowed an outcome we do not understand, I hope you will find comfort in knowing that he will never leave you or forsake you. It is so clear that he has been faithful, present, and active, as displayed in the love and concern of all of your family and friends. I'm amazed by their faithfulness too.

Your love story is a testament to those who know you (and those, like me, who have not had the privilege to meet you). God is the author of love, and his love for you and Tom is everlasting ("I have loved you with an everlasting love" ([Jeremiah 31:3]). He is the only one who understands your loss and pain completely, and my prayer for you is that you will know His comfort. He is patient and kind, and He loves you dearly.

For those of us in Christ, there are no good-byes—only, "See you later!" Your good-bye is for now, not forever.

On behalf of my husband, Philip, sister and husband, Tom and Michelle P., and friends Jim and Mary B., you are in our prayers. God bless you and keep you.

Love in Christ,

Monica Klanderud

Written October 28, 2008, 4:34 p.m.

*** *Inserted here was the writing entitled, "All Is Well."*

Patty Betlach Russell

Written October 29, 2008, 1:42 p.m.

I'm one of the nurses from 6A. My thoughts and prayers have been with you, albeit quietly, throughout these months, ever since that night Tommy was admitted.

I wish you the best. My thoughts and prayers are still with you and will continue to be.

Julia Velner

Written October 29, 2008, 7:23 p.m.

Hi, Chris and family,

I am so sorry to hear about the loss of Tom. I feel so bad that I wasn't able to help you out at all. (What are friends for?) My thoughts and prayers go out to you and your family.

Love and friends always,

Donna Muehlbauer

***

Tom's funeral was held October 31, 2008. I have included the eulogies written for Tom here.

Eulogies

Gary Vinje's Eulogy for Tom

Tom was born August 9, 1962. This is the day that he always referred to as the "blessed holiday." (The week of his birthday was the birthday week, which became birthday month.) Tom was the baby of the family (the youngest of *six*), and he never let us forget it. And according to him he was "Mom's favorite."

When we were kids I remember running around in the rain, playing kick the can and hide and seek, and spending summers at the farm. He loved his time at the farm. This was the farm that our Mom was born and raised on—the farm where he would go out in the woods on a four wheeler, cruising through huge mud puddles and turn around to look at whoever was riding with him and say, "Isn't this fun!" We would come back covered head to toe with mud. There was one time when we were riding and Tom rolled the four-wheeler going around a ninety-degree turn and I came running because I could hear him moaning. When I got there he said, "Just kidding!" One year, in April we were up at the farm for the first time of the season. Tom decided to test the four wheelers out and found that the snow wasn't as hard as he thought. The four-wheeler went through the snow crust, which stopped the machine and caused him to fly forward in a handstand position, which failed to bring him back to his seat. The whole scene will always be slow motion in my mind, just watching Tom doing flips in the snow on a four-wheeler.

Then there's the fire pit. Tom remembered everything from boy scouts. He was the king of the fire (just ask him). He kept the fire blazing well into the night, on *many* occasions.

Tom loved children, especially his nieces and nephews. There were also kids from the neighborhood who loved Tom. You could find him in the garage watching TV, and more often than not there was a kid sitting with him watching sports or asking him to fill their bike tires. He made everyone feel so special.

One thing we will miss is the "Tommy-isms." Here are a few that we will continue to recite for many years to come. Whenever he would see a newborn, he would say, "There's a freshie!"

On one fun weekend, we were in Austin, Minnesota, for a hockey tournament, and we visited the Spam Museum. After that we had sayings that morphed into, "Hot Spam," "Spam it anyway," or anything else that could be replaced with the word *Spam*.

One of Tom's most infamous sayings is, "What now!" It meant so much and so little at the same time! The thing is you knew what it meant depending on the situation.

Tommy was such a daredevil. He was not afraid of trying anything. He did things like bungee jumping and skydiving. On his fortieth birthday he went skydiving, and it was one of the greatest thrills of his life. He was also not afraid to roll a four-wheeler, or two, or three …

Tommy loved to dance. Mom always said he had slick moves. Tommy would slide across the dance floor and be all snaky as he was dancing to GB Leighton, Boogie Wonderland, or any other type of music that moved him.

Tom and Chrissie had true love. The look on Tom's face when Chrissie was walking down the aisle at their wedding said it all. "A match made in heaven" is the look that Tom had in his eye that said, "Yeah, that's my girl!" Some of the nicknames he had for her were Turtledove, Sugarplum, and Snickerdoodle, or "Snicks" for short. From the moment they started dating they were together. They did not spend another moment apart. It was predestined, meant to be.

As we all know, Tom *loved* SpongeBob, so in closing, I would like to ask, *"Who lives in a pineapple under the sea?"*

SpongeBob SquarePants!

Betlach Family Tribute to Tom Vinje

By Beth Timm

I remember when Chris first started talking about Tom. He was this guy that she knew liked her but "you know ... it's just not there." She wasn't ready. Then one day she was ready. She decided to seek him out and spent an entire weekend trying to find him at the Hennepin Avenue Block Party that she knew he always went to (creature of habit that he is), but this time he wasn't there. It turns out he was on one of the Bud Annual Weekends. She had a party a couple of months after that weekend, and Tom went with her on his lunch hour to get the keg and set it up for her. After the party they stayed up until the morning just talking ... about music, movies, and everything else they were discovering they had in common. Thus began one of the greatest love stories that most of us have ever known.

One of the first things I noticed about Tom was "Wow! What a smile." He had the warmest, most genuine smile that most often would have been followed by that very distinctive laugh! He gave a hug like no other. He wrapped his arms around you, and he meant it.

Tom meant a lot to our family. He was fun, and he was funny. He was a prankster known for planting beer bottle caps in various places to be found later (such as purses, diaper bags, hoods …). He had a way of giving you a jibe and making you feel that somehow you must have deserved it.

Tom was a dearly loved uncle and meant a lot to every child in our family. He became a strong ally to his brothers-in-law in having to deal with the (apparently) puzzling and quirky ways of the Betlach women. He would often be seen off to the side with the others rolling his eyes, the dramatic checking of his watch, and the "okay then" over the "long Betlach good-byes."

He was a caretaker with a big heart. Not only did he take good care of our sister, but he did so much for our parents and was great to the entire family, he (along with Chris) even took in our niece Nicole for a while when she needed a place to stay. We all knew he would give you the shirt off his back if you needed it (of course, he probably didn't need it anyway because he was always so hot, Mr. Snow-Blowing-in-His-Shorts). He gave, sometimes when he didn't even have it to give. Some of us were able to repay him for all he had done for us by helping to care for him when he needed it the most. I am not going to lie, it wasn't always easy. I can tell you that we all feel very privileged to be able to have returned the favor.

They say that good things come from bad, and that is even true here. Tom's illness brought our two families together. We are bonded by tragedy, hope, and humor. We are family. Though it seems so wrong that Tom cannot be with us to enjoy it, I think we all know that when we are laughing together, he is laughing right along with us. It was probably one of the more generous gifts he has ever given, and he didn't even realize he was doing it.

Tom, you were a very special person. Thank you for giving our Chrissie the happiest years of her life. Though your time on this earth was short, we will love you forever.

CHRISSIE BETLACH VINJE

Guest Book Entries

Written November 1, 2008, 10:23 a.m.

Chrissie,

I stayed up late last night and got up early this morning to read all your beautiful journal entries. Your love and devotion to Tom through his illness touched my heart. Thank you for sharing your thoughts and feelings with us and for being strong and never giving up hope. John told me about the eagle flying overhead at the service yesterday ... I wish I could've been there to see it too. My warmest thoughts and prayers are with you! Please let us know if there is anything you need.

Jenny Ruoho

Tuesday, November 4, 2008, 9:29 p.m., CST— Chrissie's Journal Entry

Hello, everyone,

I have been itching to write for a day or two now, but I either haven't had the time or it wasn't the right time. I feel most honored and humbled by all who found the time to join us for Tommy's visitation and funeral service. I knew there would be a lot of people, but even I looked around on both days and said to myself, "Wow! Really!" It was most awesome and humbling, and most certainly something I will *never* forget. The perfect end to his funeral service at the cemetery is also something that anyone who was there will never forget. If you were not there, or haven't heard, let me tell you what happened.

As many of you know, Tom *loved* the bald eagle. We have them everywhere. We have statuettes on the mantle and pictures on the walls (in the house and garage), and he had an eagle tattoo on his left arm that I got him for his Birthday while we were dating. On Friday, after the pastor was finished, there was a "twenty-one-beer salute" to Tommy with his favorite Jamaican beer, Red Stripe. (This was a very cool thing we picked up from Davey's funeral this summer, and we knew Tommy would love it.) It entailed everyone popping open their beer cans or bottles all at the same time. Way too cool ... and most appropriate. While everyone was enjoying their frosties (Tommy's word for beer), his brother Gary looked up and said, "There's a bald eagle!" (Ironically, I had just been checking out the eagle I had put on the vault for Tom's casket.) All at once everyone looked up and started clapping, cheering, and whistling! When I first looked up, the eagle was flying kind of off to the side behind a tree, but when everyone started cheering, it came out, did one huge circle, and flew away! As it was circling, I heard in my head, "I'm free!" I knew at once that Tommy was trying to tell us that he was free and he would see us later! It was simply incredible. I had chills, and it felt like my hair was standing on end. I still get chills every time I tell the story.

I am *so, so* happy for him and *so, so* sad for us. The pain is incredible. I can't believe how much it hurts that he is gone. There are moments where I think I can't make it through, and then there are moments I am remembering and laughing. I know this is going to take a long time, but right now, I don't see an end to the pain. I can't imagine it. He was much too young to leave us and too good of a person to have gone through one of the nastiest diseases out there. I don't pretend to understand why things happen as they do, and perhaps I never will. One thing I do know, however, is that my husband was loved by many. He was charismatic. He lit up a room with his smile, his laugh, and his personality. There were a lot of "Tommy-isms," as Gary alluded to in the eulogy. One of my favorites that Tom used to say in reference to his baldness was, "God made a few perfect heads; he put hair on the rest."

He had a million of them. If anyone can think of any more, feel free to put them up on the Bridge. As I said, I will be writing for a while. Also, feel free to put a comment on the guest book for his obituary. You can get there by going to legacy.com and then searching by Thomas Vinje. You can also get there through his obituary in the *Star Tribune*. I plan on sponsoring that guest book indefinitely, so feel free to go on there at any time now or in the future.

Thanks again all of you for your tireless love, support, and prayers. I feel most honored that Tommy and I were the recipients of such energy and power. We may not have gotten the miracle we prayed for, for ourselves, but I think Tommy got his miracle. He received the miracle of freedom from a horrific disease that shut down his body in such a cruel way—a way that left us wondering what he was thinking and feeling because he could not tell us. That was the cruelest part. I said it before, and I will say it again: it just isn't right …

Much love to all,

Chrissie

Guest Book Entries

Written November 5, 2008, 9:49 a.m.

Tommy, my beautiful brother,

I'm going to miss you so! Words cannot describe my sorrow. You are walking tall, and I know you are blissfully happy. That is all that matters to me. I really do believe you are happy and flying high like an eagle. We here on earth are the ones hurting so, trying desperately to live our lives without you. Time and remembering all the great memories is the only thing that will lessen my pain for such a great loss.

I'm going to miss your smile, your laugh, your blue eyes. Sometimes one would be blue and the other one green. I find myself looking at pictures and videos to see what color your eyes are. What I wouldn't do to see them again.

I loved how you always made my kids feel special, especially Clifton. They have the utmost respect for you. They always did gravitate toward you.

Your journey these last few months has brought two families together as one. I'm so grateful for that; the more memories and shoulders to cry on the better.

I can just see you now, joking around with Dad and David, playing poker or cribbage having a few frosties, the times of your lives.

Tommy, until we meet again … I love you!

Judy Vinje

Thursday, November 6, 2008, 11:55 a.m., CST—Chrissie's Journal Entry

Thank you, Luther family, Motors Management, Jaguar Land Rover Minneapolis, and Bloomington Acura-Subaru.

Now begins a series of entries in which I would like to thank everyone for their love and support over the last seven months or so. I am going to start off with everyone you see above. *Truly*, I could not have done what I did these last months without the love, support, and understanding of the people Tom and I work for. The Luther family and the people at Motors Management astounded me with their kindness, generosity, and devotion to us and what we were going through. I was never made to feel like work was more important than taking care of Tommy, which was good because he was/is the only thing on my mind. All anyone ever wanted to know is what they could do for us. (That includes everyone, not just the people mentioned here.) I felt like I was free to do what I needed to do for my husband and myself, and that means so much more than you will ever know. You gave me the freedom I needed to deal with the worst tragedy of our lives in the way that I needed to. I know there are many companies out there who would not do the same; just ask my sister-in-law Judy.

Tom was an employee for the Luthers' for twenty-five years at Downtown Pontiac Jaguar GMC (and all the other names that store has had) except for the ten months he was service manager at Luther Pontiac where the new Jaguar store now sits. He started out as a runner/detailer and ended up as warranty administrator for both Jaguar and Land Rover. He did enjoy his position and the people he worked with. (What he didn't enjoy was that service manager position ... not his deal!) The people at Jaguar hold a special place in my heart and not just because that is where Tom and I met! But they also, showed undying love, support, and friendship to us during the worst time of our lives. I know that he is greatly missed and will continue to be for some time to come.

The people at my store, Bloomington Acura-Subaru, what can I say! Without you, I could not have done what I did. I know it was rough for a while because I was at the hospital or nursing home and not there. Later on, I was home on Fridays and only there four days a week. Thank you for your understanding and support in allowing me to do what I needed to do for my husband. And I hope I have your continued understanding and support as I begin a new life without the love of my life. It is going to suck, for sure, and I know the hard part for me is just beginning. I have been a Luther employee for almost thirteen years now, ten of them at Acura. It will always mean so much to me that I mean so much to you.

I am very lucky to work for such an amazing group of people, and I want you to know that I know it, and now, and so does everyone else! So once again, thank you all, you are a stellar group of people, and I am damn proud to know you and call you my friends.

Much love to you,

Chrissie

Guest Book Entries

Written November 6, 2008, 12:41 p.m.

You're welcome! Please don't mention it ever again—no need. You're the best boss a girl could ask for, and I'm here for whatever you need. Just say the word!

Looking forward to your return, and I'm here for whatever for you during your road ahead. Just press zero.

<3 ya, Chrissie,

Hannah Strahota

Written November 6, 2008, 1:40 p.m.

I, too, would like to thank those that Chris mentioned today. As a sister with much love and concern for Chris and Tom, I cannot express enough the gratitude I have for the flexibility that was and is afforded to Chris in both her fight and her grief. I am proud to be a former employee!

Beth Timm

Written November 6, 2008, 7:31 p.m.

We, too, would like to thank the employers for all of the support that they have shown you. That is a true gift, and we are very grateful to them. What you did for Tom would not have been possible without the support of your employers.

Mitchell would like to say a few words: I would do anything to have Tommy back. This was such a hard loss. I feel everyone would love to have Tommy back, but he is in a much better place because he is not in pain. I think of Tommy like an older brother. This was very hard for me also.

We Love you and are here for you.

Lisa and Mitchell Berry

Written November 13, 2008, 4:26 p.m.

There are so many incredible connections we make in life, Tommy was certainly no less. There are few people who have connections like him, so strong, loving, and vibrant. There will always be a place in my heart that is irreplaceable as so many others have had this "incredible" Tommy experience. I wrote a poem in high school upon a sudden death of one of my longtime (then) best friends. I would have to believe this is a good time to share it.

Overcast Days

Full of sorrow as I look through the window, I think of tomorrow.

Cause maybe as I wonder what it'll be like, the mood will soon change and there will be light.

Just like time there are always fears like the memories that endure for when I shed tears.

These overcast days may come and go, but I will never forget the people I love so.

Peace and light,

Shane Lines

***

The following is an e-mail I received from a former coworker of Tom's whom I had met several times at parties and the dealership. I burst into tears when I read it. All I have to say is, thank you, Mel. Your e-mail touched my heart deeper than you will ever know, and it is one of the reasons I decided to write this book.

From: Mel U.
Sent: Thursday, November 13, 2008, 12:50 p.m.
To: Chrissie Vinje

Hey, Chrissie,

It's Mel from the Jag dealer. I just wanted to pass on something that happened to me today. Last night, I dreamt about Tom. We were all at work and laughing as usual. When I woke up, I was listening to the KQ broadcast from Vegas. I thought of Tommy again, and I was feeling so sad. After listening to the show for a while, I was laughing, and it dawned on me that Tom is probably watchin' and laughin' too. After I got to work, our shipper runs up and tells me to call KQ because I won on the payroll! I never win anything! It kinda blew me away, but I'm sure Tom was in on this. I only worked with Tom for two years, but he was always fun to talk to.

What I really wanted to say to you was thank you. I have been married for twenty years and we have a ten-year-old daughter; after reading all of your journal entries, it made me a little ashamed that I had let my gratitude for my husband wane. Well thanks to you and your love, dedication, and incredible strength, I decided to rededicate myself to my marriage and appreciate my husband more every day. It has made a huge difference, and we have never been happier! Also we talked about medical/DNR issues that we had never talked about before, and I am so glad we did. I'm sorry I'm rambling, but I wanted to tell you this for a long time. You are one awesome person, Chrissie. Keep on doin' what you do. There's a special place in heaven right next to Tommy waitin' for ya.

Take care,
Mel U.

Tuesday, November 18, 2008, 9:41 p.m., CST— Chrissie's Journal Entry

Thank you, nurses and therapists!

There are some incredible people out there in the medical field. I have always said it takes a special person to work in that field, and my opinion has not changed. I cannot imagine working on 6A at the U of M. I was talking to Kelly the day Tommy passed, and I told her that I did not know how they do what they do in that unit. I mean, to me, that unit makes my stomach turn, and I get this overwhelming feeling of dread because that is where our world changed forever. I can't fathom seeing that on a daily basis. Those people are something special just for that alone, but what *really* touches and amazes me is that they knew Tommy was special. They knew this without even knowing Tommy when he was well.

They did not know his day-to-day personality like most of us did, yet long after we left the floor, they continued to follow our story on the Bridge and find us when we went back to the university ... twice. Unbelievable, remarkable, you guys rock! Thank you so much for making us feel like we were something special. I don't know what I would have done without all of your help and caring while trying to process everything that was happening to us in the midst of trying to make some of the scariest decisions I will ever make in my life. Words really don't express everything I feel about our experience with you guys, but rest assured, if I find the words, you will hear it here!

Another fine group of people are the nurses and therapists at the TCU. You guys also knew Tom was something special, and I will never forget you guys singing "These Boots Are Made for Walking" on the day we left. Neither Tom nor I wanted to leave the TCU to go to Providence (and for good reason). That was a *really* hard day for both of us. But we are not usually in control of such things.

It still astounds me that so many people picked up on Tom's charisma while he was extremely ill. It really says a lot about him. One of the things I wanted the most was for Tommy to recover so we could go back to see these amazing people and they could know who he really was. They would have loved him even more than they already do. How could you not! I just sit here and reflect on what I had with him, and I still can't believe that it is over. That wasn't supposed to happen to us, and I am struggling to figure out why it did. It is still not real to me, and I suspect it won't be for some time. And I thought I missed him before ...

Sorry, I did not mean to stray from the subject of the praises I was giving to the incredible medical professionals we had the pleasure to meet these last eight months. Eight months ago today our journey began, and while I lost my beautiful husband in the end, please know that all of you made the journey just that much better for us, more tolerable, if you will. You did make a difference, and for that, I will be eternally grateful. I'm sure Tommy would agree.

Much love, respect, and thanks to *you*,

Chrissie

***

I did not post this on the CaringBridge, but it was always my intention to do so. I know I covered this in the dedication but, it bears repeating.

Thank you to our family and friends for being there when we needed you most. I know that some of you may think this thank you would be unnecessary as losing Tom was a loss we all share. That being said, I truly do not know what I would have done without each and every one of you. There were many, many ways that you were there for us, each playing your own role. You dealt with your emotions during Tom's illness and grief after his passing in your own way, and you did the best that you could, given the very difficult circumstances. I know it wasn't always easy, and for that, I thank you. You all stepped up and rose to the challenge of being there for us. I feel very blessed and honored to call you our family and friends, and I love you all. Also, please know that Tom is loving you and keeping watch over all of you from the other side.

Chapter 14

My Journey— the First Year

Saturday, December 20, 2008, 2:57 p.m., CST— Chrissie's Journal Entry

Greetings, everyone,

I know I haven't written in over a month, but it's not because I didn't want to. I have been totally discombobulated, lost, and unable to concentrate. I would say to myself, "Today I will write," and then it wouldn't happen. It's like that with everything … all the time. Although I am not remotely done with my thank yous to everyone here on the Bridge, I needed to write about something else this time. I have been trying to figure out if I should talk about the things I have been feeling and experiencing. I have talked to a few people about it, and they seem to think it was a good idea. I was just trying to decide how much of myself I was going to put out there. So although I don't know where this will go until it is done, I will go forward and see where this leads.

First of all, I am trying to avoid Christmas like the plague. While I have now finished my shopping (something I started on Wednesday night), I have found myself not listening to any Christmas music … I turn the station. I am having a hard time saying, "Merry Christmas" and "Happy Holidays," etc., because I am not feeling it. I won't watch any Christmas shows, not this year. I did not decorate the house. *That* would have been *way* too painful, and I did not see any reason to put myself through that. Christmas will just be something to get through this year; having said that, I have decided to spend the holidays as if my husband were still here. I will be with the Vinjes on Christmas Eve and at my sister Beth's on Christmas Day. No matter where I go, we will all be missing Tommy.

Another day I am dreading is New Year's Eve. Since we have been together, I was always so happy that I had my honey to spend New Year's Eve with. I spent the first thirty-five years of my life without anyone to share it, and it felt so good to finally have my special someone to share (everything) with until we grew old, or so we thought.

But enough about the damn holidays. One thing that I have found is that I have *never* felt this kind of pain in my life. I thought it was painful losing my father four years ago (on December 23). Man, while that was extremely painful, that was a whole different kind of pain. When you lose a parent, you lose them, a good part of the time, as a child. You are a child losing a parent. It is a different matter losing your spouse because your spouse is someone you chose. You didn't choose your parents, but you did choose your spouse. For me, losing Tom meant I lost my every day. By that I mean I lost my everyday life, my love, my forever companion, my future. I cannot bear to say or think about the word *alone*. I burst into tears every time, and it is not because I am scared to be alone; I have done that. It is because the word *alone* now means without Tom. I can't bear to think about it. It still does not seem real to me that he is not here. It is just not the way it was supposed to be. Oh, I know some people will say that *is* the way it is supposed to be, that was God's plan, but quite frankly, I don't want to hear it. This is how I feel right now, and at some point that may change, but not just yet.

Another thing that people say is, "He is in a better place." Obviously, that is true given his physical condition, but I agree with what Billy said the afternoon of Tom's funeral when we came back to the house. He did a toast to his Bud and it went like this: "All week long I have been hearing people say that Tommy is in a better place. I say f*** that! His place is here with family and friends!" *Word,* Billy!

Much love to all,

Chrissie

Guest Book Entries

Written December 19, 2008, 4:20 p.m.

Hi, Chrissie,

I have been thinking about you, especially now around the holidays. This time of year has always been a tough time for many people who have lost their loved ones. You are lucky to have so many friends and relatives that live near you to get you through this difficult time. I would like to keep in touch with you.

Tom's time on earth seemed all too brief because you wanted him in your life forever. And although you really miss him, in your heart you know that he is at peace. Still, countless times throughout the day you find yourself remembering Tom. Although you cannot see or hear him, you know that he is with you.

You will feel Tom in the warmth of the summer sun. You will see him in the brilliance of the autumn leaves. He will be beside you in the peacefulness of a gentle snowfall and rejoice with you at the first flowers of spring.

You must be so thankful of the times that you shared and all the priceless memories too, for those memories are a comfort now when you lovingly remember your husband, companion, and best friend ... Tom.

Take care,

Gail

Written December 21, 2008, 5:29 p.m.

Chrissie, I just read your journal entry ... I must say, you are an amazing writer. Every word you have written I felt deep in my soul. I love your honesty, your amazing love for your husband and for being *exactly* who you are. I have not lost anyone close to me ... I have no idea what you are experiencing. I cannot even begin to imagine. But I feel so much sadness for you. My heart aches for you. I just wanted to let you know that I'm listening and clinging to your words and praying to God that you find *peace*. Somehow, somewhere ... Much love goes to *you*!

Heidi

Thursday, January 1, 2009, 1:50 p.m., CST—
Chrissie's Journal Entry

2009

Here we are in 2009. While I was more than happy to see 2008 go away (I will be burning all three of my 2008 calendars for a little therapy), the one fact that rips at my heart most is that 2008 will always be the year in which I last saw my husband alive. This is the only fact that is allowing me to hold on to 2008 just a little bit. While it sounds great to say that 2009 is a new year, and hopefully a much better one, the one fact about the new year is that I am going into it without Tommy, forever. You have no idea what that is doing to me inside. I can't even bear the thought of it.

I have found that I can get through events (holidays, outings, things we did routinely) just fine if my family and friends are around me. It is afterward that blows me out of the water. Sometimes it's a day later, sometimes it's longer. Depression you ask? No question. Some anxiety and panic, perhaps? Absolutely. Weight gain? Trying to stop it. I do not feel like myself. I kind of feel like a mess. The aforementioned conditions are something I have not experienced to this degree, if at all. It is unfamiliar territory for me. I feel like I am in the *Twilight Zone,* which is probably why I have my TV tuned in to the SyFy channel right now because there is a *Twilight Zone* marathon running today. It seems appropriate. (You wouldn't believe the stars that appeared on that show back in the day.)

Anyway, while I am discombobulated and more than a little lost today, I was hoping that doing a little journaling on the Bridge would help me focus a little more so I could get some stuff done around the house and not wander aimlessly from room to room figuring out what it is I feel like doing. We will see if it works. I am not feeling it just yet.

When you get a minute, take time to raise a glass to 2009 and hope and pray that it in no way resembles 2008. I pray for health and happiness for everyone. That is something 2008 did not bring to my house.

Much love to all,

Chrissie

Guest Book Entries

Written January 1, 2009, 2:57 p.m.

Dear Chris,

When we prayed our family rosary, I had you as an intention to help get through this difficult time. I hope you may receive some comfort in knowing we are praying for you.

Your cousin,

Shari

Written January 1, 2009, 9:29 p.m.

Hi, Chrissie,

I read your new journal, and I can't imagine going into a new year without the love of your life. For New Year's Eve, Ken and I were over to some friends' house for dinner and socializing. There were ten of us that have known each other for many years. Before we sat down for dinner, we all spoke up about our friendship and hoping that 2009 would be a healthy and prosperous year. When it came to my turn, I spoke about one of my friends that is going through chemo because of ovarian cancer, a good friend of mine who passed away last year who was in my life for many years, and three friends of mine who lost their spouses. It just doesn't seem fair. They were all wonderful people, and they will be greatly missed by many …

My heart pours out for you, Chrissie. Please call or e-mail me sometime. I would love to get together with you.

Gail

Written January 2, 2009, 9:08 a.m.

Hi, Chrissie,

I have been sending you hugs and caring thoughts from across the street, hoping they will help a little. Taking your girl with us to the dog park helps Bailey too! I can't even imagine what it is like without your Tom, but we are all here for you, for whatever you need!

Candace McCown

Written January 11, 2009, 7:39 p.m.

Though this tragedy is very sad,
I can't help but be mad.
I was never there.
It is very hard to share.
When he hit his head on the wheel,
He could feed himself his own meal.
He's the only thing that matters

While our words begin to shatter.
They turn into tears
As we face our worst fears.
We all knew this day would be here,
So as we say good-bye,
Letting out a silent sigh,
We say our last I love you.
He mouths, "I do too."
Sorry if it is upsetting, but I had to share it.

Love you, Chrissie.

Alyssa S.

Monday, January 19, 2009, 2:27 p.m., CST— Chrissie's Journal Entry

Greetings,

I am writing today because I am not having a good day. Since Tommy passed it seems that I turn to the Bridge to write when something is not going well. While it is a nice outlet for me in that way, I think it would be good to write when things are going okay as well. I will try to do that.

In the meantime, I find myself in the midst of another anxiety-type situation. This is new territory for me and a most uncomfortable one. I am having heart palpitations galore (which, I found out, is a symptom of anxiety). I do not feel like myself, and my stomach is in knots. I feel overwhelmed and a little lost. I know I said some of this before, but it is what it is. These feelings reared their ugly heads again. I am thinking it may have been triggered by the fact that I was having furnace problems yesterday, and they did not come out until this morning to look at it. In the process I signed up for Service Plus with Centerpoint (something that Tom would never do because he thought it was a waste of money), and then they replaced the thermostat. The thermostat was a programmable one that Tom had set up. I think that I am feeling like I am taking over and changing things that he had in place for a reason, and I might be feeling a little guilty and a lot sad. The word *despair* would also be appropriate here. I feel a lot of that. Some days I am better at pushing it away than others, and I think that is why a situation like today happens. It has to come out at some point. The fact is, there are times I know I should tap into what is going on inside of me, but I don't feel like it at that moment.

I miss him so much it hurts. It is just not right that he was taken from us. He was so fun, funny, and full of life. He loved his family, friends, and pets. He loved to take trips and just go out of town and stay in hotels. We loved going out to dinner. I miss all of that and more. Each time a "first" comes up, I just dread it. I try not to think about it until I have to. There are a lot of the everyday things that wreak havoc as well. I am avoiding getting my eyes checked because I will then have to go out and pick out new glasses (something we used to do together whenever each one of us needed them). The thought of going to get new specs without him is hard to take.

I guess I have rambled on enough. Thank you for listening.

Much love to all,

Chrissie

Guest Book Entries

Written January 20, 2009, 12:52 a.m.

I still have the first pair of shoes I bought after Brad died in a box. It's so hard for anyone to know that feeling—that, "Here is something that is now in my life that wasn't here while he was alive." Life is moving on ... *It hurts! It's not fair, and it will never,*

ever make sense. Everyone else just continues to live their lives and function, and here I am. I look okay on the outside; in fact, people treat me like I am okay. *But—I am so not okay!* Doesn't anyone get that I'm so *not okay?*

I get it, sweetheart. I wish I could tell you that it was all going to get better real soon. Sorry—it's probably not. But that's only because you love so much. If you hadn't, it wouldn't hurt. Just know—you're normal. It feels this way. I promise, it won't forever. I promise. In the meantime—we are all here, and we love you. Lean on us.

I get it … xxxxxoooo WHKP

Wendy P.

Written February 3, 2009, 8:27 p.m.

Hey, Chrissie,

Just thought I'd say hi. I noticed no one had written in the guestbook for a while. Remember, you can call or text me anytime. I'm always here for you if you need someone to talk to. Even though I may not have the "adult ears" needed, I'll always listen. No matter what, I love you, Chrissie.

Love,

Alyssa S.

Monday, February 16, 2009, 12:30 p.m., CST— Chrissie's Journal Entry

Aloha, everyone!

I am writing you from beautiful Kauai, Hawaii. I am here with my friend Terry. She has had the trip booked since last summer with her friend who was supposed to come with her, but that fell through at the last minute. So she asked me to go with her. Honestly, I didn't want to at first. I could not even conceive of taking a vacation without my precious hubby. But the fact that she and I went to Oahu together, exactly twenty years ago this month, coupled with the fact that I seriously needed a break from my life, spurred me to take a leap. So here I am. The temps are in the seventies during the day and sixties at night! Perfect, except for the fact that we have not had a whole lot of sun. I suspect I won't have too much of a tan when I return, if any. No matter—it is just nice to see the sun, greenery, and flowers. It is good for the soul.

I was hoping coming here would be a good way to escape Valentine's Day. It worked fine until later in the day when we were at the Olympic Cafe having an adult beverage and people kept talking about it. Whatever! Let's just say that I know Tommy was with me anyway, just not in the way he was supposed to be, another "first" out of the way again, whatever. This is just total BS no matter what way you look at it. I still do not believe this is really happening. He never leaves my mind. He is always there in everything I do. I know my heart has been broken, and I don't know when and if it will be put back together again. My guess is it will never be whole again. There will always be those parts of my heart that belong to him only. Ain't no one getting to them; they are spoken for, for eternity.

So before I start crying like a baby, I will sign off as I must get ready to do a little shopping. I will see you back on the Mainland! Stay warm … Aloha!

Much love to all,

Chrissie

Guest Book Entries

Written February 16, 2009, 1:40 p.m.

I want to say something, but nothing seems to sound right. Words don't express all the sorrow I have for you and Tom. I think about it often. I want to cry every time I see a picture of Tom, for the loss of someone so great, but more so for what you now have to go through. Life has really thrown some hard challenges your way, and I hate it. I hate how unfair all of this is for you. You mean so very much to me that I just always want happiness in your life. I'm so sorry that you're going through this. I love you, Chris.

Nicole Betlach

Written February 16, 2009, 2:21 p.m.

Chrissie,

I too feel so much sadness as tears are filling my eyes as I write. I'm not sure when or if it will get better; I have to believe it will. My heart goes out to you, Chrissie. Remember our saying, "Fake it till you make it." It has to get better.

Love ya,

Judy Vinje

Written February 16, 2009, 5:26 p.m.

Hi, Chrissie,

I'm happy to hear that you have been able to get out of Minnesota for a while, and what better place than Hawaii. I think of you often, wishing there was something I could do to help your sorrow. Just know you are cared about.

Dianne, Victor, Lydia, and Luisa

Thursday, March 5, 2009, 8:11 p.m., CST— Chrissie's Journal Entry

Well, it's here, the month I have been dreading, for months. I have a great deal of anxiety, and as of yet, untapped feelings. I am quite confident that by the end of this month, that statement will no longer be true. I spent most of last year pushing away all I should have been feeling but couldn't because I had decisions to make, a household to run, and a job to do so we wouldn't go broke. I am scared to death to let it all come. I don't know what I will be like on the seventeenth, eighteenth, and nineteenth. These are the days that mark our descent into hell and the days when life as we knew it was over, *never* to be the same again. Never again would I have a two-way conversation with my husband. Never again would I hear him call me one of the many nicknames he had for me. Never again would he call out to Bailey and Bud. Never again would he tease Drae and his friends by calling them "ladies" and "Sallys." Never again would he strategically place beer bottle caps in people's purses, diaper bags, and pockets without them knowing. Never again would he play with his nieces and nephews or fill up the bicycle tires of one or more of the neighborhood kids. Never again would he kid with his mom or his siblings. Never again would he joke with his in-laws and friends. Never again would he go to the farm, to Duluth for our anniversary, or on any more of his Bud annual trips. None of that was ever to be again. And here I am four and a half months after he left us for good, still not believing it and still wondering why. Why him? Not that I wish this upon anyone because I certainly don't.

You know what really sucks? Given the way everything played out from March 17, 2008, up to and including October 26, 2008 ... I/ we lost him twice. It wasn't enough that he passed away in the end. No, he had to suffer for seven effing months not being able to communicate effectively and relying on the decisions that were being made for him, at forty-six years old. What a bunch of bullshit. I sit around here at night, watching TV or whatever wondering when he is going to walk into the room and sit next to me so we can watch CSI or something together. I stand in the kitchen making dinner for one or two, not two or three, waiting for him to come home after taking Bailey to the dog park so we can eat dinner. I go to the grocery store and walk past the items I would buy for him, nearly bursting into tears because they are not on my list anymore. It's the little things, the day-to-day things that are most painful. Some days are okay; others are not.

I think it is safe to say that you will be hearing from me quite often this month. I meant to write this past weekend, but this was the first chance I've had where I wasn't too tired. I slept fine in Hawaii, but once I got home, I had a lot of trouble sleeping. I am pretty sure it is due to the impending month of March, the dreaded month of March, the very dark month of March. Since Tommy passed, whenever I thought of this month or heard it, my stomach would turn and I would push the thought out of my head. Now that it is here, I know I need to face the events of the last year. I should no longer push it away because it really isn't going away. It would come back at some point for me to face. I just need to brace myself and walk forward into the darkness and let it surround me. I need to feel it and deal with it. I don't know exactly how I will do that, and I know it is going to take one helluva long time. I know I will never get over losing my precious Tommy, and I also know that I feel very lucky to have had him as my husband, even if we were robbed of time after only eleven years together. Even knowing things like this still does not make the last year real to me. I can say these things, but I don't yet believe them. I hear at some point that will happen. I can't imagine that myself. Life goes on all around me, and on some levels I am participating and on others I am so not. Grief is an entity in and of itself and a very tricky and unforgiving one, I might add. Things can happen anywhere at any time; sometimes there is just no control, rhyme, or reason. So if I tend to ramble, please bear with me.

Last year, a week or two after our hell started, when Judy and I were in the hallway at the U, I told her, "I wish it was a year from now and we were past all this bullshit." Of course, I was thinking then that Tommy would be home and he would be fine. As we know, he is neither. So in retrospect, I take that back. I wish that year hadn't passed, and if it had, I wish that he would be okay and at home. Mick Jagger once said, "You can't always get what you want." No shit.

Thanks for listening. I will ramble again for you very soon.

Much love to all,

Chrissie

Guest Book Entries

Written March 6, 2009, 11:03 a.m.

Chrissie,

I love you so much. How can I help you ease your pain? I'll do whatever it takes. It will help both of us. I'll call you this weekend.

Judy Vinje

Written March 7, 2009, 9:19 p.m.

God damn, Chrissie! I am always so amazed by your strength and courage! You have lived hell on earth this past year, and amazingly enough, you always rise above it! Yes, you have had to push down your feelings of loss squared and all that goes with that. After all, soul mates don't come along every day. I think you have every right to feel the way you do— dread, grief, anger, despair, ughhh, and ouchhhh! Think of all you've had to shoulder this past year. It is a wonder you're not a puddle of mud!

That is what makes you so amazing! I think you know deep down, your strength comes in part, from Tom! It sucks he's not here with you in body, but his soul is eternal and he will live in you and around you forever.

I agree, you and Tom were robbed, and it's not fair he was taken from you so soon! I think it is safe to say you may never get over that harsh, bullshit reality. It is also safe to say that Tom would want you to live life to its fullest, even though it hurts like hell right now. It may take a while, but you deserve that, Chrissie. It hurts so badly right now because Tom was one of a kind. It has to be hard to think about what is ahead of you, when you planned your life as a couple. Damn it!

It is time to let it out. I'm sure you know you would have a new shoulder to lean on every day of the week, for months, hell, years to come, if you need to vent. Use 'em when you need 'em!

You are loved by many,

Trish Clancy

Written March 10, 2009, 8:38 p.m.

Ramble on, Chrissie. I'm listening. I love your entries.

Talk to you soon.

Andy Corbett

Tuesday, March 17, 2009, 7:20 p.m., CDT— Chrissie's Journal Entry

Hello,

I wrote an entry earlier today and then lost it. I *hate* when that happens. This is the first chance I have had to come back and write. I will do my best to reconstruct what I tried so hard to say this morning.

This week is proving to be as difficult as I anticipated. I have been filled with anxiety since Saturday, and I am quite certain that will not abate for a while. I keep replaying the events of one year ago like a movie in my head. It was on this day one year ago that Tom left Jaguar for what turned out to be the last time. He was never to return to work again, ever. On his way home he T-boned the school bus, and everything changed. I got a call from Tom's mom, Ginny, while I was checking out at Rainbow, telling me that Tom had been in an accident and he called her to pick him up. When she got there, he was nowhere to be found. While I was on the phone with her, she was asking onlookers if they had seen him. I finally told her that I was leaving the store and to meet me at the house. When we got there, he was standing in the alley talking to Larry. He had walked home from the scene of the accident as he had totaled his Mom's car and the cops didn't seem to think he needed a ride (something I wish I had checked into). When I saw him, I ran to him with tears in my eyes and hugged him because I was so happy that he was okay. Sure. God, I wish.

The rest of the night he was somewhat disorientated and confused. I had him come in the house and wash the blood off of his eye from where he hit the steering wheel. (He told me he hit the seat belt?) Then he tried eating the chili I made while he was lying down. After that he pretty much laid on the couch all night long. The next morning I woke him up every ten minutes and made him talk to me every time. (For a couple of weeks prior to that, he had been harder and harder to wake up in the morning.) After I got to work, I called him every hour or two to see if he was okay, and then I called his mom to do the same. When she called to tell me he wasn't himself, that's when I told my boss, Mark, that something was wrong with Tom and I had to leave.

God, I keep replaying everything wishing it had a different ending. In my dreams it does. The reality of it all is still so abstract. I cannot believe it has been a year since my husband was well. It is so wrong on every level, and while I know I am not the only one in the world who has lost their spouse, I cannot begin to even fathom life after such a loss. How do people do it and then remarry! It makes me want to burst into tears just thinking about it. As far as I am concerned I am still married. I could not even conceive of not wearing my wedding rings. Are you freaking kidding me! He just gave those to me. I look around the house and see things we received as gifts for our wedding, and I think, *But he's not here …* I see our wedding picture and think, *This year would've been our tenth anniversary, and we don't get to celebrate it. We never will.* Why does this shit happen? The pain is unbearable. I also see things around the house that we had talked about doing or projects he had started or plans we had and I realize, it's all gone. It all left with him. Our hopes, dreams, and plans. I can't frickin' take it. What did we do to deserve this? It took us so long to find each other, and after eleven years together, it was taken away. We got married later in life, with neither one of us having been married before. We just had each other. WTF?

I am going to stop this now. I've probably said too much. I plan on writing the next couple of days. If that does not happen, I would like to let you know that on Thursday night, the anniversary of his surgery, anyone who is interested can meet us at Whiskey Junction, where Tommy's benefit was held. I couldn't spend the next couple of nights alone, so I thought this was a good way for anyone who was feeling the need to connect to get together and share memories and togetherness. Please join us if are able.

Much love to all,

Chrissie

Guest Book Entries

Written March 17, 2009, 9:22 p.m.

I love you, sweet Chrissie. It seems like forever ago and only yesterday that we sat in that hospital thinking that this would all be over and better soon. What an f'd-up hand you've been dealt. We're still here, loving you.

Wendy P.

Written March 18, 2009, 7:42 a.m.

We love you, Chrissie. Both of us wish we could be there. You lost your love, your soul mate, your best friend, and everyone lost a very special person. I don't know if you ever "get over" that. You just keep moving along, trying your best to keep going. You are surrounded by people who love you and are there to help you. You are a strong woman; you have shown all of us how strong you are. I know I couldn't even begin to imagine dealing with all you have been through in the last year. You are doing what you need to do for you right now. Tommy would be proud of you. Take care of you.

Miss you and love you,

Lylis C. and Alyssa S.

Written March 18, 2009, 1:14 p.m.

Thinking of you and your daily struggle. You are trying, that's all you can do. Day by day is my best advice for you. Every day is a winding road. You probably will never get over it, but some day you will learn to deal with it in the best manner you can. Everybody falls one point in life, but the strongest learn to pick themselves back up again. You are doing a great job of that. The good news is you have support from friends and family. Keep your head up, and be strong.

Peace and God bless,

Rese Patton

Saturday, April 11, 2009, 12:49 p.m., CDT— Chrissie's Journal Entry

Good afternoon, everyone,

I know I said I would be journaling more in March, but it didn't happen. Sorry! I will try and do better. Today I am feeling somewhat discombobulated. There are a million things I need to do, and I am having trouble picking one. So I decided to write, hoping that would help me move forward with the day. I find myself just sitting here staring while my mind is off God knows where. That being said, I will do my best to say what I need to say without rambling aimlessly, which I feel like I'm doing right now …

Since March has now come and gone (thank God, I had some rough days there), I find myself, every day, going back in my mind remembering what was happening last year at this time. Some of it is too painful to dwell on. The things that are most painful to me are the things that Tommy went through. The visual of him starting to cry when he woke up from his surgery; my God, it gets me every time. (The ignorant time when we thought all would be okay despite what was going on.) Then there was the look on his face when he signed the power-of-attorney, watching him in physical therapy struggle to just throw a fricking ball. Walking in to the TCU when he was sitting next to the nurse's station in the chair they had to lift him into. I know they were trying to give him a change of scenery, but the last thing he would ever want to do is be on display like that. It broke my heart to see my baby sitting there when I walked in. Then there is the damn lift. I can't believe I had to watch my husband being lifted out of bed and into a chair and vice versa. Of course, there is also the radiation. They would take him away and radiate his head, and I couldn't be with him. That's another thing that gets me. There were things that I could not be there for. I had to leave him alone sometimes. It tears me apart inside, especially when I had to leave him at Providence Place. I think of the night at PP when I was wheeling him around in the chair and he kept grabbing the side and pulling himself forward, in pain. I thought he was trying to stretch out, but it was the blood clots that were moving. I didn't know it until the next afternoon when I walked in and saw he was in distress and they were in the room with him and didn't see it! The worst part of *all* of this is that *he couldn't tell us what was going on*! How painful was that for him! It was unbearable to me then and now … I don't know if I can ever get over that. I did the best that I could to know what he needed; I just hope that I got it right most of the time. I hope he can tell me some day that I did a good job. It haunts me to think that there may have been some instances that I could have done better.

CHRISSIE BETLACH VINJE

I love and miss him so effin' much that I know sometimes when these thoughts come up I push them away because I don't want to remember that bullshit! But I also know that I have to. I couldn't deal with my feelings then. I have to do it now and I have to do it in this way, but a person can only take so much at once. I think that may be why I chose to write today. It is helping me work through some of this. If you think that I don't sit here and cry my eyes out as I write, you would be wrong. I've taken many breaks during this dissertation. My animals come over and check me out to make sure that I'm okay. God bless 'em!

I am a little (or a lot) indifferent to Easter this year. I would rather not deal with it at all but, I will go through the motions. I am just at a loss when I think about it. It is the strangest feeling. Maybe that stems from the fact that I spent last Easter in the ICU and the ICU waiting room. God, I don't miss that *at* all. We pretty much took that place over when we were there. I sometimes felt bad for the other people. Whatever, I will get past this holiday like I will all the other ones ahead. One thing that keeps popping into my head is that it has now been over a year since my honey was walking through this house, taking his dog for walks (twice a day ... he *never* missed a day, and he was very proud of that!), calling me Schnicks (short for Snicker-doodle), living his life. It totally sucks, and it is totally wrong. There is not a goddamn thing I can do to change it, but God knows I did try. Okay I know I am totally rambling. Time to let you off the hook ...

If you didn't know, the CaringBridge was recently upgraded. One of the enhancements to the CaringBridge over the last few weeks was a larger space for pictures. From twelve pictures to fifty-one, sweet! I have added some new pictures, and I intend to add more at some point so, keep checking.

Have a safe and happy Easter!

Much love to all,

Chrissie

Guest Book Entries

Written April 11, 2009, 2:14 p.m.

Despite all the acclimations you have received regarding how ferociously you fought for Tom and the truly astounding care and love you have given him (and continue to), I know you struggle with the thought you could have done more or done it better. I know that Tom will tell you how grateful he was to have the love of his life turn out to be such a warrior for him when he needed you most. Perhaps there were things that could have been done differently or signals that may have been missed, but I know in my gut and in my heart that Tom would never fault nor blame you for it. He above anyone who bore witness to or read about your crusade for him understands the dedication and love you showered upon him. He is probably more proud and in awe of you than anyone else ever could be.

I love you!

Beth Timm

Written April 11, 2009, 4:52 p.m.

Hi, Chrissie,

We hope you'll be able to enjoy some happy memories of Tom on Easter. Our thoughts and prayers are still with you.

Dianne, Victor, Lydia, and Luisa

Sunday, April 12, 2009, 10:02 p.m., CDT—Chrissie's Journal Entry

Happy Easter, honey,

Love you long time!

Love,

Your baby

Sunday, April 12, 2009, 10:04 p.m., CDT—Chrissie's Journal Entry

What can I tell you? He is on my mind 24–7 …

Tuesday, April 14, 2009, 10:24 p.m., CDT—Chrissie's Journal Entry

Today I had to purchase a headstone for my husband. Are you fricking kidding me! I was just trying to keep it together during the whole process. How messed up is this!

I was anxious all day with heart palpitations growing more frequent as the time came for me to leave and then pretty much constant on my way to the monument place. I can't even believe that was something I had to do. It is surreal.

I did not have the opportunity to get a stone sooner as winter came on pretty quickly after Tommy was buried. I don't know that was something I could have done any sooner than I did. I am still not entirely sure I was ready to do it today. I have only been to the cemetery once since his funeral, and it was not a good scene. However, I will be going back now that the snow has gone. I want to make sure everything is as it should be at the cemetery; even though things are *not* as they should be … I need to deal with the reality.

Fake it till you make it.

Much love to all,

Chrissie

Guest Book Entries

Written April 15, 2009, 7:45 a.m.

Chrissie,

OMG, I hope someone went with you! You're right, it is surreal, but getting the headstone slams it home really hard! My heart is aching for you, for me, for everyone who knew Tom. I too have been to the cemetery, and like you, it wasn't pretty. I can't believe how much it still hurts. There are a couple of quotes I try to remember when I'm hurting. The first is, "The will of God will never take you where the grace of God will not protect you" and the other one is, "Pain is inevitable; suffering is optional." But right now neither one seems to be helping.

Fake it till you make it!

Love ya!

Judy Vinje

Written April 16, 2009, 9:00 a.m.

Hang in there, Chrissie! Fake it 'til you make it is a good motto …

Best wishes,

Dianne

Friday, May 1, 2009, 8:37 p.m., CDT—
Chrissie's Journal Entry

Greetings,

My heart has been heavy the last few days, and as I make my way through each day, I think I have come to figure out why. I am here at home on Friday night, alone. Usually on Friday nights, if we had nothing else going on, we would go out to dinner after Tommy went to the pupper park with Bailey. As I was out in the alley tonight, throwing the ball for Bailey, I was looking around at the house, the yard, the tree that we planted the year we got married, and all the while it was painfully apparent that, *he wasn't here*! He is just not here. How can that be? There are all the things we did. Places we went. Plans we made. The life we built together. All of that is still here, and he is not. As long as I live, I will never understand it. There was so much happening this week, and I just wanted to talk to him. I wanted to call him at work or on his cell phone. I miss that so much. I miss him calling me. I miss being with him … I miss *us*. I don't want to be *me*, I want *us*.

I think the reason for my funk is due to the fact that we are coming out of the dark winter and it's starting to be nice outside and I look around wondering where he is, when is he coming home? Why did our lives go so terribly wrong? Why do I have to feel this pain? It is spring; everything will be new again … Well, not everything. This is my first spring without him, for good. Last spring he was still here, and we were full of hope and the prayer of a miracle. Now this spring, I have to approve a proof of his fucking headstone. What kind of bullshit is that! Life and the promise of a new year is going on all around me, and while I can acknowledge that and appreciate that to a certain degree, there is a deep, cavernous void that can never be filled, for the love of my life has been taken from me. All year long will be the reminders that this September would have been our tenth wedding anniversary. I think about it almost daily. I watched some of our wedding video a couple of weeks ago, and then came the words ... *until death parts us*. I froze. My God, really? You don't really think twice about those words as you say them because you think that scenario is a *looooooooooong* way off. You never think you have to have your husband's funeral in the same church you were married in just nine years earlier! God, sometimes I wish it had been me because then I wouldn't have to feel this, but then, he would have to be the one grieving and I wouldn't want that either. We were robbed, totally and completely.

You know, sometimes after I write like this, I feel like maybe I said too much. Maybe, I put too much out there. There are times when it feels like the morning after you had a little too much to drink and you are embarrassed about something you did or said. It's like that. It's like an emotional drunk, if you will. It is very cathartic, and hopefully, someday, a little healing. It is a good form of therapy, to be sure. With that in mind, I think my hour is up now. (And, I'm spent ...) I don't want to be charged extra by going into the next hour.

As always, thank you for listening.

Much love to all,

Chrissie

Guest Book Entries

Written May 1, 2009, 9:55 p.m.

Hey, Chrissie,

You are always in my thoughts. You do not worry about what others think … If it helps you to put your thoughts and feelings out on the table, you go for it.

My dad is told us on Thursday that it's been fifty days since Mom died. He is just like you. You feel lost and don't know where you belong yet … but you will get to a point where Tom will come in your dreams and hold your hand or give you a sign that even though he is not here alive on earth, he will always be with you in spirit. He will let you know he will be waiting for you when it is your time. Let yourself smile once in a while just thinking about the good times. Even though memories are painful, they will also heal to remember all the good you had with him … Let the music make you smile even though your tears come.

I am going to try and give you a call soon.

Luv ya,

Julie S.

Sunday, July 5, 2009, 12:50 p.m., CDT—
Chrissie's Journal Entry

Hello, all,

In the couple of months since I have written, many memories and experiences have come to the forefront. In May, as I had to endure my first birthday without my honey in twelve years, I was forced to remember our time at the TCU and then on to Providence Place. Then, of course, in June, there was our hasty exit from PP to Riverside Hospital when his blood clots moved. After two weeks in the hospital, it was back to PP … but not for long.

As I sit here now, at the end of the Fourth of July weekend, what keeps flooding my thoughts is the fact that we are entering into the final phase of Tommy's life. *God* does it suck to say things like that! It will be one year ago on Wednesday that Tommy came home. I can't fathom that it has been a year already. I also can't fathom that he is really gone. It all still seems so surreal. I frequently ask myself, *Did this really happen … to him … to us?* All I have to do is look around the house to know that it did. I am aware every moment. The feeling never leaves me, but my brain is having a hard time wrapping itself around the idea that he is never coming back. How could that be real? What happened to the idea that this stuff happens to other people, not me, not us? It's a bunch of bullshit.

Since I wrote last, there have been two memorial services. The first one was in May. That was orchestrated by Fairview Hospice, and it was located in a really beautiful setting in Centennial Park amphitheater. There were candles in the middle of the stage while they read off the names of our loved ones who had passed. The second was just last Monday at Fairview Riverside Hospital's chapel. That was nice. This service was for the people who died at Fairview Hospitals between September 1, 2008, and December 31, 2008. You were asked to bring a picture, a memento, and a candle to light. You also were able to say a few words about your loved one. Oh, I talked big before the ceremony saying that I was going to be the one to light the candle and say a few words. Right, not so much. I couldn't do it. I was having a hard time keeping it together just sitting there. Poor Gary, we put him on the spot and asked him to fill in for me. He did a fine job despite the last-minute pressure. Love ya, Gar!

The mood that came over me while at the service on Monday night would follow me the rest of the week. Honestly, I don't know that it is completely gone yet. (Okay, it's not.) Something happened on Wednesday that seriously threw me for a loop. It is something so basic and it was so unexpected, but it shouldn't have been. These are the things that come slamming home that he is really gone. I went to the doctor on Wednesday morning, the first time since he passed, and while I was checking in, the receptionist shows me the computer screen to ask if my address and phone numbers are correct ... blah, blah, blah. Then she forwards to the next screen and asks me if my emergency contact info is correct. There, of course, is the contact name ... Thomas L. Vinje. The tears were immediate and nonstop. I said, "He passed" through my tears in the lobby of the Park Nicollet. As I tried to finish writing my check and wipe my tears, I said to her, "There are just some things you forget about." She was very respectful and nice and asked me if I wanted to think about it. I was able to compose myself for a few minutes until they brought me back to the room. After the usual blood pressure, etc., I waited for my doctor to come in, and the waterworks started again; then came the knock on the door. My doctor asked if I was okay ... clearly, that was not the case. Thus began my day of being weepy at the drop of a hat. It also solidified the fact that I need a couple of weeks off to process. I really haven't *stopped* since Tom got sick. After he passed, I threw myself into one thing and then another. I have many things that I have been meaning to do, and as we know when you are working and trying to keep everything on track, you really don't stop and take the time you need to take some very necessary steps ... no matter what they are. Now is the time for me to stop and read the grieving pamphlets, to attempt (once again) to read the books people have given me. It is time to start taking care of myself again. Even though I don't really have the willpower at the moment, it is something I want to do. Maybe the time off will get me on track with many things I've been needing to do and are so easy to put off when you can explain it away on a daily basis. I am totally exhausted, emotionally and physically. I have never been in this place before. I need to slow down and deal with things. It sounds simple enough. We will see. I don't like being in this limbo, if you will. My grieving will be forever, but it shouldn't mean that I go down with it … and I won't. You know, even as I say that, I don't completely believe me.

In the last month (maybe even since Tommy's headstone went in … there's a thought), I have been missing him so intensely. I never knew you could miss anyone like that. It is extremely painful. All it takes is looking at a picture, a song on the radio, or a thought of him. The party is over. A good share of the time I melt down in the car, while I am driving home, usually. These emotions are so intense and so raw that you barely know how to get them all out. I have said it before, and I will say it until the day I die—I know how a surviving spouse dies of a broken heart. I get it. There are days I wish I had gone instead so I wouldn't have to feel this intense pain. Don't get me wrong—I would never hurt myself, but you just want out of the pain so badly that you would think of any way, some way, to stop it. You can totally understand why an older couple, who have been together forever, would not survive that intense pain and heartbreak. It is devastating.

I am quite certain that you will be hearing from me more regularly in the coming months. I have things that need to be worked out, and if you guys don't mind backing up my primary shrink, I am sure she would be grateful for the help!

Much love to all,

Chrissie

Guest Book Entries

Written July 5, 2009, 8:13 p.m.

I'm glad you've finally gotten to the point of realizing that you still matter here. You are correct—you haven't stopped. It's time. Be good to yourself. Feel. Rest.

We're all still here … and we love you.

XXXXOOOO

WHKP

Wendy P.

Written July 6, 2009, 9:18 a.m.

Hi, Chrissie,

I just want to send you a *huge* hug and let you know you have a friend across the street. Anything I can help out with, just yell!

Thanks for celebrating the big girl's birthday yesterday. It was a good time, watching all the dogs enjoy the party! Whitney was pooped, draggin' her tail!

With the rain today, I bet Bailey's treat will melt away!

See you soon!

Candace McCown

Written July 6, 2009, 10:51 a.m.

Hi, Chrissie,

You continue to be in our thoughts and prayers. Stormer and I were just talking about the hand you were dealt with all this, and it stinks. I can't imagine the hurt you are going through. I hope in some small way it helps you to know how much we care about you and how much we love you. We will continue to pray for you through this healing process. We are only a phone call away if you need anything.

Lots of love,

Colleen and Stormer

Written July 14, 2009, 9:04 p.m.

I just read your last entry, and I have no words to tell you how sorry I am for your loss. I know you will find the way through your pain to find the peace and love you desire. Just remember, you have friends that will be there for you in your grief. Your plan to slow down and reconnect to yourself is a good start. Thinking of you and sending good energy your way!

Sue Ellen Riese

Thursday, July 30, 2009, 10:04 p.m., CDT— Chrissie's Journal Entry

Greetings, all,

I am nearing the end of the two weeks I took off from work to process my life (among other things). As usual, the time went by way too fast. I have feared that from the beginning. Since the beginning I have been very mindful of each day, taking inventory on what I wanted to do versus what I had done. It was actually overwhelming most of the time just thinking of all the things I wanted to do with these two weeks. As of this moment, while I have done a few things that were important to me, there are still a few left undone.

I have also figured out a couple of things these last two weeks. The first one is the realization that I am in a depression. Go figure. A chat with my therapist confirmed that one. It makes sense now that I know it. It makes me feel better knowing that there is a reason for my actions, or lack thereof. There is a reason that I don't care a whole helluva lot about anything and that I don't get too excited about anything, even my time off. Everything just seems blah, for lack of a better term; everything, that is, except for my grief. There is a pattern emerging, and it is one I do not like. I know it is a temporary phase, but there is really nothing I can do to stop it, and I don't think I should. It has to come out somehow, and if this is how it is going to be, I have to let it happen and push through it. I have noticed that something small will set me off. I just get pissed at the stupidest thing, spouting off and saying shit I don't normally say. Then it snowballs until I melt down. I am thinking that this is the anger part of my grief rearing its ugly head. Whichever way you look at it, it is behavior I do not usually exhibit, and it is uncomfortable for me.

I decided it was time for me to read a book or two on the grief process. I think I might be able to read the books I could not read in February on the plane to and from Hawaii, but I did pick up a new one last week. The name of it is *Widow to Widow*. Hmm, there's a concept. I have a hard time relating that term to myself although; I did say it last weekend to someone, and it took me by surprise. I am only a few chapters into this book, and already I can relate. It is startling the things I have read and already experienced as well as the thoughts that some of these women have that I have had. It does make me think that group therapy with other widows/widowers may not be such a bad idea. When I was approached about going to group therapy before, I thought, *I don't want to hear about anyone else's problems; I've got my own shit to deal with.* Well, guess what? They mention that exact feeling in the book. Un-frickin-canny.

I must say that I really do wish I had another couple of weeks to get further into some of the things I have started, but maybe I can do that a little later. Sitting home does wonders for the soul, but it does not pay the bills, God knows. I feel a little better that I have taken some time to do things that I was putting off. It all has to come together to get me through this depression because I am certainly not going to take antidepressants. That would just numb my emotions and slow down the process. The process needs to happen, and I don't want to compound my problems by adding drugs to the mix. That would really mess me up. I've got enough problems, dontcha know.

In closing, I am going to recall my favorite Kasey Kasem quote: "Keep your feet on the ground and keep reaching for the stars."

I'm trying man, I'm trying.

Much love to all,

Chrissie

Guest Book Entries

Written July 31, 2009, 7:19 a.m.

Only because I know and I love you …

WHKP

Wendy P.

Sunday, August 9, 2009, 11:52 a.m., CDT— Chrissie's Journal Entry

Greetings, everyone,

I am extremely upset because I just finished writing an entry, and I lost it all. It's hard enough writing it the first time, and now I have to try to recreate it. I just want to hit a "back" button and have it all be there, but the CaringBridge does not work that way, so here it goes.

Today would have been Tommy's forty-seventh birthday. I just went back and reread what I wrote last year. That is the first time I have done that, by the way. I am not able to read much of what I wrote previously.

Last year, at this time Tommy was in the hospital following the seizure he had on August 6, 2008. I remember it because August 6 was my dad's birthday, so I am very mindful of what was going on a year ago. Ginny called me at work so hysterical I could not understand what she was saying, and then Tony got on the phone to tell me that Tom was having a seizure. I rushed home to one of the most painful memories ever, Tommy having a seizure. I can't get it out of my mind, still. As we know, he went into the hospital and they pumped him full of fluids, and he swelled up so much, he couldn't move very well. He never completely lost all of it—another painful memory.

On Tommy's birthday last year, they pulled the vent tube out of him by my "intense insistence," shall we say. It should have never been put in to begin with. Also, on Tommy's birthday last year, I wrote my wish for this year. The wish was for us to be together celebrating his birthday while he was recovering and being grateful that he was alive and we were together. Life is cruel as hell.

I was talking to him out loud earlier, telling him, "Happy birthday." Talking out loud to him is very hard to do. I can barely keep it together most times, probably because he is not answering.

I have this huge picture of Tommy that Matt S. had made for his funeral. It is one of my favorite pictures of him. It captures the very essence of Tommy. The look on his face, that smile I miss *so very much*, and what makes it even more special is the fact that it was taken on our wedding day. I haven't had the picture out very much because it was just too hard. Then, a couple of weeks ago, my great-niece, Alexis (she is five years old), insisted that I put the picture out. I put it on the back of the couch and took her picture sitting next to it. She told me that I should hang the picture in my bedroom so I could say good-night to him every night and so that Bailey and Bud (the dog and the cat) could go in to see him whenever they want. Since the picture has been there, I find myself talking to him a little bit or saying, "Hi, honey" as I walk by him, as if he were here. In some ways it is more comforting now than it was in the beginning. I just love seeing his face. *God* I miss him.

Today, on Tommy's birthday, I am celebrating him by having a little par-tay at Whiskey Junction. It sounds like there will be quite a few people there already, and any and all are invited to join us. We will all be together celebrating his life, remembering him, and having a good time doing it. I can't think of a better way to wish him happy birthday. We probably would have gone there anyway ... So, feel free to join us if you can. We would love to see you.

Happy birthday, my love!

Much love to all,

Chrissie

Friday, August 28, 2009, 8:19 p.m., CDT—
Chrissie's Journal Entry

Hello, everyone,

Not really sure what to write except that I am going to the fair tomorrow. I am not sure how that will go as Tommy and I went twice every year. We had our own routine, and it will be difficult to be there without him for the first time in twelve years. Last year Tony offered to stay at the house with Tommy so I could go, but I could not fathom going to the fair while he was bedridden in our living room. No interest in doing that *at* all. This year, I have to go; we have tickets to Kid Rock and Lynyrd Skynyrd. I can handle that, but what will be difficult is the stop I have to make at the international bazaar …

I don't know if anyone ever knew or noticed, but you know those little black leather braided bracelets you can buy at fairs everywhere? Long before I met Tom, I always wore one with the spoon bracelet I wear on my right wrist. And long before he met me, he always wore one on his right wrist with some other type of bracelet. So when we went to the fair together for the first time, he took me to one of the jewelry shops run by a sweet little Mexican woman and her daughters. She would make the bracelets and bring them to the fair. (She only does two fairs a year, the Minnesota fair and the California fair.) When we got to the shop, it was apparent that she recognized Tom from previous years and promptly showed him where the leather bracelets were. We would then proceed to buy three or four for each one of us to get us through until the next year when we could buy more. I remember one year she forgot to bring them … *that* did not happen again! Even though she went for a few years without displaying them for sale, whenever we showed up, she would pull them out and let us buy what we wanted. Tom would always say, "Hello, Senorita!" (The mother does not speak much English, but her daughters do.) One year the mother did not make it to the fair due to illness and Tom was really worried about her but, she was there the next year and all was fine. Now, assuming all is well with her and she is there, I will be going to her booth to tell her of Tom's illness and his passing. I plan on bringing a picture because I know she will remember him. I have been thinking about this since last year at this time. I hope they are there, I hope they remember, and I hope they have the bracelets. I just have a couple of mine left and a few of Tommy's. (You know I'll have those forever!) The only thing now is that I have to buy double for me because along with my spoon bracelet, I am wearing two leather ones, one for me and one for my honey. It only seems right.

Another thing I would like to mention is that Friday, September 18, would have been our tenth anniversary. It is killing me. Every time I think about it, I burst into tears. Ten years ago right now, we were going balls to the wall in preparation for our wedding, and now, ten years later, he is gone. It tears me apart in so many ways, I can't even tell you. I wasn't supposed to spend our tenth anniversary alone—not in my mind and I am sure, not in his.

Everyone, please take care. You just never know.

Much love to all,

Chrissie

Thursday, September 17, 2009, 8:33 p.m., CDT— Chrissie's Journal Entry

Okay. It is the eve of what would have been our tenth anniversary. I can't believe I had to write that effing sentence. For the last month, at least, I have been thinking back ten years ago, remembering what was happening at that time. Now, I sit here at the damn computer struggling to get out what is going on inside me. It is indescribable pain. All this week I have had this wall up inside of me shielding me from tomorrow—shielding me from the pain and heartbreak that is awaiting me on the other side of that wall. Why? Why did this have to happen? We were just two people who finally found each other, later in life. We just had us. We weren't hurting anyone. We were just ordinary people who loved each other living our lives together. I can't fathom that ten years ago we had the best day of our lives, and now, I have to go through this day without him. I am alone, again.

I am having extreme difficulty in letting him go. My therapist says there has been no movement. I can't. I can't. I don't want to let him go. Why do I have to? He should be here! Of course my head knows the reality, but my heart is holding on for dear life—my life, my life now, not ours. God dammit! Do I really have to do this? I hate it, I hate it, I hate it. My heart hurts so fucking bad. How does anyone get through this? How do you come out on the other side? You see it everywhere, people moving on, transcending their loss. I don't know how. I don't get it. Not now. Not tonight, definitely not tomorrow.

Earlier today I was thinking how much I missed our daily phone calls to each other while we were at work, just talking about dinner or whatever. I miss his laugh (who doesn't?), his nicknames for me, his hugs, and our life; being together, being us. I miss *us*. I miss *him*.

No matter how much I miss him, no matter how utterly shitty I feel on any given day that he is not here, I know that there are other people out there feeling the same way about their loss. The problem that I am having is that for me, it is all about me right now. I don't like being like that. I am not normally like that. But dammit, I lost my husband, the love of my life! I am just trying to figure out how to be. Trying to figure out how to get through each day and maintain some of who I am (or was). There have been some not-so-pretty traits coming out the last few months or so, and I pray to God that they are temporary.

I must sound like a raving lunatic. I know I am all over the board, and while I am in the throes of despair, I know that I will come out on the other side of this like I have seen other people do. I just don't know when. I know I don't have to have a timeline. Everything happens as it should, and it takes as long as it should. Part of me wants to hurry it up, and the other part doesn't want to let go. WTF? People say time heals all. I don't think *heals* is the correct word in this situation. Maybe *helps* would be a better word. I will never "get over" Tommy. I will grieve him until the day that I die. I know that all these feelings will lessen with time, but even as I say that, my eyes well with tears thinking about our wedding day. It is almost here, the day I have been dreading for months. It would have been perfect too. Our anniversary on a Friday, the weather has been beautiful, *and* I know we would have left tonight, Thursday night, to head up to Duluth for the weekend as we did every year. On Saturday he would have participated in the North Shore Inline Marathon, as he had several times. Every time I met him at that finish line, I would burst into tears (I don't know if he ever knew that) because I was so proud of him. I couldn't even yell because I couldn't speak. Yes, it would have been an awesome long weekend in Duluth for our tenth anniversary. It will be a long-ass time before I am able to go back there. It's funny because it is September, and it just feels like "Duluth time" to me. It's that time of year—our time of year. Ten years ago on our wedding day, it was as gorgeous as this last week has been, and then the week after, it went right in the tank. Yep, it would've been an anniversary to remember. Now I will remember it for different reasons. It is such total bullshit.

I have been contemplating if I should watch our wedding video or not. On the one hand it seems like that could be worst thing I could do … or would it? I don't know. People have been asking me what I am going to do. I have been so undecided that I haven't made any firm plans. *Que sera sera*, you know; whatever will be, will be. Whatever.

Okay, I am totally rambling now. I will let you off the hook. Maybe some of the other things I have to say or write about can be done in the private online journals I have started. That just might happen this weekend.

Much love to all,

Chrissie

Guest Book Entries

Written September 17, 2009, 9:50 p.m.

Chrissie,

Hugs, hugs, hugs, hugs, hugs, hugs, hugs.

Just know that celebrating your wedding day even with him in spirit is a good thing. It was a very special day for both you!

Never run away from all the good memories. They will at some point make you smile more than cry.

It's good to keep that special day with him in it however you choose to celebrate it.

Well, I will keep you in my thoughts tomorrow!

More *hugs*,

Julie S.

Written September 18, 2009, 8:38 a.m.

We are here for you in any way you need us to be.

We love you.

Nic and Lex.

Written September 18, 2009, 10:10 a.m.

I know.

I love you.

Wendy P.

Written September 18, 2009, 5:49 p.m.

You have the right to be angry, Chrissie. It is not fair for anybody to go through what you have and are going through. Always hang on to the memories, but remember that isn't all you have. Tom's spirit will always be with you. Try your best to not think about where you have to go but how far you have come. One day there will be some sign that comes your way to remind you that you will be all right and Tom is all right.

Please don't let or allow some things that could be thrown your way to cloud your vision and memories. What is seen is temporary, and what is unseen is eternal. Keep doing what you're doing, the right things in life—sharing your thoughts and memories, occupying your time, being around friends and family, simply talking about it to others, a lot of times tell your story to people you don't even know. Maybe some people won't respond because they don't know how to respond. But then, listen and understand your hurts and feelings. Keep writing here and in your journals. This is very important so you can look back to see how far you have come. Be the nice person that you are, and one of the most important things is taking one day at a time. There will be days when you seem like you have taken two steps backward, and there will be the better days you will feel and see you have taken two steps forward, but every day is a new day forward ...

My thoughts and prayers are out for you

Your friend,

Rese Patton

Written September 21, 2009, 3:54 p.m.

Chrissie,

I wish there was something I could do or say to help you through this horrific time in your life. No one should have to go through it. I am so sorry for all your pain and your loss.

With best wishes,

Dianne

Monday, October 19, 2009, 8:23 p.m., CDT—Chrissie's Journal Entry

Hello, everyone,

One week from today is the first anniversary of Tommy's death. I *so* hate that word. I usually say "passing," but I figured I need to face the reality of what's in front of me. I have been fighting it for the last year. It will only make it more difficult to move forward if I keep it up. I am so conflicted inside with all of that, and it appears to be a pattern that I am stuck in.

A couple of weeks ago I was talking to Paula (my therapist) about the fact that there was *no way* at this point in time that I could go back and read any of my earlier CaringBridge entries. I didn't think I would be able to get through them without feeling intense pain. She then told me that was exactly what I needed to do. She was thinking that it would help me process all that happened as I really didn't have time to do that last year. So, I printed it all off two weeks ago and began reading last Friday night. I have gotten through a little over one-third of the 151 pages, and I must say that it has not been as painful as I had anticipated. As a matter of fact, I have found myself chuckling about the little stunts he would pull and smiling at some of the things he said, when he was able. I have been so wrapped up in the fact that any of it happened at all that I had buried away some of the comic relief moments that Tommy gave us. We will have to see what the subsequent pages bring. I will plow through them because I think it is a good idea to get through it all before next Monday hits.

I am in the process of trying to find a young widow/widower group to go to. I was told about a group in the Allina Hospice system, and I am about to contact the Fairview Hospice system to see if they have such a group. I really think now that going to a group will be beneficial as most of the people I see from day to day have no clue what I am going through, and it is time to be around people who get it. The whole experience of Tommy's illness and death is all-consuming. I can barely think about anything else (for too long). But what I think about most is how much I miss *him* and how much I miss *us*. My head knows he is gone, and my heart doesn't want to know. Therein lies the problem.

I cannot believe it has almost been a year. Where did the time go? What did I do? Where is he? What the hell? WTF? Indeed. That was a little snapshot inside my head; barely the tip of the iceberg.

I'm sure you'll hear from me again real soon. Until then,

Much love to all,

Chrissie

Guest Book Entries

Written October 19, 2009, 9:51 p.m.

WTF, indeed. You know how I feel about your decision ... Wishing peace for you ...

I love you.

WHKP

Wendy P.

Sunday, October 25, 2009, 10:16 p.m., CDT— Chrissie's Journal Entry

Okay ...

It is the eve of *my* honey's death a year ago. I stopped at the cemetery today and I noticed that his headstone had been moved. *Excuse me*! I will be calling the cemetery tomorrow morning. Why TF would it be moved? I am still not used to having to go there. Whatever. I buried my husband on Halloween last year (not intentional), but regardless, it is weird having to get through the day with that looming ... I couldn't care less about Halloween this year and probably next year as well. If I am home, I will not be passing out candy and stuff. I am just not there ...

Anyway, I just had a moment. I think I will sign off. Talk to you soon ...

Much love to all,

Chrissie

Monday, October 26, 2009, 8:04 a.m., CDT—
Chrissie's Journal Entry

Hello,

One year ago this very minute Tommy's life was ending. I feel as if I am on the verge of a panic attack. At about 8:20 a.m. last year, Ginny was calling for me telling me that Tommy was not breathing. I remember it like it was yesterday. I bolted out of bed to find my love not breathing and looking ashen. We called 911 and they got his heart going enough to bring him to the hospital, but I knew he was already gone. His soul had left his broken body, as well it should have.

I have been replaying the events of that morning over and over, not believing it has been one year. One year since we saw him alive but one year and seven months since we found out his diagnosis, when our lives were forever changed. Where does the time go? When you think of time in such broad terms, it kind of makes everything seem so insignificant. But it really isn't. Time marches on, and so does everyone and everything else. It is mind-blowing. I have heard that the second year of grieving is really when it all comes slamming home because you spend the first year just numb. We will see how that all plays out.

I have contemplated stopping my entries on the Bridge after the first year. I wrestle with whether or not people still want to read about what I have going on. I sometimes think it is egotistical of me to think that people still want to read about me instead of Tommy. I don't know, while I think I have other writing to do, I still may pop in an entry here and there. We will see how that plays out as well …

For now, we are at the moment where my beautiful husband moved on in his journey. While I know his actual time of death was around 12:12 p.m. at the hospital, I know he left this world right here, in our house, at the very place I am sitting writing to you now at about this time. They just kept his body going until I told them to stop because I knew he was already gone ...

Godspeed, my love. I will love you and miss you forever.

Your baby,

Chrissie

Guest Book Entries

Written October 26, 2009, 6:35 a.m.

Just want to tell you ...

Love you, Chrissie!

Julie S.

Written October 26, 2009, 8:49 a.m.

You are in my thoughts, and I have my arms wrapped around you on this difficult day. I love you, Chrissie.

Lisa Berry

Written October 26, 2009, 9:06 a.m.

My thoughts are with you, Chris, on this day. Sending you a hug. Love ya ...

Roxie Chudy

Written October 26, 2009, 9:12 a.m.

Keep those journals coming, sista! I never get tired of your voice.

Kira Martin

Written October 26, 2009, 9:15 a.m.

Chrissie,

Hard to believe it has been a year. So fast, yet Tom is very much still with us all!

I am there for you to help in any way.

Candace McCown

Written October 26, 2009, 9:32 a.m.

Hello Chrissie,

Just want to let you know that this is painful. I recently loss my father. I was told that through the writing (your creativity), you restore your heart, and that by sharing with your friends this pain it opens all of us to the love of the universe. I always think this sounds corny, but it does make us more loving to one another. My thoughts are with you today.

Sue Ellen Riese

Written October 26, 2009, 7:16 p.m.

Hi, Chrissie,

You're so right how time just flies by when experiencing trauma like you have experienced. Losing Tommy has got to be the hardest thing you'll ever have to experience in life, that's for sure; I can't even imagine losing a spouse, whom you love so dear. Tommy was absolutely a good man without any doubt! That love thing is certainly tricky. You've finally found it, got it right, and a decade becomes a minute and year of memories becomes a second while living in the moment. Things certainly change when we lose a loved one. Our lives seem to stop, and the rest of the world seems to spin even faster. It's almost as though you've ridden the Tilt-o-Whirl all day long and then got off, numbingly nauseous, asking yourself why! Well that inner answer is your blessed truth in experiencing life with a fun-loving person who cared for you as much as others in your lives. You found joy in life with Tommy, and one day without forgetting the joy with him, you'll soon enjoy your own life again among the people you have been blessed with by your joining. Well you found a fun-loving, dear lifelong friend, and you are forever blessed. My thoughts and friendship are with you, and I hope that you'll continue to live your life as if you will never lose again. In memory of Tommy, and lots of love for you, Chrissie. Love, Shane.

Shane Lines

Written October 28, 2009, 7:44 p.m.

Chrissie,

Keep writing. We care!

Judy Vinje

Saturday, October 31, 2009, 6:05 p.m., CDT— Chrissie's Journal Entry

Today is the first anniversary of Tommy's funeral, as we already know. I bought a long-stem rose to bring to the cemetery with me, and as I was pulling up I saw a quart bottle of Bud Light next to his headstone. It was frickin awesome! I needed that. I looked to see if the seal was broken to see if the person who left the Bud had taken a drink, and indeed he had. I also wondered if he had poured a little for Tommy. As I found out later … indeed he had! Nice! And, as I found out when I got home, the person who left the Bud Light was our friend Larry. I had a feeling he was the one. I love it, and I'm sure Tommy did too!

Going to the cemetery was a little harder than I expected today as I have been there several times this past year, but today was different. The minute I got out of the car with my rose, the tears were instantaneous. It was nice to see the sunflowers that Wendy left for Tommy on Monday and of course the Bud Light. Now, my big-ass long-stem rose is in the mix. As I was standing there in front of my husband's grave, I was looking to the sky hoping against hope that I would get a repeat performance of the eagle from last year. Apparently, that was not meant to be. Hopefully I will see one soon. They are so mesmerizing. Be that as it may, once again, my heart is heavy, and the same old year-long feelings are with me. As I told Tommy today, this just sucks. I hate feeling like this but, for some reason, still unbeknownst to us, this did happen to us. While he soars like an eagle, I am left to pick up the pieces here on earth, left to deal with the loss of my husband taken way too early in life. Some of us are still reeling, and my hope for us is that we will all find our way.

Until then, with every eagle you see, think of Tommy. He would absolutely want it that way. He didn't have one tattooed on his bicep for nothing!

Soar, my love, for you are free …

Much love to all,

Chrissie

Chapter 15

My Journey—the Second Year and Beyond

Saturday, November 14, 2009, 7:38 p.m., CST—
Chrissie's Journal Entry

Hello,

We are two weeks past the first anniversary of Tommy's death, and yesterday, on Friday, November 13, Tommy's uncle Donny Vinje was laid to rest right alongside him. Donny was a fabulous artist, and a few of his paintings were on display at his service. He was extremely talented. Rest in peace, Donny. You will be missed.

Also, in the last couple of weeks I have been to a couple of grief groups. One of them meets once a month, and there is no meeting in December. Hardly seems worth it, but as I was listening to people in the group, I heard them say that they attended other groups around town that met more frequently in addition to this particular group. I decided to do the same. Paula gave me some info on a few groups, and I have found one that meets every Monday night. I will try that for a while and see where that leads. Confidentiality prohibits me from talking about anything that happens in the group, but I think that some good things will come from it. I will let you know ...

I have another reason for writing this evening, and that reason is my mother-in-law, Ginny. I have decided to have this entire website made into a book for her as a gift, and I wanted to say a little something to her before I got to a good stopping point. My intent is to print off the subsequent entries so she can put them in the book after it is printed.

What do you say to someone who has had so much loss in their life and appears to take it in stride? After all, loss is a huge part of life—loss and change. Change due to loss. It can be difficult and life-changing. Loss changes a person, yet Ginny's core being remains intact. I tried like hell to make it so she would not have to feel the pain of losing a second son. That, of course, was out of my hands, but it didn't stop me from trying. I thought if I just tried this or that, Tommy's condition would reverse and he would be okay. But life, being as cruel as it can be, took Tommy from her and all of us.

What I would like to say to you, Virginia Laura May Lagerquist Vinje, is that it is a privilege and an honor to call you my mother-in-law. You are the best mother-in-law anyone could ever ask for, and I love you very much. We traveled a rough road together, you and I, and I am so glad we were there for each other, making decisions and trying to do what was best for your youngest son and my husband. It is undoubtedly a bond that will never be broken, and I am so glad life brought us together. I couldn't even begin to imagine what this journey would have been like without you. Thank you. Thank you for being the person you are, for being Tommy's mommy (I had to say that!), and know that you are greatly admired by this daughter-in-law.

Tommy brought so many people together, and it is truly astounding. I will be forever grateful for the people who are in my life as a result of marrying my beloved Tommy. Also, what is truly amazing are the relationships between the Betlachs and the Vinjes, the Betlachs, Vinjes, and Buds, the Betlachs, Vinjes, Buds, and all other family and friends. Tragedy bonds people together like nothing else can. It sucks that that is what it takes sometimes, but it is another fact of life. It is total bullshit, but there is nothing you can do. It is totally out of your control. "They" say things happen for a reason, and as a rule, I do believe that, even though it may take years to figure out those reasons, if you are lucky enough to ever get the meaning. Personally, I make no promises. I don't see it yet, and I am guessing it will be a while. But, suffice it to say, I am grateful for all the people in my life, and of course, I still wish my honey were here to share in all of it. Nothing is forever, God knows.

In closing, let me just say, this book is for you Ginny. For the most part, you have been in the dark as far as my journal entries and the guest book entries go. You don't need no stinking computer 'cause now you have the book! My gift from me to you.

Much love to you, Ginny!

Chrissie

Guest Book Entries

Written November 14, 2009, 10:38 p.m.

Hi, Chris,

What a great gift you are giving your mother-in-law! I have no doubt that she has the same amount of love in her heart for you also. You are probably more than a daughter-in-law to her … You are probably a *daughter*! The words you wrote to her are so special and honest, and she will treasure this book forever! You are such a special person, and I am glad to hear that you are going to some support groups. I have no doubt in my mind that it will help you. Your memories of Tommy will never die, but I hope for you that it just hurts less as time goes on. I love you, and I am glad to see some of the things you are doing to take care of yourself because you are worth it!

Love,

Kris K.

Written November 16, 2009, 3:46 p.m.

Virginia Vinje rocks!

Beth Timm

Written November 19, 2009, 12:43 p.m.

Grandma,

You have always been there for me through thick and thin. You never judged me, and you love me unconditionally. Whenever I needed you, ten times out of ten you were there regardless of what it was, and the times are countless. You were there.

Tom and you have been the ones to keep the family together, going to the farm, picnics, and boating.

Uncle Tom will never be forgotten and always loved!

You are the world's greatest grandma! You are the best; I love you with all my heart and will always love you for being you!

Love always, 'cause I will always love you.

Ty Vinje

Written November 19, 2009, 1:11 p.m.

Grandma,

Although I can't say how much you mean to me, I know my actions do, like when I come over to your house, I throw my hands behind my head and give you the biggest smile, telling you I love you. I put both hands in the air and wave at you. I'm saying I love you. And when I come and sit on your lap, I'm saying I love you. When I come up behind you putting my arms around you, I'm saying I love you!

I love you, Grandma!

Clifton

Written November 19, 2009, 4:26 p.m.

Grandma,

When I think of you, I think of the word *strong*, and when I hear the word *strong*, it reminds me of you because that's what you are.

Our family has had a lot of ups and downs. In the past year there have been a lot of passings in our family and around us, but you still stayed positive and kept your head held high and had a smile on your face even if you were hurting on the inside.

I'm proud to have you as my grandmother! Strong is not the only word that reminds me of you. It's *one* of the many words that describes you. I am *very* grateful to have a *strong, loving, caring, sweet, fun, fabulous, and amazing Grandma* like you in my life.

I just want you to know that I love you with all my heart, and I would do anything for you!

Love always, your granddaughter,

Tija Vinje

Written November 20, 2009, 9:19 a.m.

Ginny,

I am honored to have been able to meet you and even more honored that our two families have been combined. Your strength is incredible. Your sense of humor is wonderful. You are truly one to look up to in so many ways.

I admire you and your ability to remain as strong, positive, and compassionate with everything you do. The world is a better place because of people like you. The lives around you are simply better because of you.

I love you, Ginny.

Nicole Betlach

Written November 20, 2009, 8:43 p.m.

Mom,

I am so lucky God chose you to be my mom. You are a phenomenal woman! I can only hope I've become half the woman you are. You are my shoulder to cry on, my friend, and my hero. In this last year, we've had a lot of life-changing experiences, and I know how much it must have hurt you, but you held your head high, smiled that wonderful smile, and kept that twinkle in your eye. We have laughed together at the great memories and cried together for all the terrible sorrows of our loved ones gone. It made us stronger and closer as mother and daughter. I will cherish you forever, Mom. I love you.

Judy Vinje

Written November 21, 2009, 12:44 a.m.

Dear Grandma,

It is hard to find the words to express exactly what you mean to me. You have been one of the strongest human beings I have ever met or will meet.

I am always proud to tell my friends about all of the wonderful things that you have mastered, all the way from cooking and baking to doing some of your own plumbing and stripping. (*Ha, ha!*)

But seriously, I wouldn't be half the woman I am today if I didn't have you in my life. Your wisdom and knowledge are always there to guide me, and your humor and laughter are always there to make me smile. You are truly an angel here on earth. God bless you!

Grandma, *I love you always and forever!*

Elizabeth Vinje

Written November 21, 2009, 12:05 p.m.

Ginny,

God carved a special place in all of our hearts that he filled with Tom. His caring spirit and sense of humor will live on in everyone he touched in his life. I am honored to have known him and to have been a witness to the special love he and Chrissie shared. Take it from a mom who knows a special son when she sees one. Hold all the special mother/son memories close to your heart. With much love and continued prayers for you and your family.

Patty Betlach Russell

Written November 21, 2009, 8:48 p.m.

Ginny, where do I begin? I have to say knowing you feels like *home!* You have lived many different chapters of life. I am honored to be a part of one of those chapters. I feel blessed to share the bond that has united our families together. You are a wonderful person and a survivor. I love you, Ginny! May God bless you and keep you under his wing.

Theresa Betlach

Written November 24, 2009, 6:15 a.m.

I really got to know the Vinjes when Tom got sick.
It seems that sometimes that's how things like that
happen. I've come to know them pretty well, and I
must say it's been a pleasure. When Chrissie met
Tom, I thought, *What a perfect match for her.* He was
a great guy, and I loved him a lot. I can see why. I
knew his dad from work, and I loved him. Ginny, you
are a great person, and I can see why Tom turned
out so good. I'm glad I got to know you, and I always
look forward to seeing you and your family. Keep
your chin up and keep smiling. I'm glad Chrissie has
your family.

Marlene Trombley

Written November 27, 2009, 9:46 a.m.

About four years ago, I had the fortune of being
introduced to the Vinje family. In the few years that
passed, I came to believe there was something very
special about this family. Not just one person in
particular but the entire family. Judy, Laura, Gary,
Tom … all such caring, friendly, loving people.
Certainly there must be a very special person behind
all these bright, wonderful people. For anyone who
has spent time with the Vinjes, the answer is plain as
day … Ginny. Never have I heard Ginny speak badly
about anyone. She opens her home and her heart
to everyone she knows, and she makes you feel at
home. I can't imagine what Ginny must have endured
during Tommy's illness, having already experienced
so much loss in her life, but Ginny always kept
everyone else together, being unselfishly strong for
everyone even though her heart was breaking.

Ginny, please know that while Tom was taken too early, he touched more people in his life, made so many people laugh and feel good, and was such a good friend to so many. Tommy lived more and loved more than most people do in a very long lifetime. He was so special because of you, and I hope knowing that gives you some peace in your heart.

We think of you and your family often. We both miss all of you. We both love you all very much.

Lylis C. and Alyssa S.

Written November 29, 2009, 2:44 p.m.

Grandma,

You have brought so much happiness into my life. Words cannot explain it. You created a world for me that is more like a dream you never want to wake up from—the vacations and family picnics in the past and the barbeques and holidays of the present; the trips to Uncle Kenny's house, the sleepovers as kids, and helping you prepare the food for the holidays. These are without a doubt my most treasured memories. You created a family that I'm grateful to be a part of. I could go on and on, but in the simplest words, Grandma, I love you. And thank you for being my grandma.

Love always,

Larry Vinje

Written December 2, 2009, 7:56 p.m.

Mom, I love my time together with you at the farm. There is something about being there for us. You just seem to go back to your childhood and just enjoy being "home," like when you wash clothes and then hang them on the same line you did as a young girl. You let me go out and play after a meal. I say, "Mom, I'll do the dishes." (Or actually I say, "You kids get in there and start busting some suds," as I sit back in the La-Z-Boy with my eyes closed.) You say, "Oh don't you dare. You go out and play. It gives me something to do." I always laugh. Just the way you still want to take care of me at forty-nine says volumes about the type of person you are. You are the most loving and caring person I have ever known, and I'm not saying that just because you were in hard labor for three days giving birth to me and I'm trying to suck up to you, but Mom, you are a really special person. Anyone who has ever met you has always felt welcome and has never gone home hungry or without a smile and admiration for you.

I was sitting next to Ryan at Bob's service (Ginny's younger brother who passed), and during the time when folks were saying nice things about Bob, Ryan (Gary's son) said I should get up and talk about him. I knew that I should, but I didn't because we were fifteen minutes early (we were actually fifteen minutes late for the service). I started thinking about it, but I didn't get up, so I will say what I wish I would have said here.

What I should have got up and said after the minister told a story about Bob and dynamite was that it reminded me about the time a few years ago when we were standing outside. I mentioned I would like to get a backhoe to clear out the drainage ditches around the farm, and Bob said, "Oh you should get some dynamite because you don't have a pile of dirt alongside the ditch. The dirt sprays everywhere." Then another time we were out in the garage and started talking about the slingshots that are hanging on a nail. Bob started talking about how he and Kenny (Ginny's older brother who owned the farm they grew up on) always had a slingshot in their back pockets, made out of a Y spruce stick and rubber from an old inner tube. They would shoot gophers, squirrels, or each other in the butt. Bob was pretending to pull back a slingshot as if he was going back to his childhood when he was telling his story.

Mom, you always make sure everyone else is okay and don't worry about yourself. "Oh don't worry about me. Just never mind," you say.

So Mom, here we are with me the only boy after everything was equal. It's hard to realize it. It seems so lonely without Dad, David, and Tom to me, as well I know it does for you.

I truly do love you, Mom, with all my heart.

Gary Vinje

Wednesday, March 17, 2010, 7:36 p.m., CDT— Chrissie's Journal Entry

Greetings,

It has been a while since I have written—about four months, by my estimation. I have been doing what everyone else has been doing, which is trying to get through the dang winter. Thank God the worst is behind us! As I am writing that last sentence, it dawns on me that the same could be said in relation to my grieving process. There was a significant shift, as my therapist calls it, around mid to late February.

That shift is largely due to Facebook, believe it or not. While I started my own page just over a year ago, in January of this year, I started a page for Jay Kline Chevrolet, a dealership on Lake Street that I worked at from 1982 till 1987. At the suggestion of my friend, Lenny C., (thanks again, Len!), I set up a Facebook page for Jay Kline Chevrolet so we could share pictures and memories from back in the day. After I got it going, I started calling and e-mailing people to let them know about the page, and the most amazing thing happened. Suddenly, as I was talking to people I hadn't talked to in twenty years or more, others were planning get-togethers and talking more than they had in recent years. Things just started snow-balling, and the energy was/is incredible. (It is similar to the energy that the CaringBridge perpetuated during Tommy's illness.) I can say with all certainty that the work I have been doing on the JKC site and the old friends I have reconnected with have quite literally pulled me out of the abyss that I had been floundering in for well over a year. I feel more like myself than I have in a very long time. What's really amazing to me is that people were noticing, especially my therapist, Paula. She was truly amazed at the shift and how quickly it happened. If you had told me two months ago that I would be feeling like I am now, I wouldn't have believed you.

Make no mistake, I am not done with the grieving process, nor do I think I ever will be when it comes to Thomas Lyle Vinje. I will just learn to live without him all the while missing him until we meet again. I still have my moments, and they can be brutal. Right before Valentine's Day, I took some pictures of Tommy and me off of the picture boards from his funeral to scan and upload to my Facebook page for a Valentine present for him. *That* was not a good scene. I now know that I am not yet ready to disassemble those boards. But I did finish the two I started, and I did, in fact, create an album of Tommy and me. That way I am sharing them with friends and family and not just staring at them by myself.

Another change I have experienced since the shift is that before, when I would think of myself, I would think of Tommy and me together. Now, when I think of myself, it's just me. Sad, I know, but I have to let it happen. I have to figure out who I am without him. I am a different person than I was before I married Tommy, and for whatever reason, I am being forced to have to find who I am after him. It still pisses me off that he was taken from me, and I don't pretend to understand any of it. I was going to a grief group for a while, but since the shift I don't feel that is the right place for me anymore. I'm glad I went and a part of me does wish I had started sooner, but it is what it is and that was not meant to be. It could just be that it worked out the way it was intended.

Another *really cool* thing about Facebook is that our neighbor boy/ friend, Dylan started a page for Tom just over a week ago. I have since uploaded many pictures and videos. I have also posted a "Tom Vinje Celebration" at Whiskey Junction for this Friday night at 7:00 pm. I am doing this because today, St. Patrick's Day, marks the second anniversary of Tommy's car accident. Tomorrow, the eighteenth, marks the second anniversary of his diagnosis, and of course, Friday is the second anniversary of his surgery. I can always tell when this time of year approaches. About ten to fourteen days before I start to feel it. I get weepy, and a feeling that I can't explain comes over me. I know I am in the "zone," for lack of a better word. The same also applies for October before the anniversary of his passing.

I still find it so hard to believe that he is not here and that he is not coming back. At the same time, I know he is around me. I don't doubt it for a second. I love him so much, and that will never change. I will just carry it with me always and take comfort in the fact that I was the only lucky woman to ever be married to that wonderful man—a wonderful man who touched so many people before and during his illness and after his untimely death. (I still cringe when I use that word in relation to Tommy.) He has left me with so many amazing friends and family members I would never have known had we not met. Along with my family and friends, it is their unending love and support that keep me going. That has given me the will to *want* to keep going even during the darkest days in the abyss—the abyss that I so recently climbed up and out of due to the promise of renewed friends and connections. Life works in mysterious ways, and when it all comes down to it at the end of the day, it really is *love* that carries you. It is *love* that means everything. It is *love* that gives us the will to live. I am not just talking about romantic love; it is the love of friends, family, coworkers, and sometimes strangers that can touch you so very deeply that sometimes it takes you a while to figure it out, but when you do, man; it is the greatest feeling ever! I feel I have been the recipient of just that kind of love—the human kind. It is truly amazing! And it is a gift I will carry with me, right along with Tommy's love, for the rest of my days. And for that, I thank all of you from the bottom of my heart. You guys rock!

Much love to all of you!

Chrissie

Guest Book Entries

Written March 18, 2010, 7:33 a.m.

My Dear Chrissie!

I love this post! I am so happy to see things turn around for you, and I knew they would. You just had to do it on your own time. You are right—you will always miss Tom and feel the pain of him being gone, but we learn to live with it. You have some amazing friends and family around you all the time,

and you are dearly loved ... especially by me! Hugs
Love you.

Krissy

Written March 18, 2010, 1:03 p.m.

You rock, Chrissie!

Dianne

Saturday, April 3, 2010, 9:15 p.m., CDT—
Chrissie's Journal Entry

Happy Easter, everyone,

Tomorrow I will be hosting my first holiday without Tommy. It will actually be the first holiday I have hosted alone ... ever. I have been systematically getting ready all week, getting all my ducks in a row, as it were, when this afternoon, as I was sitting at work, I got a case of the weepies. When that happens, this feeling comes over me (I know it well) that usually lasts a day or two or three. I could cry at the drop of a hat, much like a couple of weeks ago for the anniversary of Tommy's diagnosis. There is no doubt about it, the month of March totally sucks, and now April is a close second.

You know, I have heard in the past that the second year after a loved one passes can be worse than the first. On some level, I can understand that logic. I mean, one minute I think I am okay, and the next is a whole new ball game. It's like some internal clock/demon is controlling my emotions like a damn puppet. It's like they just all of a sudden shout, "Now! Let's take her down!" and down I go, usually without warning and absolutely nothing I can do about it. Actually, now that I think about it, it started this morning while I was in the shower. For some reason, as I was showering, I started thinking about the morning my honey passed away. I was thinking about walking into the ER to talk to the doctor to find out what was going on and then telling him to *stop*! God, I replayed that moment in my mind, over and over, and *bam*, crying in the shower. I don't know why that came into my head, but man, I have to say that there are so many snippets of time that pop into my head, and there are some that I cannot bear to remember. Sometimes when that happens, I let it come, and then I talk to Tommy out loud to try to get through it. But there are some that are just too big and I suspect some that I will never get over.

I don't know what it is about writing on this site, but I start out saying one thing, thinking it will be short, and then it just leads down a whole other path; crazy. Anyway, I just had to get this out there. Maybe it will make tomorrow just a little bit easier for me. I have to give it a shot, see what happens.

Have a great Easter, everyone, and be thankful for everyone in your life at this moment because it is entirely possible they will not be there tomorrow.

Much love to all,

Chrissie

Guest Book Entries

Written April 3, 2010, 11:29 p.m.

Hi, Chris,

I will be thinking of you tomorrow as you host your first holiday "alone." Know that all of us will be with you, even if it is not in the same room. It was great to see you last weekend at my dad's party; wish I would've been able to talk to you more, but that is how parties go! Have a great Easter, and know that Tommy is still with you and probably will be sitting right next to you tomorrow with his arms around you during the difficult times!

Love,

Kris K.

Saturday, September 18, 2010, 11:02 p.m., CDT—Chrissie's Journal Entry

Long time, no hear, I know.

Hello. I know it has been a while, and I have contemplated ending my entries on the Bridge. While I think I am close, I am not quite ready to call it quits.

Today would have been our eleventh anniversary. Not gonna lie, today has been a bit more difficult than I anticipated. I have been up and down all week, but particularly the last couple of days; such bullshit. There are times that I still have a hard time believing that this all happened, that Tom is really not coming back, and then there are times that it feels like years since I have seen him or talked to him. I am envious of people who still have their spouses and their lives together. I had that once, briefly. I thought I would have it for our lifetime, but that was not meant to be, apparently. WTF! Why? I really can't stand it some days. I don't understand. I hate being without him.

It is true, I am better than I was last year, but the "anniversaries" are still painful. Our wedding anniversaries are different from all the rest because they were just ours. It's not like his birthday or the day we found out about his tumor or the day he left us; those we all share. September 18, 1999, was our wedding day, and while our friends and family shared that day with us, in the end, it was our day and not a day that anyone else necessarily would remember if they weren't reminded. And now, given that he will be gone two years next month (Are you fricking kidding me!), I am really feeling so incredibly alone that sometimes it is downright intolerable, hence the envy and self-pity. I really hate the whole self-pity thing, but there are times I feel I deserve to feel that way. I hope that goes away though …

I am well aware that I am rambling but, "Frankly, Scarlett, I don't give a damn!" Just sayin'.

Instead of boring you all with the whole pity party thing, I will just say that I miss my husband more than anyone will ever know. I know there will come a time when I will move past this particular emotion, but that is not today. I see and hear frequently about widows and widowers moving on, and while I think that will happen at some point, I am not there yet. Hell, I am still wearing my wedding rings; someday, not today.

Maybe that is my mantra for now, "Someday … not today." I think there will come a day when that will change, but not today. When it comes, I will let you know. And then, that will be the day that my time on the CaringBridge will come to an end. I was thinking that maybe I was already at that point, but I think that I will see this through until I am truly ready to move on, whether that be to another relationship or house or what have you. Suffice it to say that that time is not now. I'm glad we had this little chat. How does it feel to be inside my head right now! Good Lord! I will put you out of your misery …

Thanks for listening …

Much love to all,

Chrissie

Guest Book Entries

Written September 19, 2010, 9:32 a.m.

Hi, Chrissie,

It was so great to see you last weekend. It was such a beautiful day. I have read all your CaringBridge entries over the past two years, and what comes to mind is how blessed you are to have had someone in your life you loved so much. I will always remember the final attempts you made on Tom's behalf with the prayer groups and other things you tried, and that was truly remarkable. I didn't know Tom very well, but John told me about the memorial. Whenever I see an eagle, I think of him. May your cherished memories bring you joy!

Jenny Ruoho

Written September 19, 2010, 1:35 p.m.

Hey, Chrissie,

Thanks for sharing your thoughts about Tom, and I really love the new motto. I think it is both positive and realistic. I thought of you on your anniversary and remember the magic of your day. I feel particularly lucky to have known both you and Tom as individuals before you found each other as partners. You made each other complete, and I pray that someday … not now, you find that completeness again. Until that time, please keep sharing with us. We love you.

Lynn Robson

Written September 19, 2010, 2:32 p.m.

Love you. That's all.

Wendy P.

Written September 22, 2010, 9:30 a.m.

My thoughts and prayers are with you and a *big hug* too!

Candace McCown

Written October 13, 2010, 7:05 p.m.

Hey, Chrissie,

Haven't talked to you in a while, so I just wanted to drop a note to say hi and love ya! Hopefully I'll see ya soon.

Katie Anderson

Tuesday, October 26, 2010, 10:13 a.m., CDT— Chrissie's Journal Entry

It has been two years—two fricking years already. It is so hard to believe that Tommy left us two years ago today. In some ways it feels like yesterday, and in other ways it feels like forever ago. So much has happened since he left. So much is happening, and he's not here to see it. I think about things like that frequently. Things like all the road construction, for instance, and the new Twins stadium. I just know if he had had the chance to go to that stadium, somehow, some way, we would've ended up with season tickets. Then there are also things like all the great-nieces and -nephews that have arrived and those that will be arriving soon.

Do I think he knows about all of these things? Abso-frickin-lutely! I know he is watching over everyone, visiting here and there. I have felt him in the house all month, and I came very close to actually seeing him in the living room last Saturday. I have never talked about any of this before on here because I don't talk about it with people who don't believe the same. But right now, I don't really give a good rat's ass if anyone believes it or not. It is my experience, and I know what I see, feel, and hear. My husband is with me, and that comforts me.

In my therapy session with Paula last week, we were talking about something that I know some people will disagree with, but nevertheless, it is something I think about frequently and that I need to forgive myself for. Let me preface this by saying that I know I did the best I could during Tom's illness. By that I mean juggling everything like taking care of my husband, dealing with the medical community, work, weekly shopping for Tom's needs and for the house, making sure I had enough food and such for everyone who was caring for him, doing housework, etc. But with all of that is my one regret. I wish I had let some of that go more often than I did so that I could've nourished Tom more. While it is true that he slept a lot of the time, I am not at all completely sure that he was actually sleeping all of that time as he was known to mess with us on occasion! By nourishing I mean reading the paper to him, sitting and holding his hand more than I did while watching TV, keeping him more in the loop on life going on around him while he was incapacitated. Things like that—the important things. I really, really, really wish I had done more of all of that and more. Obviously, there is nothing I can do about it now except to talk to Tom by speaking out loud to him (which is very hard for me to get through, usually) or thinking it or just by throwing it out into the universe for him to grab up. Of course, there is always writing about it. It has always been very cathartic for me, as you all know.

Also in my session with Paula, she was saying that I needed to write, that I needed to get some things out there, that there were many people who needed to be helped by what I had to say. Since then I have been thinking about what I could say that people would need to hear, and I have come to the conclusion that all I know are my experiences and what I am thinking and feeling. That's all I have. That's why I finally came clean in the previous paragraph. It's true, it's how I feel, and now that it is out there, maybe I can forgive myself and move on from it. I am quite certain it doesn't matter to Tom at this point. Besides, I did get a message from him telling me that I did a good job.

I am sitting here knowing I had much more than this to say, and I can't tap into it right now. I think I will end this particular entry and from now on just come and go with much more frequency when I have something to say. That might even mean more entries later today because I know I haven't yet tapped what I need to tap today. It's big, it's looming, and it's here. I just need to get to it. Stay tuned …

Much love to all, and thank you for still listening,

Chrissie

Guest Book Entries

Written October 26, 2010, 12:34 p.m.

I'm still listening. And I love you and I get it and I always will.

Wendy P.

Written October 26, 2010, 1:25 p.m.

God bless you, Ving ... Guilt is such a useless emotion! And you did an *outstanding* job.

We should all be so lucky to have someone there that loves us that much in our hour of need.

Tommy was a wonderful man. And he found a wonderful woman to spend the rest of his life with. And that's exactly what he did.

That is *so rare*, Chrissie. Please don't blur it up with guilt. You sent him to heaven in the most perfect way—full of love.

Take care you. Know that Tommy was very, very fortunate to have you—*every* day. Not just on the days that *you* think you did a good job.

Michelle Notch

Sunday, December 19, 2010, 3:25 p.m., CST— Chrissie's Journal Entry

I cannot believe this is my third Christmas without Tom. The first year I was numb. The second year I was not in a good place, and this year ... Well let's see. I have found that I am more crabby and weepy as the holiday approaches. I have *no* interest in decorating and haven't since he passed. The mere thought of even going through our Christmas stuff brings me to tears. I can't even conceive of it. Then last night, we had our managers' holiday dinner for work. We have not had one of those since Tom passed, and quite frankly, I was relieved last year when it didn't happen. I didn't want to deal with going by myself. But then last night, it was time to face the music.

I was fine as I left the house and made my way down Cedar over to Washington Avenue. Driving along I passed Riverside Avenue, and up came many unpleasant memories. On that street is the hospital where we found out about Tom's brain tumor. Then, there is the memory of Tommy lying in ICU not being able to breathe after being brought over from PP. A few blocks later was SE Washington Avenue, which is the way I went to the U of M Hospital for months. Instantly some of those memories surfaced—unpleasant memories from a very dark, dark time. As I was thinking this, I wondered again why he had to go through all of that. What was the purpose? What did he do to deserve those seven months that ended his life and took him away from us forever? As if all of this wasn't enough, I passed by the abandoned building that once housed Downtown Pontiac Jaguar. The place we met, the place where a lot of friendships began and continue. And also, a place where we attended some kick-ass Christmas parties on that Jaguar show floor where Tom and I won prizes just about every year. Now, here I was on my way to a Christmas party without him, passing by an empty building with *so* many memories inside those walls. All of this was now gone, and me, all alone, at night, in my car on my way to St. Anthony Main to a party. A slight bit of anxiety started, and I wanted to burst into tears and run.

I tried to regain composure and deal with the task at hand, following the directions to get to where I was going. I, of course, missed my turn, and then I had to redirect my focus. That coupled with the fact that I had things to do once I got to the restaurant saved me. I was able to focus and get caught up in the spirit of the evening, although, there were times when I would watch everyone else with their spouse/significant other and I would feel my stomach turn, a twinge of grief, and/or a moment of sadness or all of the above.

There are times that I want to feel sorry for myself, and I do. Not that that is a good thing; it isn't. Primarily, I do want to feel better and move on. It is just so damn hard to do. I believe that will happen when it is supposed to happen and not a minute before. There is some work that goes into that, and after the holidays, I vow to actively start doing the work. Sitting in limbo is not the place to be. Tommy wouldn't want me to be there, and I am growing tired of it. Have I done one helluva lot of grieving? Abso-fricking-lutely. Am I done? I believe you are never truly done grieving; you just learn to live with it. But as it stands, I think I have some very significant grieving to do yet, and I have in mind things that I will be doing to move through some of it. Now that we have a *very long* winter on deck, it seems like the perfect time to deal with things, and maybe, just maybe, I will come through this winter with new possibilities and attitude for my next chapter.

Until then, I need to, "Keep my feet on the ground and keep reaching for the stars."

Merry Christmas and much love to all,

Chrissie

Guest Book Entries

Written December 20, 2010, 9:25 a.m.

Chrissie,

First let me say that I think you are healing quite beautifully. You have a great head on your shoulders, and Tommy is beaming from above about what kind of gal he married—of that I am sure.

Next, I just want to put in my two cents about all the tragedy surrounding his last bit of time on earth. When I wonder why people have to suffer needlessly, for some reason it makes me feel better to realize that we all have our own "stories"—our own paths that we go on when we are here—and sometimes they take a left and sometimes a right. But I really do believe that things do just happen—that there isn't always a reason, and as much as we may want to think we can influence our surroundings, sometimes we just can't.

You did such a great job with Tommy. I guess the point to my long-winded message is I really hope sometime soon you can take the deepest breath you've ever taken, and when you slowly let it out, you let go of all the guilt, all the doubt, and a lot of your sorrow. ('Cause there will always be sadness—but there doesn't have to be an unbearable amount forever, right?)

You should be proud of who you are *every day*. You're Chrissie Vinje, dammit!!

Thanks for being who you are. I know you'll be surrounded by friends and family at Christmas this year who are even more proud of you than I am! Each of them is a little blessing you can count. :)

Take care, Cha Cha!

Michelle Notch

Written December 20, 2010, 6:54 p.m.

Hello Chrissie,

First off, I would like to commend you on your progress. It is a work in progress in all the situations you have endured over the last couple of years. Remember, PBPGINFWMY (Please be patient, God is not finished with me yet.) Our lives are a work in progress. Everything happens for a reason, and we may not like the things and reasons, but it does. I looked at your past letters and it shows your progress in them up until now. It may not seem like that with you, but from the outside looking in at what you write, it really is. There are not many people who have been through what you have been through and are able to deal with it. Many would have lost it a long time ago. You're still here with, as you said, your feet on the ground, looking to the stars. Now that is a positive look on the situation you are in. It will be the small accomplishments that you can build on and go from there. Last year you stated that you wouldn't even be able to bring yourself to go to the Christmas party, and this year, with a lot of reluctance and hurtful memories, you were still able to go to the Christmas party. I noticed there were times it was hard for you to write in the journal, but you still did.

Any holiday season is not easy for many people that are in this situation, but you're still standing; so I see you have made progress. My advice would be, when you're up to it, go back and read your progress for yourself. Read what frame of mind you were in from the past to the present, and notice your progress. It works for me when I do journals from types of things that happen.

Change of pace. Just try to keep your mind off what you are feeling and the things that may remind you of it. Yes, that is just a pacifier, but it could relieve how you are feeling until you grow strong to better learn to deal with it. Yes, you may be right, you may not get over it, but you will learn to live with it, which is what I have found as time goes along. You are also right; Tom wouldn't want you to feel this way. I am sure your family and friends don't want you to feel this way, and most importantly, you!

I know it is easier said than done. Our lives are a work in progress, and not many people would be able to endure what you have gone through and still be sane and standing. You, Chrissie, have accomplished that, one step at a time, and you're doing a heck of job at it so far, up until now. There are a lot of people out there who, if they were in your shoes, wouldn't have done what you have done and stuck by your man like you did for Tom, before, during, and after. Right there that is a big accomplishment to build on for your future, in our temporary life on earth, and the thereafter.

What is seen is temporary, and what is unseen is eternal. :) In other words, there are brighter days ahead for you. Your friends in the guest book said that Tom is looking down on you, and I second that to you. I would like to wish you a blessed Christmas and blessed, prosperous New Year. Keep your head up, to the stars. :)

God Bless

Rese Patton

Friday, December 24, 2010, 9:11 a.m., CST— Chrissie's Journal Entry

Merry Christmas, Tommy! I know you will be around the next few days witnessing the celebrations. I will get through these days once again, but there is an emptiness that was once filled by you … I miss you, honey, and I will love you always …

Chrissie

Guest Book Entries

Written December 28, 2010, 3:59 p.m.

Hi, Chrissie,

I don't know where to start other than to say that I have just spent the past two hours reading over this site and marveling at what a wonderful wife, daughter-in-law, and sister-in-law you are! My parents and Tom's parents were friends many years ago. I think my dad was actually friends with Tom's uncle Don and met Lyle through him (or vice versa) back in the '50s. Maybe even the '40s. The Vinje clan and the Trombley clan used to get together every summer for a day out at Lake Minnewashta. I can remember Tom and Gary pushing us on this huge rope swing they had there.

I was thinking about Ginny this morning, I don't know why exactly. I typed her name in Google, and Tom's obituary was among the first results. I can't tell you how sorry I am for everything that happened to all of you over the course of Tom's illness, and since. It is so unbearable when we lose a loved one. Please tell Ginny hello for me the next time you talk to her. I remember her very fondly, as well as all the kids. I was the pain-in-the-butt youngest sister in my family that probably got in their way more than anything, but I remember that they were always really nice to me! Please take care of yourself.

Linda Botz

Written September 18, 2011, 9:02 p.m. by
Chrissie Vinje—Chrissie's Journal Entry

Happy anniversary, my love! On earth we would have been married twelve years today. In my heart, you are mine for eternity. I love you until the end of time.

Guest Book Entries

Written September 18, 2011, 9:24 p.m.

Chrissie,

Happy anniversary! I think of Tom often and shake my head that we lost him so soon in his life. He was a great man and loved by many!

Love you,

Lynn Robson

Written September 18, 2011, 9:46 p.m.

Where does the time go? What a beautiful day that was.

Thinking about you …

Wendy

Written October 25, 2011, 6:36 p.m. by
Chrissie Vinje—Chrissie's Journal Entry

Oh my. It will be three years ago tomorrow since you left us. There is not a day that goes by that I don't think about you, and not a moment that goes by where I don't love you as much as I possibly can. I miss you more than words can say. Until we meet again …

Guest Book Entries

Written October 25, 2011 10:17, p.m.

Chrissie,

It is still hard to believe Tom is gone three years later. He was a wonderful, sincere, and incredibly funny person. I loved his laugh and still can see that twinkle in his eyes.

You were the love of his life!

Love you,

Lynn Robson

Written October 26, 2012, 12:10 p.m. by Chrissie Vinje

I cannot believe it was four years ago today that you left us to start your new journey. We needed you, but the angels needed you more. Now you are my angel. You are with me when I need you, and I can hear your voice in my head telling me what I need to hear.

I think about you every day, and I know that I always will. Words do not do justice to express how much I miss you. I miss your jokes, your personality, our life together, your way of "rigging" things up to get them to work (except for the cutting of cords for the mini-blinds ... not missing that so much! LOL!), and *of course*, that smile and most importantly, that laugh!

You were/are one special person, Tom Vinje, and I was the lucky one who got to be your wife. Thank you for the eleven years we had together, and thank you for being there for me through eternity. We *will* meet again, and it will be nothing short of spectacular! I love you with all my heart, and I always will. We were meant to be, if only for a little while.

Until we meet again my love ... stay close. I still need you!

Your baby

Guest Book Entries

Written October 26, 2012 12:21 p.m.

Yes, sweet, funny Tom!

I miss hearing the music outside when you and Chrissie were working in the yard, my first memory of you two as neighbors!

Love and hugs,

Candace McCown

Five Years, Really!

October 26, 2013, 10:06 a.m. by Chrissie Vinje

No matter how many times I say it this morning, I still cannot believe it has been five years since you left us to start your new journey. *Five* years ... really! Where did that fricking time go? I have been out here just trying to find my way, trying to figure out what direction to go.

I am not the same person I was when you left. I have changed. My beliefs have changed. I am at the point where I need change, in whatever form that takes. Things that used to mean something to me have fallen away, opening the door for the new to come in. It is time for the new to manifest so I can continue on in my journey, knowing *all* the time that you are with me.

I know you have been around for the last week. Irene saw an eagle in the alley last week. An eagle in the hood! No reason for him to be here, except for you. The orb I saw with my naked eye yesterday, twice. Walking into the living room thinking I saw someone standing there, I could feel the energy. Then when I was out playing with Bailey, I felt there was someone standing in Karrie's driveway. I swear I saw someone! But no one was there. Or were you?

I love that I know you are here, and I pray you never go away. After five years it feels like the right time to get on with really living again. I know you would want that for me. You are probably hanging out watching everything saying, "You got this! Move on! I will be here waiting!" I can only assume this is true, and I will act accordingly.

I think of you with every eagle I see. I think of you with every day that passes. I laugh when I tell and hear stories of you. My heart melts when I hear your voice or your laugh on a video. Thank God for those videos! I love you with every fiber of my being, and I cannot wait until we are together again. (Not that I will rush anything in that regard! LOL!) I miss you with each passing day and I suspect that will never change, and that's okay. The fact that I miss and love you so much is all because we had a great, true love that many people never experience. We had it. We had each other, if only for a while.

Five years. WTF! It doesn't seem real, but I am living that reality. Thank you, Thomas Lyle Vinje, for coming into my life. We had a great ride, and I love you more today than ever before. Five years have passed since you were here in the physical, but you will never leave our hearts or our memories. I love you.

Chrissie

We Have Come Full Circle

By Chrissie Vinje—October 26, 2014, 3:36 p.m.

Here I am, October 26, 2014, a full six years after you left all of us. It feels as if we have come full circle, and I say that because we are now going through the weekend as it was when you passed. I remember that weekend very well. That Saturday, October 25, 2008, was a beautiful fall day, and all of my family was at the Anoka Halloween Parade. I normally would have been in attendance, but not this year. A couple of my family members who had now come to help us on Saturdays were at the parade on this day instead of at our house helping out. In their absence Tom's beloved mother, Ginny, was taking on the Saturday with me.

I remember the sun shining and a couple of windows being open. Tom had not been conscious on this day, and his chest was rattling. Karrie came over with Tyler's nebulizer so we could try to clear his lungs as best we could. Later in the day I noticed his fingertips turning blue. Of course, I knew what that meant. When hospice stopped by, they told me that meant he was dying. I said, "No, he isn't!" To which she replied, "Okay, he isn't." Telling her not to patronize me was just an initial reaction to hearing out loud what I already knew.

The next morning, Sunday, October 26, 2008, Ginny came at her usual time, around six in the morning, to help me with the morning rituals. When she came in, I got up off the couch where I slept on the weekends, and we proceeded to give Tom his meds and other normal duties surrounding his care. I then went to bed to sleep for a couple of hours. About an hour later I heard Ginny scream, "Chrissie, he's not breathing!" I bolted out of bed and came into the living room to see Tom looking ashen and I knew ... I will not go into the entire day from here, except to say that we called 911, who came out and got his heart going again. We then went to the U of M ER, and the rest is history.

This particular Sunday in 2008 was complete contrast to the day before. It was now cold and gray, and when we left the hospital after Tom passed, there were snow flurries. The weather was matching what had just happened in our lives. The memories are so very vivid from that weekend. My sister Beth has said that they felt bad for not being there that Saturday but thought that perhaps it was meant to be so that Tom could spend his last couple of days on earth with his two favorite gals.

Fast forward to this weekend; again, we have Saturday, October 25, and Sunday, October 26. This Saturday was a beautiful day as well, *and* I was at that parade, as evidenced by the many pictures and videos on Facebook! It was a lot of fun, and it just felt so great to be there on such a gorgeous day. (As I found out, I was not the only one that had the dynamic of these dates on their mind.) On the way up to Anoka on Saturday morning, I did have a few episodes in the car thinking of my beloved husband and what was happening six years ago that day.

Now, it is Sunday, October 26, and instead of being cold, gray, gloomy, and horrendous, it is yet another gorgeous day, adding to one of the most spectacular autumns I can ever remember. And of course, the memories of this day are present. The difference, this time, is that I see a future full of promise and new things on the horizon for me. I have learned so much more than I ever could have imagined and have changed as a result. Situations such as this dictate that change is necessary. On my journey, and especially in the last couple of years, I have started exploring spirituality and the like more than I ever had before. It has helped me in my grief, understanding, and knowing of the big picture.

Who knew a few years ago that I would even be able to write the words that are spilling out of me now? Yes, time has passed. Does it heal? Healing is such a broad term. I would say it gets easier, but you never quite heal; you learn to live with it. You learn to live with the void their absence has left. You find new coping mechanisms. The sooner you realize that change is the only constant in this life, the better off you will be. You learn to roll with life and not get too caught up in the petty and small annoyances of everyday life. If you are lucky you learn that the sky is the limit here in the physical and you should not put limitations on what you or anyone else can achieve. It is up to each one of us to dream big, live big, love big! That is my wish for each one of you.

Much love to all,

Chrissie

XOXOXO

***

I received this e-mail from a good friend of ours. As soon as I read it, I knew it was the perfect ending to the story portion of the book, and I think you will agree:

Kari Kovall   March 6, 2012, at 9:54 p.m.

Hey, Chrissie,

Okay, I've been torn for the past hour debating whether or not to tell you this. I don't know if you'll get angry with me if it brings tears, but while I was in the shower after my nap my gut just told me I needed to tell you the dream I just had.

I have had many dreams about being back at Downtown Jaguar. I was the most happy there. I loved the work, and I loved the people I worked with. It was one of the most fun times in my life. I probably haven't had that kind of fun since, so naturally I dream about it a lot. Tom has been in many of the dreams, but this time it was different.

I was sitting at my accounting desk, and Tom came through the service door and shouted, "Waiter! Chop chop!" I went back to the cashier office as usual, but this time as I grabbed the repair order, he put his hands on the sides of my shoulders and said, "Tell her I'm happy."

Then I woke up, but here is the weird thing; I still felt the pressure of his hands on the sides of my shoulders as it just slightly kind of faded away.

Now please remember this could have been in my head as part of the dream. Besides, why would Tom choose me to talk to? Was tonight's "nap" just another dream or more than that? I am sure Tom has channeled you or sent you signs in many different ways, and maybe this is just one more way. I just know when I woke from the nap, I felt happy and kind of at peace. I never really forgave myself for being too sick to attend Tom's funeral. I will never forget him. Heck, I met you guys in 1997. You trained me in, remember? I just think about it, and I'm so happy to have seen you two evolve from becoming friends, then dating, engagement, and marriage. Whatever you take away from my dream is up to you, but when I wake up still feeling the way I felt in my dream, I think it means something.

I love you, Chrissie, and I miss you … a lot. Maybe someday we can go for a drink. I would really love that. Once again, I hope this e-mail was appropriate to tell you and hasn't made you too upset but maybe has made you happy.

Love you,

Kari

***

I replied to Kari's e-mail by telling her that she did not just have a dream; she had a visitation from Tom. I also told her that I thought the reason he chose her was because he knew she *would* tell me about it. I assured her that I was not upset in the least, but rather I was ecstatic to hear the words, "Tell her I'm happy." Now I ask you, who wouldn't want to hear that from their loved one?

Chapter 16

Epilogue

And Now ...

This book has been a long time in the making, despite the fact that the majority of it was written as life was happening. It was sitting out there in cyberspace, on the CaringBridge, waiting for the whole story to be told. But in order for that to happen, I had to be ready. And, as you have read, that took one hell of a long time. I would work on the book for a few days or a week or so and then stop for months at a time, letting it sit until I was ready again. There were times when I just couldn't or wouldn't tap into the emotions the writing demanded. These are painful memories, and I had to have the right mind-set to be with them. I think it is a better book because I did not rush to finish it. The more time and experiences I had after Tom's death, gave me a different perspective. God knows, I have read and relived all these entries numerous times now, and each time I seem to learn a little bit more.

There are a couple of issues that penetrated my soul as I was immersed in this part of our lives. I still struggle with my feelings about what Tom went through, especially without being able to know what he was thinking and feeling. I cannot imagine being in his position, and it still breaks my heart to think of it.

As I was revising the book, I recognized that in my desperation for our lives to return to normal, I rode Tom's ass to wake up and do whatever was being asked of him. I don't know whether or not he could have done any of it, even if he hadn't been so sleepy. Whether it was right or wrong, I will never know. It's something I just have to let go.

One of my motivations to write this book was to share the following principles:

o   "It" can happen to you. This is a reminder that life is unpredictable and can change in an instant.
o   It was scary when some of the medical staff were of the opinion that Tom was not at the surface when I knew he was. You have to be an advocate for your loved ones as well as for yourself when dealing with the medical community. They don't know their patients like friends and family do. You need to be aware every step of the way. Speak up and ask questions if you are unclear. Push back if you need to. Medical professionals are human too; mistakes and misconceptions can occur. I would also recommend that if a loved one is in a state such as Tom was, or worse, that you create and maintain an environment that suggests they are aware of their surroundings because you never know.
o   Know your partner's wishes regarding living wills, funeral arrangements, and the like, in the event he or she should become ill and/or pass unexpectedly.
o   Both partners should know as much as possible about all finances, insurance policies, wills, etc., so if something happens to one of you, the other will know what to do. This is especially important in this digital era, with online and smartphone bill paying and banking. (You need to know

websites and passwords, and believe me, that is only the tip of the iceberg.)
o   Appreciate your partner; don't take him or her for granted! Life is too short to be in a bad or unfulfilling relationship. Seriously. Be true to yourself, and follow your dreams; you are in control. Everything will fall into place.

As I continued editing, I read what I went through after Tom passed. My God, the despair! I felt so bad for that poor woman. I cried many times. Had I not written these words, I never would have realized how far I've come. When you are in the throes of such grief, it feels like it will never end; you can't imagine that it could. How could life ever be happy again? How do you gather the strength to live again—I mean *really* live again—or to care about anything, ever again? It seems so far away, an unreachable destination. Then you start to look around and see other people who have gotten there. They actually made it to the other side of their grief in one piece. How is this possible? Could it happen to me? During the first year or so following Tom's death, I truly felt like I had been dead myself. The best way I can describe what I mean by that is to say that I had been numb and felt like I was on the outside looking in at all that was happening around me. I was not participating in life. It was all just passing me by, and sometimes I was angry that the people around me were going forward while I was stuck. How could they go on with their lives while I was spinning my wheels just trying to exist? How is that fair?

Then one day, it happened. The fog started to lift. I started to wake up, slowly. Not to be weird, but I liken it to Frankenstein coming to life. It was as though electrical shocks intermittently ran through my body, kick-starting my emotions and my will. These jolts happened more and more frequently, and I wondered what the hell was happening. My therapist told me that I was coming back to life ... literally. I remember the moment she said that to me. It made sense, but I was still stunned by the process. It took some time, but eventually I found my way back. Lord knows it is different for everyone, but that was my experience.

There are no two stories alike when it comes to losing a loved one. Losing a parent or a child is different than losing a spouse. Even when siblings lose a parent, each child grieves differently. I bring this up because I had an experience in March of 2014 that rocked me to my core, and I wanted to share it here. This is my Facebook post from that day (with names and such omitted to preserve anonymity):

> I had an appointment after work today, nothing unusual, and this person and I were talking. She asked me a lot of questions about Tom, his illness, whether or not we tried to have kids, etc. I have nothing to hide whatsoever. Then she told me about a man she knew of who had passed suddenly at the age of forty-four from a heart attack. He left behind a wife and three kids. This person then proceeded to tell *me* she thought that family's situation was worse than mine because kids were involved. (So my pain should be less because I didn't have kids?)
>
> I sat there for a minute not believing this was actually being said to me, and then I said, "Well, is it worse than Tom's mother losing two sons or his siblings losing another brother?" And then I added, "At least when her husband died she had her three kids. I had no one. I was alone." The subject was dropped after that.
>
> Now let me just say that I don't think my situation was worse than the other family this person was speaking of, and I really do like this person. We have had many cool conversations. But the ignorance of that statement really shocked me. Everyone's situation is different. For *me*, losing Tom was the worst thing that could have happened, and it did. Maybe for people who have kids that is the way they think, although I tend to think that losing a child may

be worse, from what I hear. I will never know. I guess
it just makes you wonder what people are thinking
when they open their mouths sometimes. I am not
mad, just stunned. Thanks for listening ...

The point I am trying to illustrate here is that pain is pain. There are
no qualifiers or exceptions. Every individual has his or her own story,
relationships, and emotions, and it's not anyone's place to judge or
tell a person who is grieving what he or she should or should not be
feeling, thinking, or doing. That is unacceptable. Everyone moves
through grief at their own pace and in their own way.

If you will indulge me, I would like to share some of the ways that
helped me move through my grief. Hopefully someone will benefit
from even one of the following suggestions:

- Get professional help. I don't believe I would have accepted
  Tom's death and my life without him had I not sought
  professional help with my therapist, Paula.
- Surround yourself with family and friends. Do not push
  them away; let them help you.
- Feel the feelings. You have to experience the feelings to get
  past them. Let them out. Don't keep them inside or they will
  eat you up.
- If you absolutely need medicinal help to get through for a
  little while, consult your doctor about antidepressants. (I
  chose not to use pills for various reasons.)
- Journal. Write it down. This is especially helpful if there is
  no one to talk to, or if there is a moment that is particularly
  difficult and you need a way to release your emotions.
- Celebrate your loved one on anniversaries and birthdays. For
  the first couple of years after Tom passed, I had celebratory
  get-togethers either at my home or a bar for his birthday, the
  anniversary of his surgery, and his passing. I did this just to
  get through that particular day. I knew that if I had been at
  home alone, it would have been much worse. Although, I
  will admit that on the first birthday after his passing, I was

not doing well and a public meltdown ensued, more than once. So be it. I did what I had to do for me, and I got through the day, one way or the other.

I would also like to touch on the subject of benefits and fundraisers. If it hadn't been for the benefit, the garage sale, direct donations to the bank account, and the generosity of Tom's colleagues, who organized a fundraiser at the dealership (which included donating vacation days to Tom), we would have been in dire straits. The generated funds helped pay uninsured medical expenses as well as the supplies for Tom and food for his caregivers when he was home. What a blessing that medical bills did not force us into debt. A tip regarding medical bill management is to pay attention to the explanation of benefits (EOBs) that you receive from your insurance company. Check them closely against the actual billings to prevent overpaying. If you have any questions, make a phone call! Do not assume everything is correct, because errors do happen.

Many people have asked me if Tom knew or told me that something was wrong before the car accident. The answer is both yes and no. He seemed to know something was wrong but was unable to identify or express exactly what it was. For example, on Valentine's Day of 2008, about a month before the accident, we were at one of our favorite restaurants when Tom said to me, "I quit taking all my prescriptions." (He was being treated for high blood pressure, high cholesterol, and anxiety.) When I asked him when he had stopped, he said, "A month ago." When I asked him why he had stopped he replied, "Because I didn't like the way they made me feel." He then looked out the window, turned back to me, and began, "And I'll tell you another thing ..." With tears in his eyes, he broke off and couldn't go any further. I asked him if he would tell me later, and he nodded his head yes. He never did.

Over the next few weeks, I did notice some odd behaviors. One night after work, I was almost finished making dinner when he said he was leaving to go wash his truck. I said, "Now? Dinner is almost ready." He said he would be right back. I was a bit miffed and thought it was weird. He had not done anything like that in the past. He was gone for at least an hour, maybe longer. I was getting worried, and by the time he finally got home, he still seemed a bit out of sorts. We just ate dinner, and I let it go. Another observation I made was that his drinking was escalating; I had suspected he was hiding it at times. It was something I was beginning to be really concerned about as he was getting angry, agitated, and belligerent on occasion. This definitely was not normal behavior for my husband.

As we know, hindsight is twenty/twenty. However, with a little bit more time to connect the dots, I would have been able to note further odd behavior and discuss it with Tom, so we could have taken action to find out what was happening. Woulda, shoulda, coulda, is a dangerous game to play, though, and it's not worth it in the end. I have found all we can do is play the hand we are dealt, with no regrets, knowing that we did the best we could.

After having been through the worst thing imaginable, I have come to realize a few things since Tom's passing. The first is that I no longer take myself or life as seriously as I once did. Life is way too short for that kind of pressure and drama. I have no problem making fun of myself or blowing off the bits of drama and pettiness that accompany everyday life. It just rolls off of me now like water off a duck's back. When you stop and realize how little time we actually have on earth, you don't want to spend it worrying about the small stuff. It becomes abundantly clear what really matters in this world, and that is love and the relationships with the people in your life. There is nothing more important.

Another thing I have realized is that I don't really care anymore what people think about me. I have neither the time nor inclination to worry about things I can't control. It's none of my business anyway. I have lived through some traumatic times. I made it through to the other side, and I didn't let it take me down. There are way more important things to be concerned about in life.

Now, as I sit on the precipice of a new future, I am praying that my greatest wish for this book will come true. I hope that by telling our story, I can help people. Hopefully our experience can make your journey easier in some way, or maybe you will come away with a better understanding of the dynamics and the part they play in the everyday life of someone with a serious illness. If that happens, all the documenting, remembering, pain, and tears would be more than worth it. That would be the greatest gift I could receive.

Much love to you all,

Chrissie

CPSIA information can be obtained at www.ICGtesting.com
Printed in the USA
LVOW08*1503010816

498604LV00007B/55/P